THE COUNTRY OF LOST
An Australian An?

From stories of colonial children lost in the bush to the recent cases of Graeme Thorne, Azaria Chamberlain and Jaidyn Leskie, the figure of the lost child has haunted the Australian imagination. Peter Pierce's original and sometimes shocking study *The Country of Lost Children* traces this ambivalent and disturbing history.

In the nineteenth century the idea of losing one's child to a strange and silent country reflected the depth of white settlers' distrust of their new land and its Aboriginal inhabitants. Thus it offers insights into the passing of a vital early opportunity for reconciliation between European and indigenous Australians. In the twentieth century the lost child continues to torment the national consciousness, but no longer as the bewildered wanderer in the bush. The emblematic lost child of modern Australia is a victim of white society itself; of abuse, abandonment or abduction. Drawing on a wide range of sources, from poetry, fiction and newspaper reports to paintings and films, *The Country of Lost Children* analyses the cultural and moral implications of the lost child in our history and illuminates a crucial aspect of our present condition. At its core are confronting, often troubling, questions about childhood itself.

Educated at the University of Tasmania, Peter Pierce went to Balliol College, Oxford as a Rhodes Scholar in 1973. He subsequently taught at the University of Tasmania, the University of Melbourne, the Australian Defence Force Academy and at Monash University. He is currently Professor of Australian Literature at James Cook University. His books include *Australian Melodramas: The Fiction of Thomas Keneally* (1995), *Clubbing of the Gunfire: 101 Australian War Poems* (1984), *The Oxford Literary Guide to Australia* (as General Editor) (1987), *The Poets' Discovery: Nineteenth-Century Australia in Verse* (1990), *Vietnam Days* (1991) and *Xavier Herbert* (1992). A prolific reviewer, he writes for the *Bulletin, Canberra Times, Sydney Morning Herald, Australian Book Review, Eureka Street* and *Australian Literary Studies*.

In memory of my mother
Phyllis Pierce (1916–1997)

THE COUNTRY OF LOST CHILDREN

An Australian Anxiety

PETER PIERCE
James Cook University

CAMBRIDGE UNIVERSITY PRESS

PUBLISHED BY THE PRESS SYNDICATE OF THE UNIVERSITY OF CAMBRIDGE
The Pitt Building, Trumpington Street, Cambridge, United Kingdom

CAMBRIDGE UNIVERSITY PRESS
The Edinburgh Building, Cambridge CB2 2RU, UK   http://www.cup.cam.ac.uk
40 West 20th Street, New York, NY 10011–4211, USA   http://www.cup.org
10 Stamford Road, Oakleigh, Melbourne 3166, Australia

© Peter Pierce 1999

This book is in copyright. Subject to statutory exception
and to the provisions of relevant collective licensing agreements,
no reproduction of any part may take place without
the written permission of Cambridge University Press.

First published 1999

Printed in Australia by Brown Prior Anderson

Typeface New Baskerville (Adobe) 10/12pt. System QuarkXPress® [PH]

A catalogue record for this book is available from the British Library

National Library of Australia Cataloguing in Publication data
Pierce, Peter, 1950– .
The country of lost children: an Australian anxiety.

Bibliography.
Includes index.
ISBN 0 521 59440 5.
ISBN 0 521 59499 5.

1. Missing children in literature. 2. Missing children in
art. 3. Abandoned children in literature. 4. Abandoned
children in art. 5. Children in motion pictures. I. Title.

700.452054

ISBN 0 521 59440 5 hardback
ISBN 0 521 59499 5 paperback

Contents

Illustrations	vii
Acknowledgements	ix
Introduction	xi
Part I In the Nineteenth Century: Discovering the Lost Child	**3**
The Lost Child Introduced: Henry Kingsley's *The Recollections of Geoffry Hamlyn*	11
'Come let us sing of this fair child heroic': Jane Duff and her brothers	16
Alfred Boulter	29
A Monument at Daylesford	34
Marcus Clarke's Lost Children	40
The Case of Clara Crosbie	46
Frederick McCubbin's Images of the Lost Child	54
Fairytales of the 1890s	60
The Bush Balladists' Turn	65
Mrs Praed and the Punishment of Mrs Tregaskiss	71
Henry Lawson and 'The Babies in the Bush'	77
Joseph Furphy's 'Perfect Young-Australian'	86
Part II In the Twentieth Century: The Child Abandoned	**95**
In the Theatre	99
Ray Lawler: Bubba and the Baby Dolls	99
'They wasn't in our line': The Lost Children of Patrick White	104

CONTENTS

In Fiction	114
'Our dread of the coming society': Thomas Keneally's Fiction	116
'Keeping control of the young': Frank Moorhouse and the Lost Child	121
Leone Sperling's *Mother's Day*	128
Home Time with Beverley Farmer	133
'Who would bring kids into this world?': Ian Moffitt's *The Colour Man*	135
'I've had my children': Jennifer Maiden's *Play with Knives*	138
'Infected by Lost Child disease': The Fiction of Carmel Bird	143
The Lost Child's Unwelcome Return: David Malouf's *Remembering Babylon*	146
Book into Film	151
The Back of Beyond	153
Walkabout	156
Picnic at Hanging Rock	159
Manganinnie	164
Fortress	168
Evil Angels	172
True Stories	179
Peter Carey's Testaments	181
Abductions	184
'Little boy lost in a lost town'	188
Talk of the Devil	192
Orphans of the Empire	195
The Stolen Generation	198
Works Consulted	202
Index	206

List of Illustrations

'Lost in the Bush'	4
Samuel Calvert, 'Children Lost in the Bush'	5
'The Black Trackers'	10
William Strutt, 'Found, Mr. Duncan, Roderick, Bella and David'	26
Jane Duff's grave in Horsham	28
Samuel Calvert, 'Alfred Boulter'	30
Samuel Calvert, 'Finding the Remains of the Daylesford Children'	36
Monument at Daylesford	40
'Finding Clara Crosbie After Three Weeks Lost in the Bush'	52
Frederick McCubbin, 'Lost' 1886	56
Frederick McCubbin, 'Lost' 1907	57
Garret & Co. after William McLeod, 'Tracked!'	67
Dot and the Kangaroo	152
The Back of Beyond	155
Picnic at Hanging Rock	161
Crossing the creek	166
Joanna and Manganinnie at the cave	167
Christmas comes early	169
Police diver recovers Jaidyn Leskie's clothes	191

Acknowledgements

Anyone trying to understand the phenomenon of the lost child in Australia is indebted to the pioneering work of Leigh Astbury in *City Bushmen*. He is also a mate, and one whose detailed criticisms of sections of this manuscript saved me from embarrassment. Parts of the book have appeared in print in different forms before: I thank the *Age Monthly Review*, *The Critical Review* and *Eureka Street* for the opportunities to test ideas while the work was in progress and – in the first instance – before it had been fully conceived. It was a significant help to have been able to lecture on aspects of this subject thence to profit from the comments and suggestions of audiences at James Cook University, the State Library of Victoria (at the annual Redmond Barry Lecture for the Friends of the State Library), the Sydney Writers' Centre, Rozelle and at the Australian Defence Force Academy.

I would like to thank the staffs of the State Library of Victoria, the Monash University library, the James Cook University library, the National Library of Australia, the National Film and Sound Archive and the National Gallery of Victoria for the unfailingly kind and constructive assistance that they have given me. For permission to quote from her poem 'Precipice', I thank Judith Wright. For permission to use stills from their films I wish to thank John Heyer and John Heyer Film Company Pty Ltd (*The Back of Beyond*), Patricia Lovell and Picnic Productions Pty Ltd (*Picnic at Hanging Rock*), Sandra Gross and Yoram Gross and Village Roadshow Pty Ltd (*Dot and the Kangaroo*), Ian Pearce and the Archives Office of Tasmania (*Manganinnie*), Don Famulenok and Crawford Productions (*Fortress*) and for arranging for their reproduction, Tamara Osicka of the National Film and Sound Archive. Jeff Doyle came to my aid with material on *The Back of Beyond* and *Walkabout*, while Michelle Boaler assisted in the search for permissions.

My colleagues at James Cook University and Monash University have greatly assisted in my thinking about this book. In particular I wish to thank Robin Gerster (for the title), Richard Lansdown (for clarifying the notion of the child as surrogate for the parent in nineteenth-century narratives), Gina Mercer (for suggestions on Beverley Farmer and Leone Sperling), Tony Hassall (for directing me to Peter Carey's 'A Small Testament'), Greg Manning (for explaining to me the good reasons why what looked as though it should have been the middle part of the book was missing) and Carmel Lloyd for technical, but more importantly moral support throughout the time I have been in Townsville. I am grateful for the Chair establishment grant that I received from James Cook University: it was a vital aid in this research. My thanks also go to Heather Jamieson for her meticulous and good-humoured editing of the manuscript and to Phillipa McGuinness of Cambridge University Press, for commissioning the book and loyally supporting it thereafter.

My gratitude goes as always to Rae and Catherine, who know better than anyone the difficult circumstances, of absence and anxiety, in which *The Country of Lost Children* was written.

Introduction

In a riddling passage of Bruce Chatwin's *The Songlines* (1987), the Russian-born Arkady – whom the author has met during his travels into the interior of Australia – questions an Aboriginal elder. Arkady is in search of knowledge of the kind of which Chatwin's book will often presume to speak, and to comprehend. In particular, he inquires of the Aboriginal sacred sites that might be trespassed upon in the event of the construction of the proposed railway line between Alice Springs and Darwin. The elder, who is the last of his clan in this part of the country, chooses to tell Arkady something of what is sacred to Aborigines in the region. He relates the story of the Babies. Born following a transgression of Akuka, the Bandicoot Man, the Babies fell into floodwaters near Lizard Rock and melted. Without reckoning the cryptic character of this answer, which seems to indicate the sacrifice of children because of the guilt of one of their parents, Arkady reaches for a sententious generalisation. He says, 'slowly', that 'Australia … is the country of lost children'.

    This book, *The Country of Lost Children: An Australian Anxiety*, takes its title from Arkady's throwaway line. The notion is shocking: that Australia is the place where the innocent young are most especially in jeopardy. Standing for girls and boys of European origin who strayed into the Australian bush, the lost child is an arresting figure in the history and the folklore of colonial Australia. More profoundly though, the lost child is the symbol of essential if never fully resolved anxieties within the white settler communities of this country. The loss of their children blighted the lives of many pioneering Australians. Stories of boys' or girls' endurance and suffering, of their deaths or providential rescues, were related throughout the second half of the nineteenth century. They made vivid appearances in many mediums: painting and pantomime, fiction and photograph, verse and fairytale.

What were the meanings of these stories? Ostensibly, and poignantly, they told of the danger for children of wandering away from settled areas into the trackless bush. The abiding force of the figure of the lost child has, however, deeper and darker origins and implications. The forlorn girls and boys, bereft, disoriented and crying in a wilderness that is indifferent, if not actively hostile to them, stand also for the older generation, that of their parents. Symbolically, the lost child represents the anxieties of European settlers because of the ties with home which they have cut in coming to Australia, whether or not they journeyed here by choice. The figure of the child stands in part for the apprehensions of adults about having sought to settle in a place where they might never be at peace.

Narratives of lost children in the colonial period in Australia are concentrated in the second half of the nineteenth century. In fiction, that span can be marked by Henry Kingsley's *The Recollections of Geoffry Hamlyn* (1859) and Joseph Furphy's *Such is Life* (1903). Both those novels drew on real incidents of lost children, as well as the consequent folklore of the searches that were mounted for them, and their outcomes. There is an intense cross-fertilisation between the reported and the imagined tales of children lost in the bush. Such a process helped to ensure the indelibility of this aspect of pioneering experience in Australia. Lost children united rural communities in this country in colonial times, as desperately their members sought to find the lost ones alive. Subsequently, they might have to unite in mourning. The communal remembrances of the stories of children lost in the bush begins, in the latter decades of the nineteenth century, to take on a generic, composite air; thus to become the stuff of cautionary legend as well as of plaintive history.

Yet these are not stories confined, or peculiar to the lives of European Australians. A crucial element in many nineteenth-century narratives of lost children is the role played by Aboriginal trackers, who are summoned either just in time, or too late for their skills to have ensured a rescue. In the period covered in the first part of this book, roughly the second half of the last century, European children were often taken by the land. The lodgment of settlers in this country had always been fraught with natural perils. It was compromised as well by uncertainty about their moral rights to be here. Yet the bush was alluring, so that children strayed contentedly into it, only to lose themselves, perhaps forever. Often they were saved by Aboriginal men who had been dispossessed of this same land. Here, potentially, was a most potent image of reconciliation between black and white Australians. All too soon, it was forgotten.

The Country of Lost Children is divided into two parts. The first of them, already sketched in outline, is called 'In the Nineteenth Century: Discovering the Lost Child'. Its primary purpose is to present and to analyse a succession of narratives in different media in which the cultural significances of the figure of the lost child were imagined and interpreted. The 'discovery' is therefore on the one hand literal, because it deals with lost boys and girls, living and dead, and the effects of the loss of them on the communities from which they came. On the other hand it is metaphorical, for the figure of the lost child becomes a vital means for European Australians in the latter half of the nineteenth century to express and understand the insecurities of their position in a land that was new to many of them, and strange to all.

The second part of the book, 'In the Twentieth Century: The Child Abandoned', covers the period from the 1950s until the century's end. That is, there is an hiatus between this span of time and that of 'Discovering the Lost Child'. It is not the case that the lost child altogether disappears from artists' or reporters' views in the first half of this century. For instance, there are lost child episodes in Mary Grant Bruce's novels *Glen Eyre* (1912) and *Grant's Hollow* (1914). They end happily. Charles Chauvel's novel, *Uncivilised*, which he filmed in 1936, is a lost child story too, although it owes more to Edgar Rice Burroughs' Tarzan tales (which began with *Tarzan of the Apes* in 1914) than to indigenous Australian traditions. In Chauvel's story, the son of white missionaries, who has been lost as a child in the wilds of Australia, is brought up by an Aboriginal tribe. On reaching adulthood, he becomes its chief. Such a result is utterly incongruous in the history of relations between black men and white children in earlier Australian lost child narratives, however gratifying an imperialist fantasy it may have been.

Put schematically, and without any attempt at an inclusive cultural explanation, the first period covered by this book (from the 1850s until the turn of the century) describes how European children were taken by the land. In the missing half century (in this analysis, at least), from c. 1900 until the 1950s, much imaginative writing, both fiction and poetry, was concerned to offer a retrospect on the taking of the land from its Aboriginal inhabitants by European pioneers and settlers. This is the material of the saga fiction of Eleanor Dark, Brian Penton, 'Barnard Eldershaw' and others. Children lost in places they might not belong focussed anxieties not only over legitimacy of land tenure, but of European Australians' spiritual and psychological lodgment. While these anxieties were over-ridden in the narratives of progress that the saga literature favoured, by the mid-1950s new and sharper versions of that old anxiety were again being expressed in Australia.

With the lost child stories of the previous century, they shared an ambivalence about the future. Their essential unlikeness was that the agency of loss of children was now the human rather than the natural world. That is, it was purposeful, rather than accidental. The narratives of the book's second part, 'The Child Abandoned', tell of terrible crimes against the young, whether these were committed by institutions charged with their welfare, or as the result of individual malevolence, or simply out of heedlessness as to the fate of children who were at risk. Considered first are theatrical treatments of the lost child; then the representations of the figure in fiction; next the adaptation of books into film. Uncommon angles of view on these genres and the authors working within them are opened. The figure of the lost child has the power to reach into unexpected quarters; freshly to illuminate some reputations, perhaps to revive others.

The final section of this part of the book, 'True Stories', traverses terrible ground. Its subjects are actual incidents of the abduction, murder, sexual molestation, abandonment and brutalising of the young in Australia. So severe and disturbing are many of these episodes, that it can seem that a kind of national death wish has overcome Australia. The last of these stories concerns the experiences of Aboriginal Australians. In treating of the children of the so-called 'stolen generation', the book has turned full circle; gone back in truth and in metaphor to the Aboriginal 'lost child' of whom Charles Tompson's poem 'Blacktown' (1826) had spoken so long before.

The stories of these people, children long lost to their families, is one among many narratives in this book, albeit one of the most significant and harrowing of them. Where once the land indifferently took lost Australian children of European origin, now Aboriginal children were systematically taken away from their land. If these bodies of suffering and story can be connected, then the process of reconciliation between European and Aboriginal Australians, which can be glimpsed at times in the colonial tales of lost children, might be advanced in ways that do not allow regression to an age that once we thought of as less enlightened than this.

To speak specifically of an 'Australian anxiety' in the course of retelling and interpreting this selection of lost child narratives from two half centuries of the history of this country, might seem unwarrantably to privilege this national experience. What might be gleaned from the comparison of Australian with European and American accounts of lost children? First, that the differences between them are more striking in

INTRODUCTION

the nineteenth than in the twentieth century. Thus, among the collections of tales that the Brothers Grimm made early in the last century, the forests in which children were lost were perilous places, not because of any natural threats that they posed, but for the malevolent people who lived within them, better to prey on the young. Australian tellers of fairy stories in the 1890s, necessarily writing with the Grimms in mind, naturalised the Germanic material earnestly, but often incongruously. They neither found, nor fabricated, plausible human threats to lost children.

Writing in the present time of a medieval legend – that of the monstrous Bluebeard – in *Gilles et Jeanne* (1983, translated into English in 1987), the French novelist Michel Tournier imagined a connection between the martyr Jeanne d'Arc and the nobleman Gilles de Rais (Bluebeard). After the Maid of Orleans was burned at the stake, Gilles's obsession with her was perversely transferred to the exultant capture, sexual abuse and murder of children in his castle, Tauffages. This short novel gives us more of the sense of historical analogy than of period fiction. As it describes a rigorous, intellectualised cruelty towards the young, Tournier's novel resonates in our age, whatever the motives of its murderous protagonist may have been long ago.

Gustav Mahler wrote his *Kinder-totenlieder* between 1901 and 1904; they were first performed in the following year. These 'Songs on the Death of Children', based on poems by Friedrich Rueckert, were an immemorial lament, freed from the present time, the more deeply to encourage grieving. For example the fourth song, *'Oft denk' ich, sie sind nur ausgeganen'*, is an attempt at consolation which knows itself to be in vain:

> I often think they have only gone out,
> And soon they will be home again!
> The day is lovely! Oh, be not afraid!
> They have only gone out for a long walk!

The fifth and last song, *'In diesem Wetter!'*, is reproachful, although it is not clear who is being blamed for the loss of children:

> In such weather, in such a storm,
> I would never have sent the children out!
> They have been carried off, been carried off!
> I was not allowed to say a word!

Coincident with while altogether unaware of the late colonial treatments of the lost child material by Lawson and Furphy, the *Kinder-totenlieder*, the poems by Rueckert that Mahler set to music, are yet similarly ambivalent. Both hostile nature and malign human interference appear to have played roles in the fates of the children.

Much nearer to this century's end, there is no such ambivalence in Ian McEwan's novel, *The Child in Time* (1987). In the hotter, crueller Britain that McEwan imagines, a dictatorial female rules the country. Beggars are licensed and an official revision of benign, Wordsworthian, Romantic attitudes towards childhood innocence has been undertaken. The selfishness of children is now the publicly affirmed belief of the government. Parents are sanctioned to discipline their young. Corporal punishment is approved and 'the nation is to be regenerated by reformed childcare practice'. Among other experts, the Official Commission on Childcare Practice has enlisted the best-selling children's book author who is McEwan's protagonist. The horror of this man's life is characteristic of the modern, not of a future world. This is the loss of his daughter Kate, who was abducted in a supermarket, while her father was momentarily distracted. This irreparable, arbitrary, tormenting bereavement is, for McEwan's hero, a cruelty too mysterious to fathom. The title of the novel, *The Child in Time*, adverts not just to the loss of a loved, especial daughter, but to an institutional hardening of the line against the younger generation. This is besides the seemingly casual destruction of their lives that is a daily occurrence. McEwan was alert to many recent outrages – in public and private – against children. Rightly he suspected that there were worse to come.

In the United States, as in Europe, the modern record of the reasons for the losses of children is sadly similar to that in Australia. Adults prey murderously on the young on both sides of the Atlantic. A desperate and disappointed man killed sixteen children at Dunblane in Scotland. In Belgium, the paedophile, Marc Dutroux, abducted, sexually abused and killed four girls. Two of them starved to death in his cellar while he was in gaol for other offences. Worse even than this, perhaps, are the crimes of children against each other. In 1993, the then ten-year-old British boys Robert Thompson and Jon Venables kidnapped two-year-old James Bolger, and killed him on a nearby railway line. In the United States, the murders of pre-teenage children by those of their own age is a circumstance regular enough to have dulled its power to shock.

Earlier periods of American and European history offer differing comparative cultural evidence from the Australian accounts of lost children. For example, the signal lost child figures in North American history, fiction and folklore are the victims of Indian captivity, especially in the seventeenth and eighteenth centuries. From such durance, they may or may not have been released, after suffering whatever kinds of harm. Richard Slotkin traced the cultural reading of their narratives in

Regeneration Through Violence (1973). In *The Searchers* (1956) film director John Ford had set his favourite hero John Wayne on the trail of his niece, abducted by Comanches. In the course of this quest, the hero, Ethan Edwards, had determined that once a lost girl has been taken by Indians, she can never truly be restored to her community. In consequence, she would be better dead. This situation did not resemble the circumstances of Australian racial contact history and the literature which re-imagined it. That would, after all, have required notions of Aborigines as more palpably and threateningly human than were often conceded.

The most famous lost child in nineteenth-century fiction in the United States also bears scant likeness to his Australian contemporaries. This is the thrice lost hero of Mark Twain's novel, *Huckleberry Finn* (1884). Because of his ne'er-do-well father and his rebellious reluctance to submit to the civilising influences of the Widow Douglas and others, Huck is already an outcast within his community. He becomes literally lost when – as a means of escape from the violent, drunken Pap Finn – he fakes his own death. Previous efforts to save him, through well-intentioned attempts at his moral redemption, had never made much ground. Now Huck has freed himself for the journey – too briefly idyllic – down the Mississippi River with the fugitive Negro Jim.

In the nineteenth century, Australian children had few opportunities to be lost in this way. The unsettled country into which they might venture was markedly inhospitable and unpopulated. Thus the option of losing oneself deliberately was merely foolhardy. Huck, it needs also to be said, embraced a third kind of loss. At the end of the novel he determines to 'light out' for the Indian Territory, 'ahead of the rest'. In the colonial period, the Australian frontier offered no such prospect of anonymous vanishing into the interior. There may have been a limitless horizon in this country, but not one that offered shelter.

Neither, in the twentieth century, was there respite for those children who were doomed to be lost in cities, preyed upon by strangers, cut off from their families, often finding themselves in mortal jeopardy. A nihilistic wish to deny them a future seems to have inspired the actions of many who held responsibility for the young. What such behaviour, such a will to thwart the chances, or the very being, of the next generation might portend is the essential business, descriptive of a pervasive anxiety, that the second part of this book confronts. It does so without claiming fully to comprehend the springs of that anxiety, or to find any but partial ways of consolation.

Yet *The Country of Lost Children* is written in hope, out of a humanist belief that the rehearsal of stories of our past, with all their obscurities and complexities, can still illumine how in Australia we came to be as we are, a people persistently fearful of where we are lodged in place and time. Further, if the analysis of current anxieties concerning an Australian future, as revealed by factual and imaginative witnesses, shows this anxiety to be so deep and wretched and scarcely examined that the next generation is set at hazard, then these stories must be addressed as a matter of moral and cultural urgency. An inquiry into them can enrich us all. I trust that it may. Otherwise, Australia, 'the country of lost children', may become the place where the post-medieval Western notion of childhood dies first.

Part I

In the Nineteenth Century
DISCOVERING THE LOST CHILD

By 1803 there is a lost child story to mark the first decades of European settlement in Australia. A labourer, who had rowed with his son across Sydney Harbour from Pitts Row to Neutral Bay to gather timber for fencing, left the child unattended. Orders not to stray were ignored. As Jan Kociumbas relates in *Australian Childhood* (1997), when the man returned 'the child was gone. Eventually found by chance, he had travelled five miles and was exhausted and hoarse from crying'. His fortunate recovery still afforded an example of the dangers of becoming lost in the bush, which – Kociumbas writes – 'ran like a refrain through white settler experience'.

The first lost child in Australian literature appeared in Charles Tompson's poem 'Blacktown', which was published in the Sydney *Monitor* on 2 June 1826. Tompson's imitation of Oliver Goldsmith's 'The Deserted Village' (1770) was purportedly written 'in the verandah of the chapel at the deserted hamlet of Blacktown'. This establishment, west of Sydney on the New Richmond Road, had been created by Governor Macquarie in 1814 to civilise the Aborigines, in part by teaching them the arts of agriculture. But 'the poor heathen possessors' (Tompson seems liberally to assume prior Aboriginal ownership of the land) were allowed to abandon the place. Tompson laments their consequent fate, with a personal interjection into the poem:

> Lost child! Shall we the savage part pursue?
> Shall all despise thee for thy sable hue?
> Will Charity no warm vicegerent send
> To own thee brother, or to call thee friend?

History would give gloomy answers to those questions. In the culture of European Australia in the nineteenth century the lost children, whose fates would be lamented and stories retold, were boys and girls who had strayed into the bush, thence to be taken by the land. They were not the Aboriginal victims of white encroachment. Yet Tompson had spoken prophetically of a humane attitude that might have changed relations between the races, if widely adopted. As it was, Aborigines would retain a vital (if also transient and marginal) part in lost child narratives, though their own plight would never be at the core of them.

In successive years, the colour supplement in the *Illustrated Melbourne Post* ran full-page illustrations on themes which appear very similar. The pictures were titled, respectively, 'Lost in the Bush' (25 October 1865) and 'Children Lost in the Bush' (27 July 1866). The first engraving represented 'one of those lamentable features which characterise bush life in Australia, viz., the sinking of the lost traveller, overpowered by thirst and fatigue'. Far from 'the outposts of civilisation', the solitary bushman is caught without water. Thus he lies down – as plaintively pictured – 'to rise no more'. His remains will soon be devoured by the predators lurking at the edge of the picture. There are dingoes. In 1980, more than a century later, this animal would feature in the most famous of all Australian lost child stories, that of Azaria Chamberlain.

The second illustration, 'Children Lost in the Bush', was accompanied by a narrative so long and detailed that it might be thought to be describing a specific event that had actually and recently occurred, rather than being a fictional instance of a typical hazard of the outback.

'Lost in the Bush'
Illustrated Melbourne Post, 25 October 1865
La Trobe Picture Collection, State Library of Victoria

In the engraving, a boy – his back to a tree – has evidently been guarding his sleeping siblings, a younger brother and sister. He seems to have started up, warily, or in hope. Perhaps he has heard the sound of rescuers, as did the Duff children, who were famously found after nine days search in the Wimmera District of Victoria in 1864. Or maybe the only thing these children have to wait for is death, thus anticipating the fate of the three boys who perished outside Daylesford, also in Victoria, in 1867. The illustration leaves the children's fate in suspense. The accompanying narrative allows them rescue, albeit long delayed.

The elements of this account repay analysis, for they draw on Australian folk memories of a familiar misadventure, yet in such a fashion as to suggest that one in particular was being described, or recalled. Whether based on veritable incident or not, the writer wishes to suggest that the story which he tells is also true in a generic sense: more true, that is, than those tales propagated by mere fiction writers. He begins this way:

> the coloured engraving in our supplement vividly depicts one of those sad, but unfortunately too common, incidents in Australian life, full as it is of that real romance rarely to be exceeded by the most imaginative novelists.

'Children Lost in the Bush'
Illustrated Melbourne Post, 27 July 1866 (Samuel Calvert)
La Trobe Picture Collection, State Library of Victoria

As it happened, authors such as Henry Kingsley, Marcus Clarke, Rosa Praed, Ethel Pedley, Henry Lawson and Joseph Furphy, drawing on 'real' incidents as well as on communal memories of lost children, had – and would – see about that.

The anonymous writer in the *Illustrated Melbourne Post* in July 1866 gives examples of how, too frequently, 'on the vast plain and in the dark forests of the interior' of Australia, men have 'cast themselves despairingly down to die'. Sometimes they have been diggers, at others swagmen, or wandering stockmen, or ticket-of-leave holders, or those sent out into the bush 'by friends wearied of them', because they have become 'the victim of drink and debauchery'. If these men, with their pathetic histories, are both anonymous and typical casualties of a pioneering, frontier age, then others to have perished – Leichhardt, Burke, Wills (the latter two in 1861, only a few years before) – bear names which 'will never be forgotten in Australia so long as she has a history to be written and a youth to study it'.

From these actual examples, as sublime as he can – with difficulty – make them, the author turns to a representative, even if fictional instance of three children who, 'stolen out to play', have become lost. Now the perishing of adults is a predictable price of colonial expansion into the wilderness. Indeed, it lends a melancholy tincture (of 'real romance' in the journalist's term) to the national story. Thus many Australians knew well the folk song of 'The Dying Stockman', while in verse Adam Lindsay Gordon depicted 'The Sick Stockrider' (written in 1869) and Barcroft Boake wrote of 'The Land Where the Dead Men Lie' (for the *Bulletin* in 1891 and then as the title for his only volume of poetry). But the deaths of young Australians, of children, are terrible, and are a more than personal or family matter. Their loss plays more heavily on the fears of Australians than adult catastrophes in the bush. Perhaps the travails and sometimes the deaths of children are emblematic either of the forfeiting of part of the national future, or of an anxiety that Australia will never truly welcome European settlement. There is also an intimation of the guilt of parents for ever having brought children to such a hostile environment, which issues in anxiety (often and too readily realised) about their fate. In a related sense, the figure of the lost child may stand for the adult emigrant to Australia, disoriented and vulnerable, and far from all that was consoling and familiar in Britain or Ireland. For emigration (let alone transportation) always leads to a generational disjunction: parents are left behind, with consequent anxieties and a sense of bereftness for many of those who set out, willingly or otherwise, for strange lands far away.

An incalculable number of men and women became 'lost in the bush' in senses and circumstances other than those to be discussed in this book. Some became crazed by loneliness, or the forbidding strangeness of their surroundings, or the scarcity and incivility of human contact. They coped with their situations by madness, or by an exaggerated preference for solitude that could resemble insanity. In the 1890s there are memorable literary portrayals of such unfortunates, notably the title characters of Barbara Baynton's short story 'Scrammy 'And' and Lawson's 'The Bush Undertaker'. The latter ends with this famous crystallisation (or remythologising) of the effects of life outback:

> And the sun sank again on the grand Australian bush – the nurse and tutor of eccentric minds, the home of the weird, and of much that is different from things in other lands.

In line of descent from Lawson's 'Bush Undertaker' is Monk O'Neill, the hero of Jack Hibberd's monodrama, *A Stretch of the Imagination* (1972, 1973), an old man who has 'lost' himself far from the city to wait out the rest of his days at One Tree Hill, sustained by fanciful remembrance of his past. This vital strain of 'lost in the bush' material, concerned with tormented, isolated adults, awaits sustained attention.

But to return to the story of lost children presented in the *Illustrated Melbourne Post*: the magazine, after all, is not concerned with cultural speculation, but with exemplary incident. A scene is sketched of the fretful mother at home, while her husband is away at work splitting logs. Children who go missing in these colonial narratives almost always come from the rural labouring poor. 'In crowded cities stray children are easily found', but not 'here in the wild bush'. 'The lost ones' – Billy, Jacky and Mary (which nearly exhausts the treasury of bush children's names, Dick and Jane among the exceptions) – are 'stout and hardy, not delicately or luxuriously bred'. Nevertheless they must perish if not soon found. After a second night falls, 'darker and stormier than the first', they are still lost. The eldest, Billy, has lit a fire, but 'the loneliness of the bush' undermines even his courage. Too weak to walk, 'beyond all hope', Billy and Mary mutter prayers, while Jack 'is babbling some incoherent words about "Jesus" and "a little child" '.

The author bids the unfortunates farewell. They are 'alone, helpless, and deserted'; they 'have eaten their last meal and played their last game'. Not only will they never see their grieving parents again, but 'father and mother will not even know where their little ones lie'. With that terrible uncertainty, that intensification of loss put before us, the author elects – just in time – to reprieve the children, as though to emphasise how arbitrary salvation in such cases can be. Whether by chance or providence (each option will have its partisans), the feeble cry of one of the children is heard by the searchers. Resolved in the most consoling fashion, the story soon ends, although not before this final caution: 'The happy play hours of childhood will come to them again, but not to wipe out the memory of when they were "lost in the bush" '.

This narrative, which accompanied the colour supplement illustration of 'Children Lost in the Bush', distils many of the essential aspects of an Australian cultural commonplace. There is no clearer formulation – in fiction, journalism, or art – of most of the typical features of a generic lost child story (most, but not all: there are no black trackers in the *Illustrated Melbourne Post* narrative). Writers and artists from this point in the mid-1860s until early in the next century, would employ the figure of the lost child to explore the relations of European Australians with the landscapes that they were trying to settle and understand, and with the Aboriginal people with whom their contact was troubled, puzzling and destructive. This figure would also afford an opportunity to develop the discourse of 'young Australia', that is, to speculate on the nature of the coming race in this country, and the future of the nation soon to be. These three related uses of the lost child suggest that, in essence, the insecurity of the new Australians' own tenure of the land to which they had come lay near the heart of such inquiries. The obsessive reporting and imagining of children lost in the bush indicates an abiding anxiety in colonial Australia. In this century, in different forms, it has been no less intense.

This anxiety was supposedly the hoary emblem of the hostility of the bush and of the recalcitrance of the Australian climate and landscapes towards any adventuring spirits, let alone children. On inspection it appears more complex. In nineteenth-century fictitious depictions of lost children, the bush, which mildly entices and then swallows them up, is most often benign. Yarns of bunyips frighten or deter none of them. Seldom are they killed by actual bush creatures. Even more rarely are children kidnapped. An exception is Mrs W. I. Thrower's novel *Younah! A Tasmanian Aboriginal Romance of the Cataract Gorge* (1894) in which 'a white picanniny' is taken by an Aboriginal tribe in revenge for the abduction of a young girl of their own. Not to worry: 'the lost child', rechristened Younah and brought up by the Aborigines, 'the forlorn waif of the remote Tasmanian bush', is rescued and returned to white society where she becomes 'a beauty and an heiress'.

Another store of stories, the 'captivity narratives' of this country – whether legendary, like that of 'the Lost White Woman of Gippsland', or historical, for instance the tales of William Buckley, the convict who escaped at Port Phillip and lived for decades among Aborigines, or Eliza Fraser on the Queensland island to which she gave her name – all treat of adults. Once lost, children seem to fall asleep and to slip gently into death, or they are found just as that passing is about to begin and can still be averted. But for the adults who brought them to Australia there is no rest, it appears, and no end to guilt. A profound unease about their presence in this continent is the source of the fascinated dread with which these stories of lost children were retold, variously depicted and remembered.

The first section of this book examines both the collective, communal understanding which developed of the lost child in colonial Australia, and individual representations of this figure, so frequently mute and hence waiting – it would seem – to be spoken for by eager commentators. As Imré Salusinszky tartly remarked in his introduction to *The Oxford Book of Australian Essays* (1997):

> Fledgling communities huddled together in a hostile environment specialise in cautionary tales about the anticipation of danger and, more rarely, heroic tales about the overcoming of danger ...

The representations of lost children come in many forms. There are newspaper reports and the coverage – in engravings and written accounts – by the illustrated magazines that flourished in Australia from the 1850s until the late 1880s. Novelists, poets and painters take up the theme and there are even personal appearances by such famous survivors of their bush ordeals as Clara Crosbie, who was on the stage at the Australian Waxworks in Sydney at Christmas 1885. Her theatrical performance had been anticipated the previous Christmas, when John Hennings's pantomime *The Fairy Home of the Waratah* (an adaptation of the Red Riding Hood story) was staged at the Theatre Royal in Sydney. In that production, a little girl loses her way while gathering wild flowers, but fortunately finds herself under the protection of the fairy who watches over the waratah tree. In real life, many of her counterparts were not so lucky.

The authors or artists who treated this material may have been the anonymous newspaper and magazine reporters of incidents such as Alfred Boulter's disappearance in Tasmania in 1866, or famous painters such as Frederick McCubbin, who created a series of indelible images of children lost in the Australian bush. Other notable artists and illustrators were drawn to this subject: Samuel Calvert, S. T. Gill, William McLeod and William Strutt among them. The usually anonymous artists of illustrated magazines also command our attention. Until the 1880s their images provided crucial, popular representations of lost children. The magazines for which these artists worked (McCubbin for instance) did not long survive the introduction on 26 July 1888 of the half-tone process whereby photographs could be used in print. Besides these artists, authors of fairytales sought in a benign spirit to accommodate

'The Black Trackers'
Illustrated Australian News, 24 February 1864
La Trobe Picture Collection, State Library of Victoria

stories of lost children as well as to naturalise this genre in Australia. At the turn of the century, Lawson and Furphy undertook an ironic re-inspection of the lost child material. This was a moment when 'realist' eyes were turned upon one of the prime subjects of Australian romantic literature and art, and of our folklore.

Aborigines feature in many of these varied kinds of representations, often as the secular agents of salvation. Indeed, stories of lost children – in fact and fiction – are a means by which Aborigines are re-admitted to mainstream narratives in, and of, Australia. Aborigines had literally been edged out of the frame of early colonial paintings. At first doleful spectators at the margin, they disappeared altogether, to become instead the concern of anthropologists (and photographers) rather than artists. After mid-century some of them reappear as a valued occupational group – the black tracker. In this guise, the *Illustrated Australian News* gave them prominence in its issue of 24 February 1864. Although the writer conceded that 'the various attempts which have been made to civilise the Aboriginal natives of Australia ... have proved failures', yet they had shown themselves to be 'invaluable aids to the police in tracking criminals through the bush'. The Aborigines were treated with a generally respectful ethnographic interest, and a local and particular admiration for their bush skills.

There might have been so much more. Lost child stories afford the most poignant links between Aboriginal and European Australians. The white child who has wandered away into the bush and cannot find his or her bearings is regularly searched for by black men who have been dispossessed of this same country. Sometimes their labours were rewarded. Aborigines found the Duff children just in time. That image of happy conjunction was sadly transient and soon occluded, yet its moral and cultural import, properly conserved and understood, might have been immense.

That is one of the meanings, and potentials, of the narratives that are analysed below. Of so many stories which might have been retold, a dozen cases of lost children are considered in this first part of *The Country of Lost Children*, 'In the Nineteenth Century: Discovering the Lost Child', beginning with Kingsley's account of the death of young James Grewer in his novel *The Recollections of Geoffry Hamlyn* (1859). Whether ostensibly factual or fictitious, these narrative, dramatic and pictorial representations reinforce and complicate what such figures stand for in colonial Australia. Some of them also anticipate the twentieth-century revision of a familiar topos, discussed in the second part of this book 'In the Twentieth Century: The Child Abandoned', wherein the fate of the lost child, and the anxieties surrounding it, become more bleak and terrible than they had been before.

The Lost Child Introduced: Henry Kingsley's *The Recollections of Geoffry Hamlyn*

The first notable work of romance fiction to be written about Australia, which Henry Kingsley completed after his return to England, was *The Recollections of Geoffry Hamlyn* (1859). It would be warmly praised by two of Kingsley's most important successors, 'Rolf Boldrewood', who spoke of 'that immortal work, the best Australian novel' and Marcus Clarke, for whom it was 'the best Australian novel that has been, and probably will be written'. Another attentive reader, one conscious of the myth-making power of *The Recollections of Geoffry Hamlyn*, was Tom Collins, narrator of Joseph Furphy's novel *Such is Life* (1903). For Collins, Kingsley's novel was 'exceedingly trashy and misleading'. He proceeded radically to revise Kingsley's dominant myth, in which Australian pastoral plenty, once it has been exploited by English sojourners, can buy back their lost acres in the old country: 'I don't want to be young Sam Buckley of Baroona. I want to be the Buckley of Clare', as one character infamously declares. While Kingsley grants this wish, Collins does not, imagining instead a comically grim decline in the antipodes for the man whom he styles 'Hungry Buckley'.

The Recollections of Geoffry Hamlyn is a portmanteau novel. For instance, one of its chapters, the 36th, has to accommodate 'An Earthquake, A Colliery Explosion, and an Adventure'. Besides these episodes of vivid local colour, the narrator of the novel (all of which is told in the form of a protracted yarn by the garrulous old Hamlyn) is prompted by the earthquake to think of the past and the future of Australia. Once 'the great sea heaved and foamed over the ground on which we stand'. In the future (so goes his vision):

> I see the sunny slopes below me yellow with trellised vines. They have gathered the vintage and I hear them singing at the wine-press. They sing that the exhausted vineyards of the old world yield no wine so rare, so rich, as the fresh volcanic slopes of the southern continent, and that the princes of the earth send their wealth that their hearts may get glad from the juices of Australian grapes.

Kingsley happily entertains twin myths, which are serial rather than contradictory: of Australia as source of material replenishment for the old world, and as the pastoral paradise to come, when that aged, European world is worn out. It was in this novel that Kingsley coined the memorable phrase the 'working-man's paradise' for Australia. Yet it is the pre-Gold Rush, rural era of the newly settled continent that nostalgically enchants him. Claiming land, the English squatters remind him of 'the patriarchs moving into the desert', of 'the first and simplest act of colonisation, yet producing such great results in the history of the world'.

Kingsley conscientiously naturalises Australian incidents and scenes for the use of his, and subsequent, romance fiction. His characters live in a borderland, beset by outlaws. The Aboriginal inhabitants also do battle with them, although they are both violently subdued and reduced to material for art. Hamlyn casually recalls a punitive massacre, while Harding, an Oxford man, half-owner of a station 'and an inveterate writer of songs', mocks the yells and curses of an Aboriginal woman: 'What a sweet song that old girl is singing! I must write it down from dictation and translate it, as Walter Scott used to do with the old wives' ballads in Scotland'. Introducing his own romance improbabilities, Kingsley has Hamlyn deride those of Alexandre Dumas. What follows, among much else, is a very early literary assessment of what the convict era in Van Diemen's Land may yield for romance.

Thus Mary Hawker, one of the many characters whom Kingsley translates from England to Australia, is married to a criminal. However she believes herself to be a widow, having no reason to doubt the report that her convict husband George had died while on the chain-gang in Van Diemen's Land. Hamlyn dilates on its terrors: 'Men would knock out one another's brains in order to get hung, and escape it. Men would cry aloud to the judge to hang them out of the way!' The ex-convict servant, William Lee, now entreats a chance to tell Mary a story (whose upshot will be that she is not a widow: the bushranger Touan is her husband George), but before he can, Tom Troubridge relates how he has just unwittingly sat for half an hour in the public house at Lake George with the notorious bushranger who styles himself Captain Touan. (The strange name purportedly comes from that of a little grey squirrel which only begins to fly about at night.) To alert Mary to the dangers that this outlaw poses to their community, if with more than necessary relish, Tom describes Touan as:

> the most damnable villain that ever disgraced God's earth, and that is the truth. That man, cousin, in one of his devil's raids, tore a baby from its mother's breast by the leg, dashed its brains out against a tree, and then – I daren't tell a woman what happened!

But will leave her to guess: apparently child murder will be less offensive to Mary's ears than rape. Another curious aspect of the scene, at least for modern readers, is that Touan's outrage against the child might recall European vigilante massacres of Aboriginal communities in Australia. They may also have done so for Kingsley, whether from stories that he heard in the colonies during his stay from 1853 to 1858, or from material which Evangelical Christians such as his brother Charles Kingsley, the novelist, clergyman and Cambridge history professor, had gathered in England. It is not clear whether Kingsley has condemned such atrocities by transference, making evil bushrangers the agents of them, or is unaware of the resonances of the scene that Tom paints.

Certainly the author thinks the incident sufficiently important to warrant a footnote, which neatly conflates fact and fiction. Tom, we are told, was confusing Touan with Michael Howe, one of the most feared of the bushrangers of Van Diemen's Land in the first two decades of the nineteenth century: 'The latter did actually commit this frightful atrocity; but I have never heard that the former actually combined the two crimes in this way'. Where he heard about Howe is uncertain. The dashing of babies' brains is not among the catalogue of offences in T. E. Wells's account of 'The Last and Worst of the Bushrangers of Van Diemen's Land', *Michael Howe* (published in Hobart in 1818 and perhaps the rarest of all Australian books). For the sake of verisimilitude, one supposes, Kingsley informs us of how

> We must remember that barely four years from this present time (1858) a crime, exceeding this in atrocity, was committed in Van Diemen's Land, in open day. I refer to the murder of a lad returning from school.

In what way was the second, and much later child murder more excessive? Sparing us details, Kingsley (rather than Clarke in *His Natural Life* (1870–2) or than Caroline Leakey, whose novel of the convict system in Van Diemen's Land, *The Broad Arrow*, was published in the same year as Kingsley's) made Van Diemen's Land for the first time a separate, special province of horror. Several chapters later, the man-eating exploits of the escaped convict Alexander Pearce are recalled in the person of 'Moody the cannibal', one of the members of George Hawker's gang, whose boasts of his deeds lead Hawker to exclaim enviously: 'My God! That's worse than I ever did'.

While the novel includes emblematically violent incidents from the pioneering history of Australia, mainland horrors are less lurid, it seems, than those of Van Diemen's Land, although they are bloody enough, whether in the hunting of Aborigines and kangaroos, or the showdown with the bushrangers. The Van Diemen's Land material, however, appears to belong to another order, or kind of fiction; it is known nightmarishly at second hand, by near legendary report, rather than as one of the predictable accidents of any day. One of the latter is described in the 30th chapter of the novel: 'How the Child was Lost, and How He Got Found Again …'. This is one of the earliest, and – for later writers – perhaps the most influential of all the colonial narratives of the lost child, though to say that is to ignore how such narratives began to take on so many stock features, scarcely individuated, for all that significant elements of their interpretations of the events in question change.

Captain Brentwood is interrupted by a 'lithe lad' who bluntly tells him 'child lost, sir'. It is 'James Grewer's child … at the wattle hut'. Already lost for two days, the eight-year-old boy is the only child of a shepherd and his wife. Evidently he had crossed the river and strayed into the bush. While Mrs Buckley hopes that 'the black fellows may have found him', Brentwood reckons that by now the Europeans would have been informed. So the search is, literally, mounted. The nature of the missing boy is elaborately described by Kingsley, as if the child is an embryonic type of 'the coming race' in Australia:

> A strange, wild little bush child, able to speak articulately, but utterly without knowledge or experience of human creatures, save of his father and mother; unable to read a line; without religion of any sort or kind; as entire a little savage, in fact, as you could find in the worst den of your city, morally speaking, and yet beautiful to look on; as active as a roe, and, with regard to natural objects, as fearless as a lion.

The ambiguities of that 'savage' are hard to resolve. Having no experience of any intercourse beyond that with his family, the boy is hardly one of Fagin's foster children, which makes the insinuation peculiar. He is almost a child of nature, as the similes suggest. Is it, by implication, the uncivilised character of the 'strange, wild little bush child' that makes him susceptible to the blandishments of the natural world, especially of the land across the river? In that place, he fancies, other children – such as he could never have known – are 'beckoning him to cross and play in that merry land of shifting lights and shadows'. The question of why he strayed is essential for a reckoning of the symbolic significance of this account of a lost child.

For this is not a parable of parental delinquency. Although ultimately to no avail, the boy's mother warns him that the river is too deep to cross, that 'the Bunyip lives in the water under the stones'. When he asks who are the children who play there, she responds 'black children likely', but emends that to 'pixies' who will 'lure you on, Lord knows where'. Finally, and prosaically, she tells him that he might drown. Seeking to keep this only child safe with her, the mother has unwontedly encouraged him to venture away. Thus 'next day the passion was stronger on him than ever'. The river is low. He strips naked and crosses. In this forbidden land, this region that he means to 'penetrate', fruits abound – 'such quantongs, such raspberries, surpassing imagination'. As an adventurer, now dressed again, the boy thinks of the satisfaction of homecoming: 'What tales he would have for his father tonight'. It is as though this adventure will be a rite of passage, the first stage in making an adult of him. Soon the boy is in contact with creatures that will do him no harm – a kangaroo, a snake, an eagle and a native bear. Entranced for a time by this idyllic natural scene, he is then suddenly shaken to find that 'He was lost in the bush'. In Australia, that phrase would have a terrifying and abiding resonance.

Now it is, Kingsley comments, that 'a strange madness' comes upon the child such as even strong men feel when lost – 'a despair, a confusion of intellect, which has cost many a man his life'. Therefore, Kingsley adds, 'Think what it must be with a child!' Crying 'Mother!', the boy nurses the native bear, that incidentally he has taken away from *its* mother. Meanwhile the community rallies, as it always will in those disastrous episodes of fire, flood, drought and lost children which would come to assail so many generations of characters in Australian literature. It is the conventional wisdom of 'old bush hands' that lost children climb from height to height. Kingsley gives a footnote in support: his knowledge of a child found dead two to three thousand feet up in the mountains outside the township of Avoca in the Eastern Pyrenees region of Victoria. The boy had been lost while his father was shooting on the flats below. Subsequent 'real' events – as reported in newspapers and pictured in such magazines as the *Illustrated Melbourne Post* – would both confirm and elaborate elements of the kind of story that Kingsley chose to tell.

Sam Buckley and Cecil Mayford (incidentally rivals in love, but united in their purpose to locate the child) climb on upwards, until at last the shepherd's lad is found by the faithful dog Rover:

> There he lay, dead and stiff, one hand still grasping the flowers he had gathered in his last happy play-day, and the other laid as a pillow, between the soft cold cheek and the rough cold stone. His midsummer holiday was over, his long journey was ended. He had found out at last what lay beyond the shining river he had watched so long.

If the boy has indeed found 'what lay beyond the shining river', Kingsley intimates no religious consolation. And if the child is depicted as though he were asleep – or so he could seem to sentimental eyes – Kingsley tells us first and sharply that the boy is 'dead and stiff'. Insofar as the child does survive, it is for the way in which his death inscribes a soon to be typical and already familiar moment in the history of the European pioneering of Australia. Rather than the solemn legend-making of Charles Harpur's poem 'The Creek of the Four Graves' (1853), where the slaughter of a party of explorers by Aborigines gives a name to a place, Kingsley prefers a mawkish mode of inscription. The native bear, a living lost child as it were, is taken back to the Brentwood household, of which – in time – it becomes a venerable part, prompting parents to tell their children of 'the little boy who lost his way on the granite ranges, and went to heaven, in the year that the bushrangers came down'.

According to Stan Mellick, in his biography *The Passing Guest* (1983), Henry's more famous brother Charles, author of *The Heroes, Westward Ho!* and *The Water Babies*, 'particularly swore' by this episode in the romance. Henry's London publishers, Macmillan, were also sufficiently impressed to publish Chapter XXX separately in 1871, as an illustrated book for children with which to introduce young British readers to one of the characteristic perils, or excitements, of life in colonial Australia. Macmillan titled the book *The Lost Child*. Many works for a similar market would follow, while in Australia the representations of the lost child would continue and consolidate their long and strange career.

'Come let us sing of this fair child heroic': Jane Duff and her brothers

The most famous of all stories of lost children in colonial Australia might be regarded as untypical of them, for it had a happy outcome. On Friday 12 August 1864, the three Duff children – Isaac (nine), Jane (seven) and

Frank (three) were sent out by their mother, from the shepherd's hut in which the family lived on Spring Hill station, west of Natimuk in Victoria, to cut brush from which to make brooms. They lost their way in the scrub at Nurcoung. It was not until Saturday of the next week that an extensive search, assisted in its last stages by three Aboriginal trackers, miraculously found the children alive. The *Illustrated Australian News* of 24 September 1864 judged that

> the painful account of the loss and subsequent discovery of three children near Horsham, in the Western district, is perhaps the most remarkable in the history of such cases in this colony.

That estimation has been reaffirmed in the many years since. But why was the story of the Duff children especially selected from so many? And in particular, why was the role of the girl, Jane, singled out for celebration?

Two years after the Duffs' rescue, British readers were treated to a verse narrative of *The Australian Babes in the Wood*. This 'True Story. Told in Rhyme for the Young', 'by the author of *Little Jessie* etc' was published in London in 1866 by Griffith & Farran and illustrated by various hands. This was not so much 'a record of a family's hopes and fears' as an homiletic construction of the tale so that it reinforced 'the faith divine'. The author purportedly based his story on incidents that had been reported in the Melbourne *Argus* late in 1864. Three children who lived with their parents in the district of 'the Mallee Scrub' had been missing for '*nine* long days and *eight* weary nights'. The landscape of their trial was abstract and moralised, rather than antipodean or naturalistic. They 'wandered a dreary heath', endured a 'desert atmosphere'. In this wilderness (in fact the Wimmera, not the Mallee) they were without 'a morsel of bread to allay their hunger, or a drop of water (save *once*) to quench their thirst'. This must be the evidence, the author concludes, of 'one of the most amazing acts of Divine preservation which we have had brought under our observation'. Not that it was uncalled for or undeserved: the girl whom the writer calls Jeannie recited 'Gentle Jesus meek and mild' to her brothers every evening.

The poem proper opens with a father telling his 'little children three' of how another 'three sweet children lost themselves/Amid a wilderness/Of yellow broom and bursting flowers'. The author seeks to situate the Australian story that he is about to relate by comparison with familiar European fairytales that are brought to mind by his title (numbers of which, it should be noted, involve children who are stolen or abandoned, rather than lost – 'Hansel and Gretel', 'The Lost Son' and 'The Changeling' among those that the Grimm brothers collected). It is a story in this mode that the writer recalls: 'the pretty babes left in the wood/By their wicked uncle's will'. They never woke again, but there may be better news from the Antipodes, to which now he returns: 'Away across the western main/On far Australia's strand'. We focus on an isolated, cloyingly happy 'home of love'. There, one morning, Frankie and Edwin persuade their mother to let their sister Jeannie accompany them as they go off to pick broom. The girl loves to look on the fair things of nature, but 'mentally/I see another sight'. One fears that heaven is in prospect and that the child has had a premonition of her end. It is indeed not long before 'Their homeward path is lost!' The brothers' 'wild cooeeying cries' bring no response, but Jeannie is undeterred and 'upward turn'd her gaze,/For God, she knew, was there'. A recitation of 'Gentle Jesus' follows.

The children wake in the morning and miss the comforting routines of home, but they are 'still undaunted, full of hope' as 'They trod the endless waste'. This is a setting for spiritual testing. A poisonous snake hisses through the grass, while 'an omen-bird/With black-spread wing' flies overhead. Hopes that a path may have been discovered are dashed. In the second part of the poem a search is mounted, and in the third Aboriginal guides are enlisted. Perfunctorily named 'Dick, Jerry, Fred – three blacks scan/The hidden path'. In the accompanying illustration, one of them looks suspiciously like a Red Indian, with his boomerangs in a quiver. He has no need of the weapons, however, for he and his companions are called upon only to read the trail left by the children. They do so to such effect that the lost ones are recovered. In the poem their father reaches them first. It remains only for the poet to emphasise a conclusion that has already been drawn:

> And still those wand'rers may be seen
> Upon Australia's distant strand,
> A living testament of love,
> A living test our faith to prove
> In God's almighty hand.

There are some unintended ambiguities in these last lines. The Duff children may indeed still be seen because – unlike many lost before and since – they have survived. They are 'living' now, but in addition the poem guesses at how their fame will outlive them. *The Australian Babes in the Wood* was one of the first of many redactions – in prose, verse, in illustrations in various forms and ultimately in film – of the story of the Duff children. It had been preceded by William Stitt Jenkins's poem, *The Lost Children: in Perpetual Remembrance of Jane Duff* (1864), whose title indicated clearly that the girl would be given an emblematic prominence:

> Come let us sing of this fair child heroic,
> And let her name in Austral history glow!

Jane was therefore one of the earlier instances of the type of 'young Australia', prefigured in important respects by Kingsley's account of James Grewer's son, the child who is precious because it bears and stands for a national future as well as for the qualities of a developing Australian type. Therefore, his or her imperilment threatens a loss to a whole people, and not just to her family. The child's story is forced to carry a weight of implication out of proportion to its events. The unprecedented and unrepeated religious outpourings, the discernment of the finger of providence or even 'God's almighty hand' in the salvation of the Duff children, is the counterpart – more traditionally expressed – of a secular anxiety aroused by their disappearance, and the subsequent intense relief that their being found alive occasioned. The Christian significance so relentlessly imposed on the children now seems exaggerated. As Robert Holden commented in 'Lost, Stolen or Strayed' (*Voices*, Autumn 1991), 'their salvation virtually becomes a resurrection experience'. In its own time this may have betokened something more like surprise at the providential happy ending, than the belief that in a land such as Australia rescue of this kind was very often likely to occur.

The Duff children quickly became a favourite subject for illustrators. For example, they posed for studio photographs that re-enacted their ordeal. The artist Nicolas Chevalier depicted 'The Lost Children' for the *Illustrated Australian News* of 24 September 1864, and with the caption 'Lost in the Bush' for the *Illustrated Melbourne Post* two days before. In the latter illustration, little Jane selflessly places her cloak over the sleeping brothers. *The Australian Babes in the Wood* had four illustrators: Hugh Cameron, J. McWhirter, G. Hay and J. Lawson. S. T. Gill had drawn 'The Duff Children (August 20, 1864)' in *The Australian Sketchbook* for that year. He depicted their father on horseback lifting his hands and presumably about to fall into prayer with relief. The children are on the ground before him, two of them asleep. The blacks are relegated to the distance. William Strutt, who had returned to England two years earlier, was nevertheless captivated by the story. His earliest sketch of 'The Little Wanderers' dates from 1865. He was to have much more to draw and write of them.

In O. F. Timms's novel, *Station Dangerous: or, The Settlers in Central Australia, a Tale Founded on Facts* (1866), the children are renamed Ames, but essential moments in what is supposedly their story are carefully preserved. Thus they are lost while gathering broom. Jane takes off her dress to cover her little brother William. Rescue comes just in time.

Sophia Tandy's *The Children in the Scrub: a Story of Tasmania* (1878) transposes the setting of the incident and rechristens the children Edward, Janey and Tommy Mullings. They are lost while gathering sticks and eventually found five days later by an elder brother. In this colony, there were, of course, no black trackers to be had. At the rescue of their children, the parents are converted to Christianity. Tandy's book was published by the Religious Tract Society. Capitalising on the religious emphasis that the tale had nearly from the first been given, Tandy ensured that the Duffs' story became the property of proselytisers. What, however, had the first newspaper reports and the subsequent accounts in the illustrated magazines made of these events?

On 3 September 1864, a fortnight after the recovery of the children, the *Geelong Advertiser* proclaimed that

> the story of the 'lost children', of the Spring Hill station, their wanderings and sufferings, and subsequent restoration to their friends, has been read by every one, and will by many be remembered to the last day of life.

It was reported that on the down train from Melbourne the previous afternoon, a group of gentlemen fell into conversation on 'the heroic conduct of Jane Duff'. Therefore it was resolved 'to give something more substantial to the little maiden than simply praise'. Accordingly a memorial fund to commemorate 'her self-denying and self-sacrificing love' was established and by Monday evening £62 had been raised. The author of *The Australian Babes in the Wood* reports the amount (at a later date) as £226, money dedicated to providing for all the children 'a better education than their parents were able to afford'. Thus the heroics of the Duffs became the opportunity for charitable condescension. The solicitude for Jane in particular is harder to explain unless perhaps one guesses that an aspect of the feverish relief at her preservation was the allaying of sexual anxiety at what might have befallen her, that is, satisfaction at how her chastity had also survived the ordeal. Even after her struggles in the wilderness, Jane emerged an intact young Australian maiden.

Fuller accounts of what happened to the children, such as the *Illustrated Australian News* printed, made less of an exception of the girl. Chevalier's drawing 'The Lost Children' shows Jane cautioning the excited black tracker who, with his fellows, has burst into the clearing where the children are. She is enjoining him to be quiet, because her two brothers are still asleep. The lengthy written account that accompanied the illustration revealed that the three children lived in a hut on the home station of the squatter Dugald Smith, near Horsham in the Wimmera District of Victoria. On Friday 14 August their mother sent them to cut broom. They did not return. The father began a search on horseback, soon assisted by other men from the station. That day and the next brought no result. By Sunday 30 men were out 'but no traces were seen of the children'. A systematic search by a line of men turned up no clues, until one Mr Alexander Wilson found and followed tracks for nearly twenty kilometres the next day. But by Thursday night that trace of Isaac, Jane and Frank had been obliterated by rain. The father would not give up and sought the help of Aborigines, although he had to travel some distance to near modern day Kaniva to the north to find them and it was Friday night before they could reach the scene.

On Saturday morning Wilson, Duff, his stepson Keena, and three unnamed Aborigines 'recommenced the task of following the children's tracks'. The trackers found where they had spent the previous night from the evidence of 'a little pillow of broom on which their weary heads had rested'. The magazine gives in detail the blacks' reading of the tracks, for instance of how one child had carried another for a considerable way. Then, an hour before sunset, they found the three children sleeping in a clump of trees. The writer assumes that the rescue was just in time, though without giving his warrant for that: 'It is probable the little ones would never have travelled from this last resting place, unless discovered on this night'. Woken, the oldest said 'father', the youngest, reproachfully, 'father, why didn't you come before?', but the girl – of whose 'Gentle Jesuses' so much would later be made – 'seemed utterly powerless and could not speak'. Jane's turn to be spoken for would soon come.

The writer now attempts to fill in the blank period of the children's stay, from the accounts that they themselves gave. Their socks having been stolen by wild cats, they slept with their shoes on. It may have been on the fourth day that

> they came to a hill, which they thought was near their own home, and they again gathered some broom to take with them; but after carrying it for some time, and finding they were deceived, they threw it away.

The children claimed to have had no food at all, and water but once. No sceptical eye is turned on that assertion. Meanwhile, their job well done, 'the blacks were rewarded for their valuable help, without which the poor children must have perished; one squatter gave them five pounds, and the father gave them ten pounds'. There was a moral left to be drawn:

> Seldom has a tale been told, which relates so much patient suffering as these little children underwent. Seldom has brotherly or sisterly affection been so beautifully illustrated.

Jane's doffing her dress is the instance in mind in this tribute, whose language may hint at, but refrains from making explicit, a Christian interpretation of the Duff children's story.

The most significant detail to be omitted in this account concerns the parentage of the children. The father of two of them, Isaac and Jane, was in fact the deceased Joseph Cooper. After his death, the widow married a man named Duff, himself a widower, who worked as a shepherd on Spring Hill station. Frank Duff was the child of this second marriage. The three loving siblings, whose story would become legendary, were the product of a family history fractured by the deaths of parents, and as such of a kind common enough in the colonial period.

There is a curious footnote to the tale of the recovery of the children. One of the Aboriginal trackers achieved another, and less anonymous kind of fame than contemporary reports had afforded him. This was Dick-a-Dick. When the Duffs went missing he was one of the three Aborigines brought to search for them. Dick-a-Dick, or King Richard, was also among a number of Aboriginal cricketers who played regularly in the Western District of Victoria. Early in 1866, he was a member of a team that travelled as far as Sydney. There, at an athletics meeting, Dick-a-Dick threw a cricket ball 114 yards, 'the best recorded by any Aborigine', according to D. J. Mulvaney's *Cricket Walkabout. The Australian Aboriginal Cricketers on Tour 1867–8* (1967). The team was back in Sydney, destitute, in May 1866, and Dick-a-Dick was seriously ill. Yet in the following February, he embarked with the Aboriginal cricket team which was the first from Australia to tour England. Between 25 May and 17 October, it played 47 matches, of which Dick-a-Dick missed only two. His batting form was moderate, but he excelled at the ancillary entertainments which the team staged to raise funds. In particular, he was adept at dodging cricket balls thrown at him from close range, aided only by a parrying shield and wooden club. That club is still in the Lord's cricket curio museum, but – as Mulvaney relates – Dick-a-Dick 'vanished back into his tribal bushland, the area in which he had located the lost Duff children in 1864'. He was last sighted at a race meeting on Mount Elgin station in 1884. At that time, Isaac and Jane Duff, thanks to Dick-a-Dick and his companions, still had almost half a century to live.

The Duff children's story became an obsession of William Strutt. Born in Devon in 1825, he was the son of a cleric and amateur painter, grandson of an author and antiquary. Strutt began work as an illustrator, but so strained his eyes that a long, recuperative sea voyage was recommended. On 5 July 1850 he reached Melbourne on the *Culloden*. Shortly afterwards, he began work as an artist for the *Australian Illustrated Magazine*. Apart from a brief trial of life in New Zealand, Strutt lived in the colony that became Victoria (and whose ceremonial separation from

New South Wales he painted). He had gone back to Britain in 1862. His most famous painting was of a natural disaster endemic in south-eastern Australia – a bushfire. This was the catastrophic event that he captioned 'Black Thursday, 6 Feb. 1851'. Strutt had success back in England, exhibiting at the Royal Academy from 1865 until 1893. The first of his paintings to be hung there was a scene of the antipodean life that he had left behind and of events of which he had no first hand knowledge (although he may have seen Chevalier's illustrations). Strutt's 'The Little Wanderers, or The Lost Track' announced his decades-long preoccupation with the Duff children.

In the late 1950s, the National Gallery of Australia acquired Strutt's preliminary sketches for the painting as part of the Rex Nan Kivell collection. In 1967 it purchased the manuscript of Strutt's narrative of the lost children and the drawings to accompany it. Strutt evidently began the book in 1876, then set it aside for a long while, only completing the task in 1901. This work, *Cooey: or, The Trackers of Glenferry* was sold to a magazine in 1906 but was never published there. Eventually, in 1989, the National Gallery printed its own edition of this long forgotten, profusely illustrated text.

In his preface to the book, by-lined from Tunbridge Wells in May 1901, Strutt claimed that what he would relate was, 'in the main, a true story'. There are two objects of praise in what will follow, first 'the endurance of the lost children ... and their devotion to one another', second the 'not less extraordinary ... sagacity and intelligence shown by the Australian Aborigines'. Yet there was a plangent undertone to the second remark. Strutt subscribed to the theory, analysed by Russell McGregor in *Imagined Destinies* (1997), that the Aborigines were a doomed race. In fact such reckoning was under challenge by the time that Strutt wrote this of them:

> Much is it to be regretted that these poor Aborigines, in many ways so keen and clever, should soon become only a memory in the land of their ancestors, notwithstanding all the benevolent efforts made to save their race from extinction.

The comments show a well-meaning, if perverse desire to write a threnody, to dignify the Aborigines because Strutt assumed (as had many commentators before him) that as a race they would soon cease to be. To borrow a term deployed by Anne McLintock in *Imperial Leather* (1995), her study subtitled 'Race, Gender and Sexuality in the Colonial Contest', for Strutt and others the Aborigines occupied an 'anachronistic space'. That is they were 'prehistoric, atavistic and irrational, inherently out of place in the historical time of modernity'.

An introduction follows the preface in which Strutt contends that while children lost in the city are invariably soon found, 'with children lost in the backwoods of some of our Colonies, it was a different matter indeed'. The result, 'not unfrequently, means death by starvation'. The Duff case, on which he will concentrate, was 'fortunately exceptional'. Their story begins – not as if it was once upon a time – but with a specific designation of the season and the year. It is a spring morning in 1863 (a year earlier than the events on which the story is based, which looks like a minor mistake). The three children are renamed Roderick, Bella and David, the youngest of them 'a ruddy little fellow and every inch a Caledonian'. Whether that provenance makes him more prone to become lost in the bush, or more likely to survive, is not clear.

The children become lost because of their hurry to get home, thus they get 'into an unused track which in reality was no road at all'. They cooee, but receive no human reply; only the song of the white cockatoo is to be heard, and then 'the rollicking peals of the laughing jackass', as if in mockery of their plight. For the bush will not provide for them:

> There was nothing for them to eat; indeed there are few countries naturally so destitute of anything edible growing in a wild state as Australia; yet it is a land which, with very little effort on the part of man, can be made as it were to flow with milk and honey.

Why the effort has not been made by 'man' in Australia, and whether it ever will be, is not discussed. Strutt is anyway more interested in the dangers of the land to his little wanderers. In one of the peculiar interpolations in his tale, the children come upon a brown snake that is attempting to squeeze an eagle to death. The bush children are not disconcerted by the peculiar behaviour of the local fauna. Roderick kills the snake and frees the bird, so that Bella sighs 'Oh, could we but fly like the eagle we should see our home'.

Shortly afterwards they lie down to rest. That is the occasion for Strutt to remind us of the piety which will see these children (if not all others in a similar plight) to safety. They sleep 'with the beautiful childlike trust in the promise of help which they had ever been taught to cherish in a loving Saviour'. That flourish done, Strutt sets to work to fill in the characteristic blank spaces in the story of the lost children, that is, those between the time they go missing and their discovery. 'Native companions' lead them to water. But Strutt believes that his British readers deserve incidents as well as local colour. Therefore he provides another bizarre insertion: the children steal upon a group of Aborigines who are dancing a corroboree. Bella's reaction is immediate. She cannot stand them. The author mildly reproves the child, for she 'little thought that some of these very blacks would be ultimately the means of their rescue'. But not yet: the children depart, undetected.

Thereafter their movements are desultory and faltering. Strutt tries to inject some excitement, from which the children might have wished to have been spared, by raising the possibility that a dingo could have scented, and then attacked them, had one been around. One was not. A key scene in the narrative of the Duffs that had long since congealed into legend comes next. Bella wraps little David in her frock. Having recounted this, Strutt cannot help himself: 'Brave, loving, Bella, this deed of unselfish love and sisterly affection shall never be forgotten!' In a way, he has been proved correct, though his own belated literary contribution had little to do with it.

Strutt turns now from the wanderers who have fallen asleep, perhaps for the last time, to the action which is being taken to find them. Their father has reproved his wife for not looking for the children earlier. The reproach makes scant apparent difference because 'she found comfort through her strong simple faith in God'. Meanwhile the gentry rallies. The man who manages the station for 'the worthy Squatter', Mr Dalrymple, turns up, together with 'Old Tom (a trusty servant)'. Their ranks are complemented by 'Mr Macrae the beau ideal of a Squatter of the old school'. It is this paladin who detects the clue of the scattered broom. Notwithstanding his bush skills, the blacks are called upon to give assistance. This is a scene which Strutt evidently found hard to imagine, distanced as he was by so many decades from Australian life. On hearing of the loss of the children, 'one poor wizened lubra' whines 'poor piccaninny!' Strutt goes on to explain that she was 'Perhaps thinking that Duncan himself was one of her deceased children resuscitated in his present form – for these people believe in the transmigration of souls'. Such superstitions are set apart once Strutt has ventilated, or invented them. That is because, in the present extremity, 'all seemed to depend on the keenness and sagacity of the Children of the Desert'.

Following the signs, the Aborigines interpret them in broken English, thus constructing an account of the errant movement of the children. What they see was 'plain as living words to these marvellously sagacious Sons of Nature's own domain'. And before too long, or before it is too late, first the Aborigines and then Macrae proclaim that the children have been found. Strutt now cuts back to the forlorn homestead of the Duff family, and does so with another interpolation, with reference to that familiar circumstance of an adult worker dying of thirst in the bush, so regularly pictured in magazine illustrations and imagined in verse and prose. Thus it is that

William Strutt 1825–1915
'Found, Mr. Duncan, Roderick, Bella and David', c. 1876
Pencil and wash drawing
15 × 19.2 cm
National Library of Australia

> the general impression of gloom was not lessened by a piece of news just then reported in the papers of a neighbouring Colony, stating that an unfortunate man who had lost himself in the bush had lain down with starting eyes and swollen tongue, just able to scratch his name on his tin pannikin, and had there died, parched with thirst, famished and starved.

The news is prudently kept from Mrs Duncan, but not from the readers, many of whom would have recognised another generic portrait of the fatal possibilities of life outback.

But the Duff children have avoided that fate. Strutt briskly wraps up his version of their story. The boys soon forget their troubles. Bella, it seems, will always be reminded of how she surmounted hers: 'Her self-denying love for her younger brother was on every tongue, and a handsome present from her numerous admirers was her reward'. Posterity's less tangible reward has been the memorialising of Jane Duff, but it is not with her name that Strutt ends. Considerately, and in farewell, he gives his last illustration to the three Aboriginal trackers, whom he calls Nimrod, Corungiam and Minight.

It was Jane Duff, however, who came to dominate the interpretation of the story that she shared with her brothers. What were descried as her Christian fortitude and self-sacrificing love were soon seen as qualities that had triumphed over the implacable hostility of the natural environment of Australia. Her brothers were reduced to bit players. The Aborigines who helped to find the children were granted an important subsidiary role in the story, although for Strutt theirs was one of the last heroic acts of a dying race. Providentially, an emblem of young Australia had survived one of the most common and terrible trials of bush life in this country. That so much was made of her survival is a sign of the deep and ultimately unassuageable anxiety concerning the fate of the youngest generation in the land. It was an anxiety, in Jane's case, that may have had a sexual undertone as well. More broadly, it spoke of a deep insecurity about the present and an intense fear of the future, for all that these responses were sometimes muffled in the rhetoric of an idealistic proto-nationalism, and of an obliged, conventional Christian piety.

In this century, the meaning of the story of the Duff children has been steadily secularised, although the episode has been kept alive in many mediums as an edifying example of fortitude and courage in adversity. As Robert Holden has shown, the Duffs featured in various school readers, from M. A. Pitt's *Australian Second Book* (1868) to the *Victorian Readers' Fourth Book* in 1930. Six decades later they returned in Pat Edwards's 'Lost in the Bush' (1989), which was also part of a reading scheme for schools. In 1973 the Duffs' story was made into a film intended for school children. This was *Lost in the Bush*, directed by Peter Dodds and filmed on location near Horsham with local citizens participating in the search-party scenes. While it had travelled far from the time of its origins, the main elements of the tale survived more or less intact. No other narrative of children lost in the bush has been so tenaciously maintained in Australia.

On Friday 22 January 1932, the *Horsham Times* gave front page coverage to the death of Mrs G. Turnbull (formerly Jane Duff) under the heading 'Bush Heroine Passes'. She had long been ill, but it was 'her indomitable will and courage, so characteristic of the Wimmera folk and of Australia in particular, that kept her spirit aflame in days of much darkness and suffering'. The news of her death (on 20 January) 'awoke the echoes of a dim past to the surviving pioneers of Horsham'. Jane had been one of them. Born near the Wimmera River in Horsham on 7 January 1857, she had confided to the 'Women's Interest' columnist of the *Horsham Times* that this region 'will always do me, and I never want to leave it'. That wish was emphatically granted.

Jane Duff's grave in Horsham

The newspaper included a verse 'Tribute' by J. M. H., which spoke of one 'Born to the Wimmera's smiling plains' and concluded:

> The story's ne'er too often told
>   Of hunger, pain and thirst
> Endured by one with courage bold
>   Who thought of others first.
> And tho', alas, the heroine dies
>   Who lived that we might gain,
> For ever 'neath our southern skies
>   Her valour will remain.

In its prose tribute, the *Horsham Times* judged that 'Her name will go down in Australia's eventful history as the heroine in the Australian version of the nursery story (though in this instance a real life episode) "Babes in the Wood"'. Under that heading, the Duffs' story was retold, but with details that the child Jane had not provided for contemporary accounts.

The three of them survived, she recalled, by eating quandong berries and licking dew from leaves. 'Forget I never can. Wasn't it wonderful we were saved!' A photograph accompanies the story, of an elderly Mrs Turnbull looking wistfully at the lilac dress, still preserved, that she had worn during her ordeal. Other mementoes had been kept by the family: a Bible, inscribed to Jane Cooper, from the children of Tasmania, and a marble statue of Jane and her brothers, sent to them by an anonymous Londoner. Mrs Turnbull was survived by six of her eleven children, and by her brother Isaac, then living at Nhill.

Noting that a subscription for a memorial had been conducted as long ago as 1905, the newspaper felt that 'The period is opportune now for the public of Horsham and district, the Wimmera, the Commonwealth and admirers overseas to make a tangible recognition of Australia's heroine'. And, at last, this was done. A granite memorial (to Jane alone) was erected in 1935 and is now incorporated in the Jane Duff Highway Park, on the road between Natimuk and Goroke. Its legend runs 'In Memory of Jane Duff who succored [sic] her brothers Isaac and Frank while lost in the bush near this spot'. Two kilometres back along the road to Natimuk, a replica of the family's hut has been erected. In 1943 a headstone was placed over Jane Duff's grave in the Horsham cemetery. On it she is described simply as 'Bush Heroine' and goes by her childhood, not her married name. Her husband's remains lie under a low mound of earth, marked by no headstone. A few paces away is a neglected and unfenced grave, with the barely legible headstone of Jane Duff's father, Joseph Cooper.

Alfred Boulter

By the time that the *Illustrated Melbourne Post* related his story, in its issue of 27 September 1866, Alfred Boulter had been safe for more than three months. The narrative of 'Extraordinary Sufferings of an Infant' ran around the borders of a large illustration by William Calvert, from 'a photograph by Frith'. Clad in tartan, the pictured child sits with a twig in his mouth, pensively waiting to find out how long or how truly lost he will be. The magazine's report explains that this infant of two years and four months had strayed from his father's cottage on the afternoon of Monday 18 June. He was discovered at 11 a.m. the next Wednesday. What were the circumstances?

First, young Alfred was a typical Australian lost child, in that he was born of poor, rural workers. In Alfred's case he lived eight kilometres from New Norfolk, in Tasmania. This is a hop-growing area north of Hobart, 30 kilometres up the Derwent River. The search for 'the unfortunate child' was promptly begun by the local police. There were, of course, no black trackers at hand. Throughout Tuesday the bush was scoured without result. Next morning, though, the child was found alive. The interval during which he was lost was relatively short, but as the writer remarks:

> What made the preservation of his life the more extraordinary was [that] the weather was intensely cold, and the nights were more severe than had ever previously been known in Tasmania. The salmon ponds were frozen over enough to bear the weight of a man.

'Alfred Boulter'
Illustrated Melbourne Post, 27 September 1866 (Samuel Calvert)
La Trobe Picture Collection, State Library of Victoria

Thus it appeared that nature collaborated in the intensification of a lost infant's ordeal. No worse weather had ever been reported in which to be lost. Alfred Boulter accordingly suffered frost-bitten feet, 'but they recovered with the timely application of spirits'. The 'sympathy' excited by 'this miraculous preservation' led to the Boulter family receiving 'some handsome presents from their more wealthy neighbours'.

The *Illustrated Melbourne Post* gave the apt, wintry, Tasmanian inflections to the lost child's story. Otherwise the narrative had little to distinguish it from others where the outcome was happy rather than sorrowful. More immediate reporting of this incident, in the Hobart *Mercury*, was altogether distinctive, in particular in the context it thought appropriate to supply as background for the child's disappearance. On Friday 20 June the paper announced: 'Lost Child Found'. The correspondent gave an account of events upon which the Melbourne magazine would substantially draw. 'The lost child of John Boulter has, we may say, most miraculously escaped the death which was thought to be inevitable'. His exposure to two nights of bitter cold, while scantily clad, is noted. Like some other lost children, Alfred had not strayed far, being found only a couple of kilometres from home. Bread moistened with tea revived him, and he 'knew his father instantly'. The correspondent turned next to praise of 'the inhabitants generally of the neighbourhood', before concentrating on the deeds of the gentry. He singles out Mr Richard Thompson of the Union Inn, the police officer Superintendent Evendon and Dr Moore who happened to be 'humanely riding down' when the child was located. The lost child thus becomes the occasion for social notes which confirm the *noblesse* of the propertied classes of the Derwent Valley.

That would be an over-interpretation of the blandness of this account, were it not for what had been printed in the *Mercury* the day before, on 19 June. Under the heading 'New Norfolk' (and as part of the newspaper's regular regional notes) the correspondent observed that 'the weather in this neighbourhood has indeed been unprecedentedly cold. Hoar frost has remained on the shady side of the hills all the day long.' Yet there was 'sadder news than this'. Rather as an afterthought, the writer mentions the loss of the poor little child 'named Boulter, whose father works for Mr York, at Sorell Creek'. Alfred Boulter (although without a given name here, as is his father) had 'wandered away yesterday afternoon into the bush, and by this time has undoubtedly perished'. That certainty had not prevented 'a diligent search'. Even as he writes (on the Tuesday evening) 'the bellman is parading the township and soliciting volunteers to meet tomorrow morning to renew the search'. As we know, that search would save the child.

The essential curiosity of the report is what follows, in an insouciant juxtaposition. The correspondent cuts to the news of the last two Thursday evenings at the Public Reading Room in New Norfolk. Most recently Mr Frederick Sharland, son of W. S. Sharland esq., Member of the House of Assembly, 'entertained a highly intelligent audience with selections from Tennyson'. Following him was Mr William Shoobridge, who 'made his first attempt to entertain an audience from "Leaves from the book of nature"'. The author hopes that such exercises as this might call forth 'the latent talent of young men ... thereby preparing them for future and more exalted usefulness'. Presumably that might include riding out in search of the strayed children of the rural poor, thus incidentally to gain more practical experience in reading the book of nature.

The *Mercury* column sharply contrasts the varied prospects of native youths. While the battler's child is forlorn, impoverished, at grave risk of never growing out of infancy, the sons of the gentry are mounted and schooled in Tennyson. They are physically and culturally prepared for a future whose prosperity depends, in part, on the labours of the likes of the Boulters, father and son. Thus there was a practical as well as a humane purpose to finding the lad alive. Almost certainly by accident, the *Mercury* reveals a class element in the classic form of the lost child story in Australia.

The deference of the correspondent to the esquires who joined in the search for the Boulter boy, of ill-omened name, is the counterpart of that pathetic gratitude shown by shepherds and other rural workers for their kindly bosses' assistance in numerous lost child narratives of the colonial period. For example, in his final version of the saga of the Duff children, *Cooey: or, the Trackers of Glenferry*, William Strutt applauded Mr Macrae as a 'beau ideal of the Squatter of the old school', one who devotes himself to the discovery of the three lost children of his station hand Andrew Duncan (Strutt having changed the family names). In 1901, when he wrote this prose complement to the many illustrations which he had made of the ordeal of the Duff children, Strutt evidently could still call to mind the episode of Alfred Boulter. Appeasing their hunger with grass, the lost children of his story perhaps had heard:

> that a very young child, lost for several days in the Tasmanian bush, was kept alive by doing this and, when discovered, was found so employed and apparently not much the worse for its long fast.

In fact the young Boulter had gone missing two years after the Duff children.

The complex interfusion of lost child stories, the passage which they make across genre boundaries so that their source seems a legendary one in common, is exemplified here. Strutt's narrative interspersed his illustrations from the 1860s with an empurpled moralising tale that would have seen in the new century, had he found a publisher. The Duff children were his primary inspiration, but he saw no need to exclude other and similar stories, such as that of Alfred Boulter. Rather Strutt took pleasure in the factual reinforcement that the Tasmanian boy's travails gave to a narrative that was lodged uncertainly between fairytale and documentary. At the same time its ideological basis was clear. The Duffs (or Duncans as Strutt calls them), Alfred Boulter and many more lost children were passive victims, reliant for rescue on others. There is a ghostly trace of political desire here, a sense in which the lost child stories had a cryptic, economic component, further that they reinforced class stratifications, and the scarcely questioned habits of deference and dependence that they inculcated.

There is a dreadful postscript to the story of young Alfred Boulter. On Sunday 29 June 1997, another man named Shoobridge, also from a land-owning family in the Derwent Valley (they came from a property called Cleveland, near Ouse), murdered his four children as they slept. He was the self-styled poet Peter Shoobridge, whose daughters Rebecca (eighteen), Anna (fourteen), Sara (twelve) and Georgia (ten) were staying with him for an access weekend at his house, Southernfield, near Cambridge, east of Hobart. After cutting the children's throats, Shoobridge wrote notes to friends and family to explain himself. Detective Sergeant Tony Bennett said that some of the letters spoke of 'a cruel world' in which to bring up children. On 1 July, under the headline 'Why I Did It' (the previous day's had been 'In Cold Blood'), the Hobart *Mercury* quoted from one of the letters, addressed to Wendy (his estranged wife), and the world. Shoobridge wrote that

> because of deep, very deep graphic images from the past, present, future, I did not want our girls to face the hardships, tests, rigours, trickery, risks, uncertainties, fears, anxieties of wrong choices legacies, left behind responsibilities, problems, pressures.

And he added: 'I urge every young person to think deeply before bringing children into this world such responsibilities such commitment such pressure'. Yet in the preface to his volume of verse, *A Bush Wedding*, Shoobridge's dedication had been to 'my ever-caring and supportive wife, and four beautiful daughters who provide all the beauty a human being could wish to have'.

After he had finished writing the letters, or those that had not been completed earlier, Shoobridge drove into Cambridge to post them. Stained in blood, they began to turn up at various addresses on the next morning, Monday 30 June. That task completed, Shoobridge returned to his home. There he took an axe and cut off his offending right hand. When police arrived in response to a 000 emergency call made at 6.51 a.m. on the Sunday morning, the hand was found on the chopping block outside his furniture-making workshop. By the time that police reached Shoobridge's property, he had shot himself. As another Shoobridge, one who may have been a distant ancestor probably rode out to search for Alfred Boulter, who was ultimately rescued, so Peter Shoobridge had perhaps sought to 'save' his children in a different and terrible way. The late twentieth century in Australia would see expressed in literature and in such acts as this, a desire that a next generation should either not come into being, or have the lives of its young people shockingly and violently terminated.

A Monument at Daylesford

On 16 September 1867, a central Victorian newspaper, the *Daylesford Mercury*, reported the clearing away of a 'great' mystery. The remains of three boys, lost as long before as Sunday 30 June, had been found 'about a mile and a half from Wheeler's saw mills on Musk Creek, and about three miles from Specimen-hill, where they were last seen alive'. Had they only known, the boys were desperately close to salvation, being but 200 metres from the hut of a splitter named McKay, and the same distance 'from a road in daily use by splitters and men engaged in carting wood to the saw mills'. Two bodies were found inside a hollow tree, in which the children had evidently sought shelter. The bones of a third were scattered about. The writer speculates that the children were 'tired and exhausted'. Moreover they had gone missing in midwinter, in 'bitter cold', so that they 'lay down and slept the sleep that knows no waking'. On their disappearance the efforts of the residents of the town, assisted by police under Superintendent Smith and black trackers (one at least of whom was given a name – Jemmy), had been unsuccessful. Nor did a government reward bring a breakthrough.

A detailed and gruesome account of how the boys came to be discovered follows, one that showed no interest in sparing the feelings of the bereaved parents, or in missing the opportunity to titillate readers. McKay, the splitter, went out with his dog to fetch a bucket of water from Fern Creek. He met a neighbour, Charles Stewart, with whom he chatted for a while before they parted. The dog was busy elsewhere. Observing that the animal had something in its mouth, McKay found 'a boot with part of a child's foot in it'. He guessed that the bodies of the three lost children must be nearby and recalled Stewart to help him search for them. This was unavailing, but at nightfall the dog brought a human skull to the hut. Darkness and heavy rain prevented any action until the following morning, when a search party was formed. Uncooperatively, the dog refused to leave the hut. Bones and clothes were, however, soon discovered, then the two bodies in the tree. Of the remains of the third, the writer conjectures that when 'the knee joint, locks of hair, ribs and pieces of broken bone were found', this surely indicated 'that they had been gnawed by dogs'.

The missing boys, now found at last, were William and Thomas Graham and Alfred Herbert Burman. The younger Graham's and Burman's bodies were in the tree. Their 'position' and 'general appearance' inclined the reporter to judge that 'their spirits passed away peacefully and gently while in sleep'. They are pictured for readers (in a fashion which would have recalled illustrations of the Duff children, who were found alive three years before), 'lying closely cuddled together, as if the children had by the warmth afforded each other endeavoured to ward off the bitter wintry cold'. Yet this account of a peaceful end, which intends to be reassuring, soon unsettles itself. The third boy had probably also been in the tree, 'but had been dragged thence by dogs and devoured'. The newspaper story veers between conventional consolation: death as a welcome sleep, and the recounting of horrors, whose purpose can hardly be an injunction to children to be more careful when wandering off into the bush in search of wild goats (as apparently the three boys had been).

As the bodies were placed in coffins that had been brought out from the town, the extent of their deterioration became clear. The hand of the elder boy

> was white, plump, and apparently undecomposed; but the whole of his features were gone, and nothing remained but a ghostly skeleton outline, with the lower jaw defaced and fallen. The face of the younger boy was, however, in a state of preservation, but perfectly black. The members of both bodies were much attenuated. The trunks, however, were swollen with gas, and corruption was claiming them for its own.

This is material which would be too sensational for any present-day newspaper to print, for it seems pruriently to dwell on the horrible aspect of the corpses. At the least the report presumes a greater familiarity with dead bodies on the part of readers of the 1860s than can be taken for granted among those now. The cliché of death as sleep is shockingly disestablished by the figure, and the consequences, of a triumphant 'corruption'. After the inquest, which was held at the Farmer's Arms Hotel, the cause of death was plainly agreed and stated: 'they died from exposure and want'. One might conjecture that the apparent relish with which gruesome details are recounted was in part intended as an antidote to the pious outpourings with which the salvation of the Duff children had been greeted.

The funeral followed the next day, attracting 'the most numerous assemblage that has ever congregated in that town on such an occasion'. After a funeral procession that had passed along Vincent, Howe and

'Finding the Remains of the Daylesford Children'
Illustrated Melbourne Post, 26 October 1867 (Samuel Calvert)
La Trobe Picture Collection, State Library of Victoria

Raglan Streets, one thousand people came to the cemetery. The Reverend Main from the Scotch Church read the 90th Psalm ('Lord, thou hast been our dwelling place in all generations'), the fifteenth chapter of 1 Corinthians (Paul's account and interpretation of the resurrection of Christ), and then finished with the seventh chapter of Revelations, which ends 'and God shall wipe away all tears from their eyes'. At the closing of the service, the mourners filed by the single, open grave, 'taking a farewell look in their resting place of the little ones, whose wanderings had formed so prominent a part in the public mind for the past eleven weeks'. The borough council agreed to collect subscriptions for a fund 'having for its object the erection of a monument to the children and enclosing the grave in the Daylesford Cemetery' (as the *Daylesford Mercury* noted on 26 September). That monument still stands in Daylesford, mute testimony to lost children who – unlike the Duffs – did not providentially survive their ordeal of exposure in the bush.

The *Illustrated Australian News* of September 1867 and the *Illustrated Melbourne Post* of 27 September 1867 both reprinted the *Daylesford Mercury* story in full, although the latter did so without acknowledgement. A month later, each of these magazines followed the story up, in particular with drawings of the scene in which the bodies were found in the tree. In the *Post* illustration of 26 October, by Samuel Calvert, 'Finding the Remains of the Daylesford Children', a lone searcher starts back from the hollow tree in the centre of the picture in which human forms can be glimpsed. Behind is a forest of tall straight trees, sentinel, funereal, stern. Yet the decorum of this illustration, which is in its way a commemoration as well, is disrupted by another which occupies the top half of this broadsheet page of the *Illustrated Melbourne Post*. This represents a 'Massacre of Missionaries in the Fiji Islands'. The accompanying story explains how recent and vigorous attempts by missionaries from the Australian colonies 'to Christianise the savage aborigines of the Fiji group of islands have been temporarily checked by the massacre of a party of eight'. That is what the picture shows. The story enticingly adds what the artist refrains from depicting: 'horrible to relate – there is strong evidence to support the belief that cannibalism was subsequently resorted to by the savage murderers'.

Taking their cue, design and arrangement of contents from the *Illustrated London News* (which had been established in 1842), the *Post*, *Sketcher, Australian News* and other illustrated magazines in the colonies in the second half of the nineteenth century treated heterogeneous, often sensational episodes from around the world with a semblance of scientific disinterest. Their focus was frequently ethnographic. Strange people and customs were literally pictured, and were regularly juxtaposed. The Fijian massacre and the deaths of the lost children in Victoria were alike in being typical and symptomatic dangers of those places. As the missionary massacre catered to what the audience thought it knew of Fiji, so the lost child narrative is a defining and familiar element for Australian readers of their larger, proto-national story, as it was for those overseas readers who took the *Australian News* each month. Anne McLintock's notion of 'panoptical time', adumbrated in *Imperial Leather*, is also relevant here. By panoptical time she means 'the image of global history consumed – at a glance – in a single spectacle from a point of privileged invisibility'. That is the kind of vantage given to readers of the *Illustrated London News* (published from the centre of an empire that encompassed Australia and Fiji) and its antipodean imitators.

The *Illustrated Australian News* had a varied coverage of the loss of the Daylesford children in its October issue. It featured an engraving by W. H. Harrison from a photograph of the scene, presumably taken later, rather than at the time of the discovery of the bodies. More circumstantially accurate than Calvert's, this picture showed four men around the tree, which looms gloomily above them, in the centre of the composition. The magazine had also followed up the story, to the extent of printing a communication from the splitter, Michael McKay, on how the children's bodies were found.

In more detail this elaborates the story already related of what the dog brought back to the hut: the boot with a foot inside it was muddy, leading McKay to search by what he calls the Fern Tree Creek. After the first, fruitless efforts with Stewart, McKay was about to leave for the town to tell the police when the dog turned up with part of a skull. Presumably to remove it from harm's and the dog's way, McKay put the skull in a bucket which he hung on his clothesline. Next morning, with the assistance of more neighbours, a search was begun again in a north-easterly direction from the head of the creek. Shortly afterwards more bones were found. McKay never speculates on whether his dog too was guilty, along with others, of eating the remains of the elder Graham boy. After Ninian Bryan found the two bodies in the tree, word was sent to Daylesford to summon the police. There ends McKay's deposition, 'a true statement connected with the finding of the children'.

In the column to its right sits a report of the Cadell expedition to the Torres Strait coast of North Queensland. Not only has its camp been rushed by alligators, with the loss of two horses, but 'a white man with a very white beard reaching to his waist' has been sighted. It is conjectured that he may be the last survivor of the expedition of Ludwig Leichhardt, which left the Darling Downs in 1847. On the far right of the page is an account of the Aboriginal cricket team which is preparing to go to England: 'if the blacks do not succeed in beating English cricketers, they will certainly astonish Britain in their other games, such as throwing the boomerang, spears and cricket ball'. Dick-a-Dick, who had helped to save the Duffs, was one of them. This random collection of news items, respectively familiar, legendary (and probably spurious) and exotic, is a snapshot of a country exploring, and tentatively approving, its own strangeness.

The *Illustrated Australian News* had not altogether done with the Daylesford children. McKay's column was filled and completed by a poem from 'Alice' of Richmond, dated 26 September. This was 'In Memoriam. The Lost Children of Daylesford'. The particulars of their plight are almost altogether erased. Only 'the old hollow tree', with which the poem concludes, is an allusion to the circumstances of their deaths. Interestingly, 'Alice' leaves God out of her poem. She remarks how hard it is 'to lay the little ones/Down for their final rest'; speculates on 'the heart wrung agony' of the stricken parents; imagines the events which led the children to their deaths. If 'they started full of rosy health' on their wanderings, they 'found in sad despair/That they had lost their way'. 'Anxious searchers' passed by, but did not find them 'locked in that last embrace'. Although 'Alice' gestures at the world to come – 'passed in painless sleep/Up to a brighter home' – she quickly turns back to earth to praise the searchers who, 'fruitless efforts past', now gather around a grave. Sentimental on first appearance, and stilted in measure and diction, this 'In Memoriam' nevertheless does not make any easy lapse into religiosity.

Such outbursts had greeted the salvation of the Duff children. The deaths of the Daylesford boys were met more soberly, if perhaps with an excess of realism. No account of perished lost children would ever again be so publicly graphic. The happy story of the Duffs would become better known – retold in many mediums for the next century – but the tragedy of the Daylesford children would seem the more typical and dreaded outcome of such events. It was the grim fate of the little boys that was suggestive for Marcus Clarke when he wrote the story of 'Pretty Dick' soon afterwards. And it was this sad ending that writers following him – like Lawson, Praed and Furphy – found truer to the circumstances of the Australian life that they imagined.

Visitors to Daylesford these days, coming from Melbourne and approaching the town from the south, pass a sign that says only 'Historic Marker 2km'. Then, on the right, comes the Daylesford cemetery, which was established in 1861. It is here that the boys are buried and that their memorial stands. The graveyard plan directs those who might be interested to a single column above the grave of the three children 'Who Wandered From Their Homes at Table Hill on Sunday June 30th 1867'. The rest of the story is tersely related on one panel of the memorial: 'After An Ineffectual Search Their Remains were found by accident in A Hollow Tree near Musk Creek on September 14th 1867 and After a Public Funeral were here Deposited'.

For a long time, that was almost it for the lost boys. William Graham, father of two of them, later went on to strike it lucky, discovering rich leads of gold at Allendale. In 1889 he established scholarships in memory of the lost children for the best boy and girl pupil at the Daylesford State School. Their story was never forgotten, but hardly publicised until it was revived for tourist consumption in the 1980s as part of a Bicentennial community project. Near Connells Gully, to the north-west of the town, the area from which the boys had strayed, is a cairn in the Three Lost Children Memorial Park. From the Daylesford Information Office the curious can obtain a map and accompanying narrative for 'The Three Lost Children Walk', a fifteen kilometre journey that reconstructs – as far as is possible – the route which the boys took. It goes south, skirting the edge of the town, passing through what would have been shallow diggings, before turning east to Specimen Hill and then south-east, across Wombat Creek. Another cairn on the

> **LOST CHILDREN.**
>
> WILLIAM GRAHAM
>
> AGED 6½ YEARS.
>
> THOMAS GRAHAM
>
> AGED 4 YEARS
>
> ALFRED H BURMAN
>
> AGED 5 YEARS.
>
> WHO WANDERED FROM THEIR HOMES

Monument to the lost boys at Daylesford: 'In Memory of the Lost Children. William Graham Aged 6 ½ Years. Thomas Graham Aged 4 Years. Alfred H Burman Aged 5 Years. Who Wandered From Their Homes'

Wheelers Hill–Quines Road (the Historic Marker as it turns out), directs one to the spot, six chains east, where the boys' bodies were found. Not far away, there are still thick stands of timber, of box, peppermint and stringybark, such as those in which the children lost themselves. On the site itself, no hollow tree remains. It has long since been cleared, and in the summer of 1998 was covered by a golden field of grain.

Marcus Clarke's Lost Children

Marcus Clarke's most famous contribution to the literature of the lost child was the story 'Pretty Dick'. It appeared first in the *Colonial Monthly* in April 1869, less than two years after the Daylesford boys had perished. When it was published in the collection *Holiday Peak and Other Tales* in

1873, Clarke had made alterations, notably to the age of Dick Fielding, the lost boy. The *Argus* reviewer in 1869 had reckoned that Pretty Dick was too old at twelve to have suffered such a fate: 'Bush lads of that mature age are generally strapping fellows, who do not easily get lost'. Accordingly, Dick's age was lowered to seven when he made his second fatal entry into fiction.

The story opens with an evocation of summer heat on the plains: 'the Australian sun [has] got up suddenly with a savage swoop', cockatoos scream, kangaroos seek shade back in the scrub and station dogs retreat to the lee of the huts. One of the workers on the station is Richard Fielding, a shepherd, who shares that occupation with Kingsley's James Grewer in *The Recollections of Geoffry Hamlyn*. Fielding's only child is named for its father: the boy and his name are palpable signs of belief in the future. Pretty Dick 'was the merriest little fellow possible, and manly too'. He can chop wood, drive refractory cows to milking, ride. With his parents he lives in the Log Hut on the edge of the plains, where his father is in charge of five thousand sheep. While Dick's mother, who had been a maid in a rector's family in Kent, was 'a little above' the labourer whom she married and with whom she emigrated to Australia:

> they were all three very happy now in their adopted country. They were alone there, these three – Pretty Dick, and mother and father – and no other children came to divide the love that both father and mother had for Pretty Dick.

Those are words that seem to doom the boy. The parents will suffer for their dependence on this only child. That hot morning, Dick ponders his father's inevitable discomfort at work, and seeks to cool himself 'by thinking of the Ranges'. They are invested with terrifying story:

> Had he not heard how men had been lost in that awesome scrub, silent and impenetrable, which swallowed up its victims noiselessly? Had he not heard how shepherds had strayed or slept, and how at night the sheep returned alone, and that search had been in vain, until perhaps some wandering horseman, all by chance, had lighted upon a rusty rag or two, a white skull, and perhaps a tin pannikin, with hopeless scratchings of name and date?

This appears to be the lively and detailed working of an imagination schooled in romance fiction, and much more like that of a twelve than a seven-year-old boy. In particular, the child sketches the end which he may fear for the shepherd, his father, when he is alone in the bush. Deeper into the ranges are to be found the lair of bushrangers, their stolen money 'hidden away behind slags and slabs of rock', and the site where a travelling hawker had his brains beaten out by swagmen to whom he had inadvisedly offered hospitality. Imbued with none of the benignity that Kingsley's errant child had hoped to find, this is a terrain of natural as well as human menace, as Dick knows well:

> What stories had he not heard of wild cattle, of savage bulls, red-eyed, pawing and unapproachable? What hideous tales of snakes, black, cold, and deadly, had not been associated in his mind with that Mountain Land? What a strange, dangerous fascinating, horrible, wonderful place that Mountain Land must be, and how much he would like to explore it.

Explicitly, the beckoning land is a place of potential adventure. Unlike many children who become lost, Pretty Dick does not stray, but sets out deliberately.

Having scorned his mother's caution, 'half in jest, half in earnest', not to get lost, Dick walks down to the creek, tarries there, crosses, and then 'plunge[s] into the bush'. At once his beguilement by the unfamiliar begins:

> There was a subtle perfume about him now; not a sweet, rich perfume like the flowers in the home station garden, but a strange intoxicating smell, evolved from the heat and the water, and the many-coloured heath blossoms.

Entranced, intoxicated by the bush air, he is ready to be lost, as many others had been and would be. In an essay in *Studies in Classic Australian Fiction* (1997), Michael Wilding has contended that the 'sustained passages of natural description', 'the foregrounding of landscape' in 'Pretty Dick', serve to delay the pains of its ending. Thus 'the "study" of bush scenery' which Francis Adams noted in his commentary on the story in an article about Clarke, 'is the acceptable subject that displaces the unacceptable death of the child'. Wilding adds that 'the more scenic description the later the inevitable facing of the end', which is, of course, the discovery of Pretty Dick's body. Like the three Daylesford boys two years before, whose story would have been familiar to Clarke when he wrote 'Pretty Dick', he fails to survive his ordeal. In 'Pretty Dick' Clarke emphasises the allure of the bush, its fatal role in the straying of Pretty Dick, the ways in which it abets the child's inclinations. This is also to vindicate Clarke's conviction, notably expressed in his famous pages on the 'weird melancholy' of the Australian landscape (a notion first formulated in 1875 and revised in a preface to the poems of Adam Lindsay Gordon in the following year), that this is a country replete with possibilities for Romantic art. Insofar as the scenery of the story is 'foregrounded', it is with a more polemical purpose than Adams, or Wilding discerned.

Nor is Wilding attuned to how – in this story as in other narratives of the subject – the landscape is symbolic as much as scenic. The creek to be crossed, the allure of the bush, the trespass that seems unavoidable, are all vital constituents of the structure of the lost child story, whatever its outcome. Disobedience takes Dick across the creek, but more important is his desire, inchoate as it must be, for sensations and experiences which have thus far been beyond or forbidden him. At the margin of the settled and the unknown, Dick stands at a point where his society is most vulnerable. But he dares to go on: this step begins a rite of passage from which the youthful venturer will not return.

The child sleeps, and when he wakes 'the place [seems] quite changed'. It is late in the day: 'there was sunlight where no sunlight had been before, and shadow where there had been sunlight'. Resolved to follow a way home that he thinks he knows well, Dick sets off 'sturdily', but it is not long before 'a terrible fear came into the child's heart. He is "Lost"!' Almost at once, Pretty Dick suffers from a predictable misfortune of the country. The overseer, Mr Gaunt, rides by, but while he may have heard Dick's cooee, he does not respond. The cry was 'mistaken, perhaps, for the scream of a parrot, the cry of some native bear, or strange bird, but in his present strait, the departure of the presence of something human, felt like a desertion'. There is 'no mother to help him'. The mocking answer to his cry for help comes from 'a hideous black crow'. Dick is oppressed with all that he may have lost forever:

> No more mother's kisses, no more father's caresses, no more songs, no more pleasures, no more flowers, no more sunshine, no more love – nothing but grim Death, waiting remorselessly in the iron solitude of the hills.

Dick's prayers to God to take him home go unanswered.

That imaginative facility which had led Dick towards the ranges now torments him. The form that it takes is expressionistic, summoning terrors for which before he had only had names. Thus the boy

> was dimly conscious that any moment some strange beast – some impossible monster, enormous and irresistible, might rise up out of the gloom of the gullies and fall upon him, – that the whole horror of the bush was about to take some tangible shape and appear silently from behind the awful rocks which shut out all safety and succour.

What might seem 'the nameless terror of a solitude' is, for Dick, 'a silence teeming with monsters'. No author of the colonial period in Australia went further than Clarke in investigating and envisaging the mental torments of the lost child. This was, in an important sense, part of his Romantic programme for Australian literature: the sensibility of the child is given the central place which might have been accorded it in the poetry of Blake or Wordsworth. Typically, Australian authors abandon lost children to their fate. Once strayed they are ignored until found, alive or dead. The narrative interest is in those outcomes, and the lessons to be drawn from them, as well as the search which went before. Far from deferring the pains of the child's death, Clarke's story intensifies them by its depiction of Dick's dreadful fancies, by filling a blank space in the conventional form of the lost child narrative. Dick conjures up a monster of whose lineaments literature and folklore have given him foreknowledge: 'He pictured the shapeless Bunyip lifting its shining sides heavily from the bottomless blackness of some lagoon in the shadow of the hills'. Feeling suffocated, Dick screams to break the silence, only to hear his cry echoed 'by strange voices never heard before'.

He staggers on, his strength deserting him. Falling asleep, he dreams of the 'happy boy' he once had been. At dawn, Dick has an uncanny experience. If the text offered any more than the most perfunctory religious consolation, it would be as if his soul had already left his body. Seemingly detached from that body, 'up in the pure cool sky, looking down upon a little figure that lay on an open space among the heather', Dick is attempting to release himself from earthly pains. Yet that relief is temporary. The discovery that the figure whom he has been observing is himself is a 'terrible shock, and he was Lost again'. There is a further shock for the reader. Dick has been given an eerie premonition of how his body will appear when it is found. In another disturbing and literary sense, he has seen himself in the form of the lost child which conventional narratives of this business construct: abandoned, possibly beyond help, voiceless, lying as if or in fact asleep. In all these respects he is far from the hyperactively, tormentedly imaginative creature whom Clarke depicts.

Heat, hunger, terror, loneliness wear Dick down. Clarke suggests that the child loses the sense of who or where he was: 'He had almost forgotten, indeed, that there was such a boy as Pretty Dick. He seemed to have lived years in the bush alone'. Moreover, this is a condition that has come to feel natural to him. He has given up the wish to get away. Before much more time passes, and while 'crooning a little song', Dick goes down 'into the Shadow'. On the sixth day of the search his body is found, head on arm as if asleep, 'in the long grass at the bottom of a gully in the ranges'. Clarke looks here to be pitting his bush lore against Kingsley's. It was, after all, asserted in *The Recollections of Geoffry Hamlyn* that lost children sought out and therefore would be found, in whatever condition, in high places. One also suspects the last words of 'Pretty Dick' of irreverence, if not of outright insolence: 'God has taken him home'. The gesture at comfort is self-mocking. No easy closure for such tragic accounts of lost children is plausible, or kind.

Clarke's two versions of 'Pretty Dick' appeared on either side of the serialisation of his novel *His Natural Life* in the *Australian Journal* from March 1870 to June 1872. Near the heart of this book, in the section of it which is set in the 'natural penitentiary' of Port Arthur, is an episode which has aggrieved Tasmanians ever since, although not to the extent of preventing it from becoming part of the marketing of the convict site for tourism. The incident in question, which however congruent with the cruelties of the place is wholly fictional (as David Young discusses in his study of 'The Evolution of Convict Tourism in Tasmania', *Making Crime Pay*, 1996), concerns the suicide pact of two boys, William Tomkins and Thomas Grove, who are among the three hundred boy prisoners at the convict out-station called Point Puer – Child's Point.

Captain Maurice Frere has been called from Hobart to head an inquiry into the death by flogging of the convict Kirkland. A bank clerk transported for embezzlement, and himself hardly more than a boy, Kirkland was on a charge of insubordination after objecting to the foul language of the commandant, Captain Burgess. Locked up over night with hardened prisoners, Kirkland was sodomised. Trying next morning to escape, he was captured and died of heart failure during the punishment of 500 lashes to which he had been sentenced. Burgess has no cause to fear the outcome of the inquiry, indeed he 'was in high spirits at finding so congenial a soul [Frere] selected for the task of reporting on him'.

Burgess supposes that Frere's wife Sylvia will enjoy a visit to Point Puer, across the bay from the main prison site, in the course of her husband's tour of the settlements, but the moment is ill-chosen. That morning, as all soon learn:

> A refractory little thief called Peter Brown, aged twelve years, had jumped off the high rock and drowned himself in full view of the constables. These 'jumpings off' had become rather frequent lately, and Burgess was enraged at one happening on this particular day.

Clarke suggests that if Burgess could have brought the child back to life, 'he would have soundly whipped it for its impertinence'. Frere is nonchalant. He knows 'those young devils. They'd do it out of spite'. The child's 'iniquities' are now read out from the punishment book. With a Dickensian explicitness Clarke angrily interpolates: 'Just so! The magnificent system starved and tortured a child of twelve until he killed himself. That was the way of it'. To emphasise the hypocrisy of that 'way', Clarke at once shows us 'a long schoolroom, where such men as Meekin taught how Christ loved little children'. The reverend's name mocks Christ's Beatitudes, as does the proximity to the schoolroom of 'the cells and the constables and the little yard where they gave their "twenty lashes" '. Here, Clarke judges, 'Her Majesty's faithful Commons in Parliament assembled, had done their best to create a Kingdom of Hell'.

It was the young Sylvia Vickers's, as it is now the married Sylvia Frere's fate, to be disquietingly accosted by characters who summon up her past. When some time ago she had seen the convict hero Rufus Dawes again in a garden in Hobart, she was obscurely troubled by memories that she could not retrieve, of his role in saving her life at Macquarie Harbour. At Point Puer, first Tommy and then Billy move her deeply. Tommy wants to know whether his dead friend Cranky Brown looked happy. Having no answer, she kisses him, as he remembers his mother who is still in England used to do. Summoned by Tommy, Billy is kissed in turn. Weeping, Sylvia may be grieving for her lost childhood, or for the children that she has never had, thus intensifying the distress which the innocent supplications of the boys have caused her. That night, however, Frere almost convinces Sylvia, 'by so many illustrations of the precocious wickedness of juvenile felons', that she has been duped.

The events of the next day prove otherwise. Resolved that death cannot hurt more than a whipping, and remembering Sylvia's plea that the Lord should have pity on these two fatherless children, Billy and Tommy jump off the cliff to their deaths. Burgess is outraged at the news. Sylvia despairs that they have been driven to suicide. Meekin 'piously' notes that the children have condemned their young souls 'to everlasting fire'. Clarke makes sure that he, as author, has the last word. An inquest into the boys' deaths is held, but nothing comes of it. Why should anyone have bothered? 'The prisons of London were full of such Tommys and Billys'.

The episode in *His Natural Life* that treats of the end of two lost children is exceptional in this literature, in that it argues an uncontestable case (in its own terms) for a clear, indictable, institutional cause for the loss, through suicide, of the boys. Literally, 'the system' is to blame. Whether Clarke's writing reflects his growing political and social radicalism (as Wilding contends) or its mainly rhetorical imposture, the lost children of Australian legend have never before been so trenchantly co-opted for the criticism of injustice, even if it is for the soliciting of a pathos whose particular cause has since safely passed into history.

The Case of Clara Crosbie

On Christmas Day 1885, the following advertisement appeared on the second page of the *Sydney Morning Herald*:

AUSTRALIAN WAXWORKS
opposite the cathedral
CLARA CROSBIE, aged 12 years,
will explain to the public how she was lost in the Bush
and lived for
THREE WEEKS WITHOUT FOOD

New Scriptural Group
'CHRIST BLESSING THE LITTLE CHILDREN'
Curios from the late Soudan War

Admission 1s; Children 6d Open from 10 a.m. till 10 p.m.

The New South Wales contingent had returned from the Sudan on 23 June 1885 after an adventure in which scant military glory had been won and because of the commitment to an imperialist cause, that the *Bulletin* had devastatingly ridiculed. But the home-grown story took top billing: the narrative of the lost child was an essential Australian adventure, the Sudan had been the sideshow.

On 12 May 1885, the then eleven-year-old Clara Crosbie went missing from her home at Cockatoo Creek, some twenty kilometres from the township of Lilydale. This territory is now part of the outer eastern suburbs of Melbourne, which are reclaimed from or set among pockets of bush in the foothills of the Dandenong Ranges. If Clara Crosbie had disappeared a century later, there would at once have been fears of a grisly, modern, especially urban crime – abduction. Psychologists, not Aboriginal trackers, would have been enlisted to find her. But Clara Crosbie had not been kidnapped. Instead she had wandered away, evidently of her own volition, to become another incarnation of that stock figure of Australian colonial culture, the child lost in the bush. Yet while there have been better known stories about the lost child, both before the Crosbie episode and since, there are few as curiously and contradictorily reported, or so conflicting in their evidence and implications. The stock elements of other, earlier narratives here become ambiguous.

The newspaper and magazine reports of the child's 23-day travail in the bush are replete with emotional embellishments, but uncertain (or maybe too sure) of facts. The girl's surname is variously spelled Crosbie and Crosby, sometimes both ways within the same account. Her father is not mentioned at all, and the mother appears very briefly in one report, without reference to any of her reactions. The reasons for Clara having become lost are never clearly established. Eventually the child was discovered and succoured by strangers. There is no agreement on how, or in what condition, she came to be saved.

The Melbourne *Argus* of 4 June 1885 related how Clara Crosby (as the paper spells her) had been found near Cockatoo Creek the previous day, about five kilometres from where she had gone missing. In fact she was located on 2 June. This is the newspaper's narrative of her discovery:

> Two men, named Cowan and Smith, who were engaged on a road contract, while looking for a strayed horse, heard a faint coo-ee, and soon after discovered the child in an emaciated condition and unable to stand. She was without clothing, and her limbs and body were badly lacerated. She could not have lived another day.

The men wrapped her in a coat, gave her warm food, and 'removed her to the Woori Yallock Hotel'. Medical assistance was sought from Lilydale. The child was said to be doing well, 'and is able to talk'. Thus she could tell her rescuers that 'she lived on gum leaves and water the whole of the time'.

There, abruptly, the *Argus* report ends. Its apparent matter-of-factness is incongruous, for strange inferences are encouraged throughout. For example, Clara's discovery seems to have been the merest, happy chance. If her faint, plaintive cooee had not been heard (as presumably it had not been before), then Clara Crosby would have perished: 'She could not have lived another day'. Yet that suggests a providential intervention, masked as chance. And how had she survived, through to the first days of winter? The road builders or menders found her naked and emaciated. Her diet is so meagre as to be incredible – or fanciful. The gum leaves and water might have sustained a marsupial, but hardly a child. Yet no doubt is vented as to this crucial aspect of Clara's trial. Apparently she was at no risk from predators. With rare exceptions (the boy fatally bitten by a snake in Rosa Praed's novel *Mrs Tregaskiss*, 1895, is one of them) the child lost in the Australian bush is in no danger from its wild life. Indeed he or she – at least in fiction – is more likely to find the fauna to be companionable.

At the end of the month, on 29 June, *The Australasian Sketcher* gave an extensive written and pictorial coverage of the recovery of Clara Crosbie (as she appears in the caption to the half page illustration, Crosby as she features in the text). The *Sketcher* reports the date of her discovery as 2 June, at the start of a more circumstantial and suggestive account than the *Argus* had provided. A brisk observation – 'the child's story is a record of remarkable endurance', which is intended to excite readers' admiration – is followed by the contention, more extreme than in the newspaper, that 'during the whole time she was in the bush she was without food'.

But what ensues is more surprising. Evidently Clara had only recently arrived from Melbourne and was staying at the house of 'Mr Haines, a selector, about a mile and a half from where her mother lived with a man named Leech'. The implication here, snide as it may be, is of maternal delinquency. Moreover, the *Sketcher* maintains that Clara had started out at 10 a.m. on Tuesday 12 May 'to see her mother, after promising Mrs Haines that she would return the same evening'. Not until two days later did Leech inquire after the child. Presumably Mrs Haines had not checked on her whereabouts either. A search was then instigated, but it will pay first to examine some of the odd and opposing implications of the account so far.

On the one hand, it enfolds Clara within a fairytale, and naturalises for Australian readers stories such as those the Brothers Grimm collected near the beginning of the nineteenth century. Here the child sets out on a woodland journey from the home of a surrogate mother to that of her real mother and a stepfather figure (whether either is wicked or not is uncertain). As in fairytale so in the newspaper: causal explanation is elided. We are not, apparently, to learn how Clara came to be staying with the Haines, near but not with her mother. Nor do we learn why it was that she strayed, never to reach her destination – if, indeed, she ever really set out for it.

On the other hand, an ironic edge has come into the narrative. It is not, purportedly, the blandishments of the bush that have enticed Clara away from the right path – as it was for Marcus Clarke's 'Pretty Dick' for example. Rather, the insinuation of parental absence and neglect raises the issue of human blame. This may have been a neglected child, emotionally bereft before she was literally lost. The re-readings of the lost child topos at the start of the new century by Henry Lawson in a poem and a story both titled 'The Babies in the Bush', and Joseph Furphy in his novel *Such is Life* (1903), are anticipated in the way that the Crosbie story hints at the dereliction of the parents, rather than the susceptibilities of the child to the charms of the bush. For instance, the father in Lawson's story, Walter Head, was an experienced bushman better equipped than anyone to have found his lost children, Wallie and Maggie. His absence from home was not, as his wife believed, because he was in Sydney on business, but rather 'on a howling spree … in an out-of-the-way shanty in the Bush'.

Once deemed lost, Clara Crosbie became the object of a police hunt. An essential element in many of the earlier lost child narratives was present in her story: 'the services of two black trackers [were] obtained, but their efforts, as well as those of a number of residents in the district, proved fruitless'. 'Eventually the search was given up', but the *Sketcher* adds a tantalising detail: 'it being concluded that the girl had either perished or found her way to Melbourne, where she had some friends amongst members of the Salvation Army'. Of this distracting hint – again suggesting a degree of family neglect – we hear no more. Something like first-hand testimony concerning Clara's early steps is given next. The view that she had set off for Melbourne rather than her mother 'was strengthened by the statement of the landlord of the Junction Hotel, on the Woori Yallock Creek, that he had seen the girl pass his house on the morning she left Mrs Haines's'. Because the hotel was on the road between the Haines and Leech houses, 'the police naturally arrived at the conclusion that she could not have been lost afterwards'. But would she not still have been a missing person who needed to be found? The magazine says nothing about this, except to add that the publican must have been mistaken. On the evidence given by the girl more than three weeks later, 'she never came near the hotel, but, on the contrary, took the opposite direction'.

The effect of these conflicting testaments is to make more puzzling the question of how and where Clara Crosbie spent her 'lost' time. The *Sketcher* relies on what, presumably, is the child's account. Although taking the track from Haines's, she must have become disoriented, for she called at a house 'for the purpose of inquiring her way'. No one was home. A man called Wilson came there only at night. The girl left 'in a direction opposite to that from which she had approached', became tired, sat down to rest, fell asleep, and then awoke to find that it was nearly dark. Is it fatigue that put her to sleep, or a kind of spell of the bush? Just because of its determined plainness, the narrative ventilates the fanciful as well as the prosaic possibility. Certainly Clara is soon to experience one of the crucial stages of fictional narratives of the lost child. Wandering away from the track, she reached Cockatoo Creek. Initially she could not reach the far bank. Therefore she lay down and slept till daylight. In the morning she endeavoured to cross on a sapling which broke. Nearly drowned, she scrambled out on the other side.

Creek crossing – leaving the familiar for the unknown – is the liminal moment in some of the most influential Australian stories of lost children. Thus in Kingsley's *The Recollections of Geoffry Hamlyn* the eight-year-old son of the shepherd James Grewer dreams of a land across the river, 'fancying he could see other children far up in the vistas beckoning him to cross and play in that merry land of shifting lights and shadows'. The sinister suggestion is that he is being lured by some morbid power to join those 'other children', long lost. Disobeying his mother, the 'strange, wild little bush child' crosses the river. It may be his uncivilised nature which makes him yield to temptation. Clarke's Pretty Dick also trespassed. Once across the creek, Dick 'plunged into the bush'. In each case, the crossing was fatal in fiction, as it nearly was in fact for Clara Crosbie. Neither author proffered religious consolation for his readers.

The blank stage of Clara's ordeal begins once she has attained the other bank of the stream. Her sufferings are much more protracted than those endured by the lost boys in Kingsley's and Clarke's fictions. Clara 'sat down in a hollow tree about 40 yards from the creek, where she afterwards remained until found'. That is, she stayed put for 22 days. Was she exhausted, or resigned to a fate which she would often have heard and seen depicted? Would movement have led to her death or to a swifter rescue? Did questions of these kinds occur to the girl herself? The passivity which overcomes children lost in both factual and fictitious narratives (to make a distinction that is hard to sustain because of their intense mutual influence) usually dooms them. In effect, these stories most often end once the initial temptation of the bush has been accepted, the dare taken. Only the aftermath, joyful or melancholy, remains. Typically the lost child narrative is limited in incident; it is minatory, yet indulgent of fancy; terrifyingly familiar without providing any compensatory reassurance. To be 'lost' is to be in stasis. The child's whereabouts are uncertain. Once the crossing or straying into unknown territory has occurred, travel is minimal. The search is conducted while the lost one is out of sight, off the stage, immobilised. The discovery (whether or not it is abetted by Aboriginal trackers) is either too late or – as in Clara Crosbie's case – just in time. The most significant burden of such narratives, as they congeal into legend and mingle the kinds of representation afforded by fiction, journalism, and the illustrative arts, may be what can be inferred, grandiosely perhaps, about Australia, the bush, the interaction of Aborigines and European Australians decades after first contact, and the essence of family relations at the margin of settlement.

Given up as lost, Clara – says the *Sketcher* – chewed some bark at first, 'but finding it bitter thought it was poisonous'. Thereafter she said that 'she had nothing whatever to eat the whole time'. Dependent, it appears, on the girl's testimony, the *Sketcher* has to explain this unlikely medical phenomenon. The course chosen is sentimentally pious, hence discordant with the obscurities and troubling intimations of her background: 'She was afraid the first three nights, but not afterwards, as she said that she prayed to God to preserve her life, and thanked Him for the beautiful clear water'. If this is what Clara said, she was a well-tutored little girl. Her bush lore did not serve so well, for her cooees went unheeded, despite the evidence – from the report of guns – that there was human activity not far from her.

At last one of her cries availed. Mr Cowan, a road contractor, and Mr Smith, 'a resident of Melbourne', were in search of a strayed horse

'Finding Clara Crosbie After Three Weeks Lost in the Bush'
The Australasian Sketcher, 29 June 1885
La Trobe Picture Collection, State Library of Victoria

(as the *Argus* had also written). When Smith stopped to examine a dead native cat, Cowan 'heard the feeble cooee'. The child was discovered. No mention was made of her nakedness. Instead, this version of the story precipitately ends with Clara being taken first to Cowan's camp, then to Mr Claxton's hotel, 'where she received every attention, and was soon rapidly improving'. For the sake of a happy ending, all the uncertainties and improbabilities of the story were foreclosed.

The large engraving in the same number of the magazine varies the tale told in the text three pages earlier. The dominant figure in this composition is a solitary horseman, glancing to his right where he descries the lost child. Arms imploringly spread, she is barefoot, but clothed in a white dress. Behind her is the hollow tree in which supposedly she had sheltered. The ambiguously worded caption informs us that this is an illustration of 'Finding Clara Crosbie After Three Weeks Lost in the Bush'. By emphasising the rescuer, the artist appears to be concerned more with the search than its object, but the waif at least has been found.

No new information was supplied by the *Illustrated Australian News* in its report of 8 July. But the story had an hortatory opening, applauding as it did 'An extraordinary instance of the physical powers of endurance possessed by some colonial children'. Was one to infer from such remarks, and from fictional narratives going back to Kingsley, that the 'coming race' in Australia was easily led by and into the harsh outback, but hard to extinguish? The explanation of Clara Crosby's disappearance in the *Illustrated Australian News* was vaguer than that of its rival, the *Sketcher*, and contradicted some details in the longer account. Thus 'she strayed from her parents' home and wandered into the bush, where she was believed to be lost'. Clara could be assumed to be dead, for the weather was 'unusually severe' and there 'seemed no possible means by which the child might hope to obtain either food or shelter'. The *Illustrated Australian News* tells us first of the rescue – she was 'accidentally discovered by a man travelling through the bush on horseback' (no names, one man – exactly, and confusingly, this confirms the visual image used in the *Sketcher* whose prose report had specified two). Unable to retrace her steps, crying out to no purpose, the child crept into a hollow tree for shelter. There she subsisted on 'berries and ground nuts', which is an improvement on the water and gum leaf diet of which the *Argus* had written or the water alone to which the *Sketcher* said that Clara had been reduced. No reference is made to the girl's clothes, but she is 'greatly emaciated' and 'must have succumbed shortly to the hardships she endured, but for the arrival of assistance'. This account leaves Clara Crosbie further afield than Claxton's hotel, placing her in the Melbourne Hospital, where she is 'in a fair way to complete recovery'.

But what, in truth, had she endured? How had she survived? There are puzzling lacunae in the girl's story. In fact the Crosbie narrative is so imbued with hints of perfidy and with contradictions that it is not only suspect in itself, but calls into question the cherished if shocking form of the classic tales of children lost in the Australian bush. There is no religious consolation after the fact, no celebration of communal, Christian values of self-sacrifice and love which followed the discovery – alive – of the three Duff children in August 1864. Nor was there occasion for the horrified reaction to the death of the three boys at Daylesford in 1867. Two of the Daylesford children's bodies were lodged in a hollow tree, which evidently did not provide them with the shelter that Clara Crosbie would later enjoy. The *Illustrated Melbourne Post* of 27 September 1867 described them in death as 'lying closely cuddled together, as if the children had by the warmth afforded by each other endeavoured to ward off the bitter winter cold'. The accompanying prose account, it will be recalled, was frightfully detailed. Yet the engraving by Samuel Calvert excised all these horrors. The hollow tree is in the centre of his composition. The bodies are scarcely discernible. The single searcher starts back from them, more in surprise than in shock. The illustration is elegiac. It functions as a benediction. Literally it has prepared the ground, limned the scene, for those who came later and who may – as in the circumstances of Clara Crosbie – have happier outcomes to describe than was the case for the Daylesford children.

In Clara's case, either her prayers, or the efficient operation of the conventions of fairytale, ensured salvation. She is returned to civilisation (if not necessarily to her family) as the Duffs had been. Like them, she enjoyed a public celebrity, although her after-life in public memory has been much briefer and we know nothing of what became of Clara Crosbie when her stint on stage at the Australian Waxworks in Sydney concluded. What her story anticipates is a darker re-reading of the lost child narrative. The errancy of the Duffs and the Daylesford boys had been innocent. Their loss was nobody's fault, or nobody's but their own. Inescapably, a reading of the Crosbie narrative hints that some rupture in the girl's family contributed to her becoming lost. Indeed, one might infer that she was abandoned before ever she became lost in the bush. Of such abandonments, the twentieth-century Australian literature of the lost child would have much, obsessively, to say.

Frederick McCubbin's Images of the Lost Child

The two most famous visual representations of the lost child in Australia usually hang side by side in the National Gallery of Victoria. They are Frederick McCubbin's paintings entitled 'Lost' (1886) (formerly known as 'The Lost Child') and 'Lost' (1907), where a girl and a boy respectively await what may befall them in the bush. The loss and recovery of Clara Crosbie (as depicted and related in illustrated magazines and newspapers in 1885 and in W. S. Stacey's 'Found' in *Australian Pictures Drawn in Pen and Pencil*, 1886), as well as fond childhood memories of pantomimes of 'The Babes in the Wood', may have encouraged McCubbin to undertake his series of paintings of children, lost and found, in the Australian bush. The first of them was 'Lost' (1886), one of the famous narrative works of his Box Hill period, a time when he also painted 'The Pioneers', 'Down on His Luck' and 'Bush Burial'. McCubbin's intention, according to Ann Galbally in *Frederick McCubbin* (1981), was 'to interpret a field of subject matter which was redolent [sic] with local and nostalgic associations'. 'Lost' (1886) portrayed 'an old colonial nightmare', one – we might add – that usually had to wait for daylight for its terrible, or joyful conclusion.

The Crosbie story was fresh in McCubbin's mind – the canvas was begun not long after her discovery – but the painting also signals a concerted, determined, programmatic effort to draw on Australian materials for pictorial narratives, thus to emulate and to naturalise here the genre of narrative painting so popular in Victorian England. Andrew MacKenzie has persuasively argued in *Frederick McCubbin 1855–1917: 'The Proff' and his art* (1990) that 'Lost' (1886) is itself part of a narrative sequence. The work, he writes, 'was painted in the bush at Box Hill, in the same year and very likely in the same vicinity as ... "Gathering Mistletoes"'. It is probable that McCubbin's sister Mary Anne (Dolly), although already 29 in 1886, was the model for the girl in each painting. In 'Gathering Mistletoes', a child is engaged in the innocent activity that had led so many others astray. The Duff children, for instance, had wandered off to gather broom. Lawson's Wallie and Maggie Head would go in search of flowers. In McCubbin's painting 'Lost' (1886), MacKenzie contends, it is 'as if the young girl has wandered into the bush in search of mistletoe and finds herself lost'. The mistletoe, slung over her shoulder in the first painting, is placed in her apron in the second. The effect of this suggestion of cause is to confirm with what gentle seductiveness the Australian bush lures children from home. In 'Lost' (1886), the girl blends in with the soft, blue-green thicket from which she may never emerge. One small patch of sky appears at the top left of the canvas. The child's way, once she moves again, will be into obscurity, and legend. The critic in *Table Talk* on 26 April 1889 enthused that McCubbin's picture was 'thoroughly Australian in spirit, and yet so poetic, that it is a veritable bush idyll – a sad one, it is true – but one that is to be seen every day'. Not every day, fortunately, but McCubbin had again shown his genius for exalting the commonplaces of the colonial era into the visual clichés by which so many urban Australians in the next century would comprehend the Australian bush.

McCubbin returned to the motif of the lost child a few years later, this time providing what appeared to be a happy ending, although one that may be more ambiguous than on first sight. The painting 'Found' (1892) foregrounded a weathered, bearded bushman, who is gently cradling a small child. The *Argus* of 20 April 1893 described the scene: 'a poor little derelict who has wandered away into the bush, and has now fallen to the ground exhausted by hunger and fatigue, has been found by one of the search party'. The girl seems to be asleep, but of course she may be dead. This is the terrible point of crisis and uncertainty at so many of the moments of discovery in lost child narratives. Dead, the child will often be said to appear as if asleep, not that such a euphemism would for long be a comfort to her family. McCubbin shows an acute awareness of the literary (and historical) tradition by leaving the resolution of the matter of the girl's fate unclear in this case. The child has been found and will come awake if that is what viewers of the painting wish to believe. In a pungent,

Frederick McCubbin 1855–1917 Australia
'Lost' 1886
Oil on canvas
115.8 × 73.7 cm
Felton Bequest, 1940
National Gallery of Victoria, Melbourne

Frederick McCubbin 1855–1917 Australia
'Lost' 1907
Oil on canvas
198.7 × 134.6 cm
Felton Bequest, 1941
National Gallery of Victoria, Melbourne

circumstantial irony, the painting 'Found' has since been lost. It is as though Australian culture adjudicated that bleak rather than happy outcomes for the lost child story were the more appropriate.

In her study of McCubbin, Galbally argues that while living in isolation at Mt Macedon, to the north of Melbourne (in a house grandiosely named Fontainebleau) in the early years of this century, McCubbin attempted 'to engage in a new, much more intense relationship with the bush. The key to this was to be the child's vision and the whole world of the childish imagination'. This makes McCubbin a belated convert to Romanticism. What is confused in the analysis that follows, is the difference between retrieving the supposed purity of childhood vision, and the depiction of the products of children's fancy (or of adults' on their behalf). Galbally argues next that:

> For almost the first time the well-worn literary theme of children lost and alone in the bush did not necessarily have a tragic outcome. Now the bush itself could be seen as a place of enchantment for a child, a huge playground where Australian bush creatures, their habits and settings, could entertain and aid the lost child.

This ignores the ways in which that figure had already been depicted. Just because the bush seemed 'a place of enchantment', children left home, crossed creeks, plunged into it, often never to return alive. For little James Grewer, for example, in Kingsley's *The Recollections of Geoffry Hamlyn*, the bush that enticed him was 'a merry land of shifting lights and shadows'.

Thus it was not 'a new attitude' to the bush that appears – as Galbally suggests – in Australian fairy stories published in the 1890s. James Grewer was consoled by a native bear bereft of its mother, 40 years before Ethel Pedley's Dot fell in with a kangaroo that was in search of its joey. This is not to dispute the coincidence of what is loosely described as 'McCubbin's search for an imagery of innocence and fantasy' and the development of 'an indigenous Australian children's literature'. Galbally discusses McCubbin's paintings 'What the Little Girl Saw in the Bush' and 'Childhood Fancies': in both of them children gaze at a point where fairies have materialised among and from the trees. In each painting, Galbally contends, McCubbin is representing 'an opening into a secret world, a world whose only limits are the limits of childish imagination'. Perhaps, but this is an interpretation that ignores the weight of the tradition of depictions of lost children in Australia. The girl and boy in the two paintings being discussed are precisely on that dangerous threshold where they might choose to leave the known and safe for the fascinations of the unknown and the perilous. McCubbin was as alert as any Australian artist in any medium has ever been to that tradition. In picturing the fairy creatures of the children's fancies, he has made visible, and also more palatable, that nameless force which had for so long attracted children across boundaries, so that they wonder and wander, then become lost. This innocent attraction to the bush can be fatal. That is the darker undertone in the paintings to which Galbally is not attuned.

McCubbin's final version of the lost child has a curious history. According to one of his sons, Louis, the figure group in a painting called 'Motherhood' was painted out by McCubbin, then 'a figure of a boy (Sid) was introduced into the landscape, and thus the first painting of 'Lost' (1907) developed'. The symbolic implications of this erasure of a family group representing motherhood (in fact Mrs McCubbin, seated on a log, with her sons around her) and its replacement by the figure of a lost child might be traced and over-interpreted in a solemn spirit and a biographical cause. More probable is that McCubbin did not like the painting, therefore he wanted to use the canvas again. In any event, as Louis McCubbin continued:

> On the advice of Walter Withers, the old man abandoned this one and reproduced it on another canvas (same size) which is the 'Lost' [1907] now in the Melbourne Gallery. The original 'Lost' was subsequently cut down to a smaller canvas and the figure of the lost boy was painted out.

The symbolism of that excision can also await others' attention. It is known that the model for the boy in the painting was Sidney, another of McCubbin's sons, who had been born in 1896. When the last 'Lost' went on sale, in 1907, McCubbin sought £315 for it. Two decades earlier, 'Lost' (1886) (admittedly a much smaller canvas, less than a third the size of 'Lost' (1907) had been priced at exactly one-sixth of that sum. The artist's, if not necessarily the subject's stocks, were on the rise. (This was nothing to compare with the posthumous valuation of his work. On 17 August 1998, McCubbin's 'Bush Idyll' set a world-record price for an Australian painting when sold at auction for $2 312 500 by Christie's Australia. It depicts a young man and woman, patently not lost in the bush: he plays the pipe while she watches dreamily.) Another of McCubbin's children, Kathleen, attested that the painting 'Lost' (1907) 'depicts the bush at Macedon close to our cottage'. There is a prophetic irony here: Hanging Rock – site of Joan Lindsay's novel about the mysterious disappearance of three school girls and their teacher, *Picnic at Hanging Rock* (1967) – is only a few kilometres away.

Rather than speaking of any person concerned, the title of 'Lost' (1907) distils a terrible human condition. In the painting a seated child, near the front, has his back to the audience. With his left hand he wipes his eyes, brushing away sleep, or tears, or both. He may just have awakened or been conscious for a time of his plight. Determinedly and perversely, Galbally seeks to invent a happy outcome for the boy, even though no rescue is in prospect. Pantheism rather than pathos is what she discerns in the painting. Thus 'the bush itself is an active life-force', while 'we'

> sense the mysterious dynamic of natural forces at work in 'Lost' [1907]: the healing and life-giving potentiality of the sun; the endurance of the great tree trunks and the frailty of the broken saplings which are placed, symbolically one feels, about the bent form of the child.

'We' are not enlightened about the nature of that symbolism. It can, however, be pointed out that to children or adults lost and dying of thirst in the bush 'life-giving potentiality' is not likely to be the way in which they think of the sun.

Galbally not only misreads this painting, she does not comprehend the cultural tradition of which it is a culmination. And this tradition, as has been argued, was one of which McCubbin was acutely aware. Writing in *The Art of Australia* (1970), Robert Hughes expressed his dislike of the painting:

> McCubbin, when it came to human values, was able to be neither oblique nor subtle, and the morasses of late-Victorian English genre [painting?] contain few scenes of more toffee-like bathos than the little boy in McCubbin's 'Lost' [1907].

This is, primarily, an objection to a genre – Victorian narrative painting in the manner of Augustus Egg, W. P. Frith, Robert Martineau and others. Hughes ignores (as the art historian Leigh Astbury, in *City Bushmen* (1985) had not) the essentially *literary* tradition from which McCubbin's painting comes, as well as the careful attention to the Australian bush setting which is the essential element in the stories of that tradition. McCubbin brought the figure of the lost child from the nineteenth to the twentieth century, with most of the hallowed features of scene and circumstance intact. The impulse of his depictions of the lost child was conservative and nostalgic, rather than revisionist. That comprises a great deal of their importance. Unwittingly, but for no reasons that he would have had to regret, McCubbin gave enduring forms to an image upon which more sceptical eyes would be turned in the decades to come.

Fairytales of the 1890s

A vital element of Australian writing of the 1890s, although one that is not usually accommodated within legends of that decade, was the upsurge in literature written for children. Intending to enchant familiar Australian landscapes, to people them with the elves and fairies that had called Europe home, this writing also made use of well-tried local narrative materials, not least stories of lost children. As the expatriate novelist Rosa Praed would tell such tales to English readers, so Australian authors of the same decade told them to their own.

Atha Westbury announced what appeared to be the completion of an ambitious project with her collection entitled *Australian Fairy Tales* (1897). It was as if some substantial body of work had waited to be gathered, rather than its being recently invented. The book was illustrated by A. J. Johnson. In the manner of Praed, and of other adherents to the view that Australia had once been home to the lost race of Lemuria (sadly vanished without any, save fictional, traces), Westbury imagined 'a vast kingdom in the centre of Australia'. Her tales were as often cruel and minatory as comforting. In 'Mothland', for instance, a naughty girl, Lily, who will not own to having broken the family clock, is punished by 'a small native race of people called "Moths"'. It seems from that description that the Moths are alternative indigenes. Of actual Aborigines, Westbury's book has nothing to show.

Deciding to punish Lily for her falsehood, 'a sin we hate and abhor beyond all things', the Moths abduct her and put the changeling, Scarlet Mantle, in her place. The child is not, strictly, 'lost', because her parents are unaware of the substitution. Consequently she is not missed. Taken from her home, miserably fretting in Mothland, Lily suffers some of the first pains of a veritable lost child, before being returned to her former estate, her penance done. It is another *stolen* child who occupies the story 'Nellie', a piece of writing undecided whether to be bleak or mawkish. We begin on a rainy Christmas Eve in Sydney. A girl is 'wearily toiling from street to street', wrapping 'her scanty rags around her wasted body', trying to sell her remaining half dozen boxes of wax matches. Wandering in a daze through streets that seem known to her from long before, Nellie has a vision of her brother Frank, then is led into the chamber of a 'lovely being' who explains that the gems which stud it are formed from 'tears of joy'.

It is time to wake up. Nellie comes to on the doorstep of a grand house. Bending over her is a beautiful woman who finds it 'tiresome that this wretched child should choose my porch, of all places', for its collapse. Nonetheless she takes her inside, this being the Christmas season. Once in the house, the child is troubled by the familiarity of its appointments. It is, of course, the home which she had mysteriously quitted as an infant. Notwithstanding that 'coldness, pride, the vigorous will, that moulds martyrs and devils alike' are strong in the woman, she collapses upon realising that this waif is her own lost daughter. The sentimental, sub-Dickensian conventions under which Westbury is operating (although there are also elements in this tale of an anti-Christmas book that never fully gets written) require that the earthly reunion between mother and daughter should not last long. Nellie is a 'stolen child'. Her brother Frank had pined and died soon after her loss. Their father 'perished at sea'. Why Nellie was stolen, or by whom, is never disclosed, nor are these questions made to feel pertinent to a parable of the softening of a (not unreasonably) hardened heart. Nellie dies: 'the tired spirit entered into rest'. Though the agency and motives of her earlier abduction are not explained (and the degree of the mother's complicity, or responsibility, if any, are not clear), Nellie's fate as an urban child who is kidnapped, rather than lost, foreshadows a crucial transformation of the lost child narrative later in the next century.

Westbury's *Australian Fairy Tales* includes some more recognisable lost child stories, although the first – 'Wonderland' – modulates from the familiar to the fairy. The setting is the Blue Mountains, where a woman is wringing her hands: 'It is the wife of the charcoal-burner, and she calls for her two children, who have wandered away and become lost in this wild region'. Fortunately a mountain goat soon turns up, announcing itself as 'the guardian sprite of this glen, which my race have occupied since the Flood'. He explains that there are two kingdoms on the mountain, of Love and Hate. If Croak and Gloom have her children imprisoned underground, in Hate, she need not worry for long because his powers are stronger than theirs. Indeed the boy and girl are soon released, almost before their trial had time to begin, and before Westbury was put to the difficulty of imagining what forms it might have taken.

The last of the lost child stories in the book, 'The Laughing Jackass', begins in a realistic mode. The cry of the kookaburra, 'the laughing jackass' of the title, mocks a child who has been sobbing underneath the tree where the bird sits. The child has an ill-omened name: 'Poor Berty Wake was lost in the bush – lost utterly'. He had been sent out by his father to hunt up an old roan mare, which had strayed into the bush. In turn the boy discovers that he, too, 'was astray in the trackless waste, with not a single point or landmark to guide him'. But he need not despair. The jackass cannot long restrain itself from breaking into serviceable English. He declares himself to be Jack the Rover, a pet of the Wake family when they lived by the Murray. Remembering the kindness of the boy to him then, the bird speedily arranges for Berty's escape on the back of an emu. When Berty is apprehensive, Jack remarks drolly, 'I thought an Australian could ride anything'. On the way home they find the horse. Berty is reunited with his family. He has been saved, although not in a way that grown-ups can be expected to believe, by the kindly intercession of the creatures of the Australian bush. There is not a moth or fairy in sight or sound this time.

The next year, in 1898, Jessie Whitfield's *The Spirit of the Bush Fire* was published. This was a collection of fairy stories (some of which had appeared before, for instance in the *Sydney Mail*) with 32 illustrations by G. W. Lambert. The title story relates how 'the good little rain-drop elves' foil the villainous incendiarist. The second story introduces mermaids, who live off the coast between Newcastle and Sydney. Lambert happily pictures these indigenes of Australian waters as going bare-breasted. There is, inevitably, a lost child story in Whitfield's book. It is 'Daisy and the Giants', in six parts. Daisy, who is ten, is now an only child, although she 'would remember that once she had a little brother, who disappeared some years ago, and that her mother never spoke of him'. Thus the lost child narrative is, literally, in the family.

Sensible of the dangers of the bush and – one supposes – of her own family tragedy, Daisy's mother enjoins her daughter always to keep to the main road. Unfortunately, the heat of the day tempts Daisy into the cool, green shade of the trees. Whitfield's reproof is sharp – no blaming the parents for her: 'this foolish and naughty little girl did just exactly what she had been told not to do – she left the main road and plunged boldly in among the ferns and trees'. Like many children before her, Daisy has found the bush to be compulsively attractive: 'bright flowers lured her farther and farther in'. But her errancy will not be punished. The travails of a child lost in the Australian bush are soon left behind in this story.

Neither fatigue, nor exposure, nor heat threatens Daisy, who soon finds herself in a different kind of extremity, pursued by a giant who roars 'I smell child ... Child soup is good'. Daisy, of course, escapes the pot, just as Whitfield had spared her the realistic and probable harms of one truly lost in the bush. What the author offers instead is a creepy fantasy of the fate of lost children. Daisy finds herself in company with others, as a toy, or plaything for Tantrums, daughter of a giant called Muncher. Whitfield is describing a monstrously large bad child as the agent of punishment for the disobedient lost little ones. When rescue is eventually afforded, Whitfield moralises:

> after this everyone was most careful, both children and grown-ups, never to stray off the road, and whether the giants starved to death or died of old age I know not, but this much is certain, there are none there now, and of their Castle on the top of the Black Spur not a vestige remains.

The terrors of being a lost child have been made a childish thing, as well as a convoluted injunction to obey one's parents.

Ethel Pedley came out to Australia as a teenager, returned to London to study at the Royal Academy of Music, and then re-established herself in Sydney from 1882 as a teacher of violin and singing. It was she who gave the most ambitious of these treatments of the lost child material that were intended for children. Illustrated by Frank Mahony, *Dot and the Kangaroo* was published in 1899, a year after Pedley's death from cancer. In 1977, a fine animated children's feature was made from Pedley's book. A century before she had written it, the English poet Robert Southey, still in the phase of youthful radicalism in which he dreamed of Pantisocracy and a settlement on the banks of the Susquehanna with Coleridge, and wrote his satirical verses, *Botany Bay Eclogues* (1794), had imagined an antipodean land that he would never see, replete with 'all the perils of a world unknown'. This was a pre-pastoral place with 'wild plains/Unbroken by the plough, undelv'd by hand/Of patient rustic'. Remarkably, Southey next outdid the Creator of Australia's fauna. For in this country, instead of 'lowing herds' and 'the music of the bleating flocks', 'Alone is heard the kangaroo's sad note/Deepening in distance'. While she was more likely to have been influenced by Lewis Carroll's *Alice's Adventures in Wonderland* (1865) than by Southey, Pedley – like the poet laureate to be – gave the kangaroo a voice. She also burdened it with the search for a lost child.

Dot wanders into what she has previously apprehended as the 'cruel wild bush' and becomes lost. However, unlike a small boy from her district whose fate she vaguely, but ominously recollects, Dot does not perish. Instead she is befriended by the animals whom she encounters, who remain as benign as almost all of those whom lost children in literature have come upon before. In particular, she is looked after by a grey female kangaroo. Sympathetic, if sententious, the kangaroo gives Dot 'small, sweet berries' to eat, so that the child is now able to comprehend the speech of the bush creatures. This awakened faculty opens Dot to admonishment by them. Humans like her, she is told, 'know no other way to live than that cruel one of destroying us all'. The platypus grouches about the many books that humans have written concerning him and he looks forward to a time when – ceasing to be creatures new to this Australian world – they will stop writing books altogether. For his native land, opines the platypus, is now a sad place because of the arrival of humans (by which he seems to mean the European rather than the Aboriginal Australians). Once it had been happy.

Thus Pedley re-imagines in *Dot and the Kangaroo* a fall from Edenic complicity between the human and the natural worlds. Sleeping in the hollow of an old watercourse, Dot dreams of a court of animals which at times turns out to be as fractious as that of Chaucer's 'parlement of fowles'. Like some other romance novelists of the 1890s, for example William Moore Ferrar in *Artabanzanus: The Demon of the Great Lake* (1896), 'an allegorical romance of Tasmania', Pedley incorporated satirical material within a dream vision. Dot is arraigned for 'the wrongs we Bush creatures have suffered'. The lost child is invited into harmony with their world which – properly understood – will be a source and place of solace and enlightenment, rather than of despair and a lonely death.

In one possible reading of it, Pedley concludes her story sentimentally, with the reuniting of Dot and her family, the kangaroo and her lost joey. The latter return to the bush, now conceived as a benign place whose creatures can communicate with the humans who stray there. Yet *Dot and the Kangaroo* also retains strong intimations of what has been lost (or of what might so much better have been comprehended) during the century of European habitation of the continent. Thus she darkens a story that is cheerfully dedicated 'to the children of Australia'. Nor did Dot's rescue announce the end of unhappy endings to the stories of lost children. Within a couple of years, Lawson's and Furphy's work would reinstate them more disturbingly than ever before. The fairytales and children's fictions of the 1890s, which have been considered here, provided consolation only on terms that elided the harshness of the lands into which the children had ventured; took them to a bush that never was, somewhere indeed like the 'huge playground' of which Ann Galbally wrote; and there provided fairy or animal protectors for them in roles that adults, and their parents especially, had signally failed to fill.

The Bush Balladists' Turn

The popular press in colonial Australia was notably welcoming of the many amateur poets among its readers, although editors often took their chances to give critical advice to them. The disappearances and discoveries of children prompted various effusions in verse, for instance the 'In Memoriam' for 'The Lost Children of Daylesford' by the Melbourne writer who called herself 'Alice'. Like most such contributors, she preferred to remain pseudonymous. The theme of the lost child also engaged professional authors. It is almost, one feels, as if they were responding to an exercise that readers expected of them, or that was compelled by the distinctive local material that was theirs to use.

Four of the most famous 'bush balladists' (a loose term that covers only a portion of their written work) – Henry Lawson, 'Banjo' Paterson, Will Ogilvie and Barcroft Boake – wrote poems about lost children. Lawson focussed on a specific incident. Paterson's and Ogilvie's works were rather generic and atemporal; they have more of the distinctive ballad qualities of drawing on folk memories and of seeming to belong to an indeterminate past time as they tell respectively of the loss of a boy in a riding accident and of the role of black trackers in searching out those who are fugitive or strayed. Causal explanation is elided in ballad. The generative incident is a given. The business of the poem is to narrate the consequences in a memorable fashion that lets the work become part of a cherished, common store of memory, however doleful are the incidents that it relates. Paterson's 'Lost', Colin Roderick claims, was 'one of his most-quoted ballads'. By contrast with Paterson and Ogilvie, Boake's performance is against this popular grain. 'At Devlin's Siding' is the story of an infanticide. The terrors for the lost child of the century to come are there previewed.

While he was in Brisbane in April 1891, contributing stories and verse to the radical paper *Boomerang*, Henry Lawson wrote 'The Babies of Walloon'. It was published the following month in his mother, Louisa Lawson's magazine *Dawn*. A note to the poem tells us that two little girls, aged six and nine, daughters of a 'lengthsman', that is a railway worker, of Walloon, near Ipswich, were sent on an unspecified errand by their parents. They never returned. Evidently

> Little Kate and Bridget, straying in an autumn afternoon,
> Were attracted by the lilies in the waters of Walloon.

Lawson follows local opinion in supposing that the girls fell into a pond and drowned. Perhaps gratuitously, he further surmises that 'The angels sing in Paradise/Of the younger sister's danger, and the elder's sacrifice', while being decent enough to concede that 'the facts were hidden from us'. The interpretation that the poem proffers hardly mitigates the father's pain, but it may keep alive, as a cautionary tale, 'the legend of the Babies of Walloon'.

'Banjo' Paterson had already written a poem about a different, but typical kind of bush tragedy. 'Lost' was first published in the *Sydney Mail* on 26 February 1887. The single, blunt word of the title could do service for so many circumstances in outback life. An unnamed 'old man' voices his anxiety about the boy Willie, who had ridden out to the Two-Mile on a Reckless filly (which, by the second stanza, becomes a 'vicious' mare): 'He ought to be home', said the old man, 'without there's something amiss'. Intensifying his concern is the fact that, ever since his father died, the boy was 'his mother's idol'. What will she say? And what will become of the only hope for a next generation in this family?

The setting of the poem cuts from the homestead, where the old man leans apprehensively on the sliprail, to the bush, swiftly and terribly to answer the second question:

> Away in the gloomy ranges, at the foot of an ironbark,
> The bonnie, winsome laddie was lying stiff and stark;
> For the Reckless mare had smashed him against a leaning limb,
> And his comely face was battered and his merry eyes were dim.

The horse has sped away 'like fire through the ranges to join the wild mob's ranks' (much as 'the colt from old Regret' would in 'The Man From Snowy River'). This becomes one of those harrowing versions of the lost child story where the body is never found. Paterson's gesture of comfort, his assertion that the boy is gently enfolded within the natural world, 'the wattle blooms above him, and the blue bells blow close by', is no consolation to 'a broken-hearted woman and an old man worn and white'.

The catastrophe is not over. Paterson's poem relates the extinction of this small Australian family. Though pining and fading, the mother 'rode each day to the ranges on her hopeless, weary quest'. In the end the loss, the searching, kill her too. She is found dead, her pale features stamped with 'an angel smile of gladness – she had found her boy at last'. This gilding of horrors is unlikely to appeal to modern tastes. In *Banjo Paterson. Poet by Accident* (1993) Roderick comments on such supposed reactions: '"Hackneyed", says our urban civilisation, knowing nothing of the truth of such bush fatalities. "Sobstuff", says the literary critic'. As indeed she might, but the comment properly invites us to inquire what Paterson meant to do, or thought that he was doing in this poem. Perhaps it was the case that a conventional, decent, but fundamentally

'Tracked!', 1884
Bulletin, 23 December 1884 (Garret & Co. after William McLeod)
Coloured lithograph
54.4 × 43 cm
National Library of Australia

unconsoling conclusion kept in balance the words of comfort that have to be given at the time of a loss that is beyond reckoning. Or maybe he chose not to tease out the more sombre implications of the yarn that he told in verse.

Earlier in the decade, in its Christmas supplement of 23 December 1884, the *Bulletin* ran a dramatic illustration by William McLeod titled 'Tracked!' The scene depicted involves an Aboriginal tracker, whose skills have led him just in time to a child who is still alive and sleeps by a pond, or stream. The Aborigine raises his hat exultantly and calls to other searchers. Evidently his efforts have saved a lost child from death. The somewhat grudging endorsement of black trackers' abilities that had been given 20 years before in the *Illustrated Australian News* now looks less conditional. They had been involved in numerous searches for lost children (and would be again the next year in that for Clara Crosbie), as well as in such notorious pursuits as that of the Kelly Gang in 1880. Will Ogilvie attempts a sympathetic inside portrait in his poem, 'Black Trackers', whose last line returns us to the figure of the lost child.

The poem begins with a brisk apostrophe; seeks similes from the animal world to characterise the Aborigines: 'Swart bloodhounds of the fenceless West,/Black gallopers that lead the Law'. The eyes of hawks are less keen, the dingo is slacker in the chase than are these trackers. Once Aborigines used their skills to hunt food. The hunters of the modern day, 'clothed and horsed and paid in gold', now deploy those skills to hunt men. Thus the trackers lead the white troopers in the pursuit of criminals. Ogilvie is uncertain what to make of the Aborigines' role. If on the one hand there has been an historical advance: from hunter-gatherer to mounted officer of the white law, on the other the trackers' pleasure in their work is atavistic:

> The hate that shaped your father's spears,
>   The wrath that armed some ancient sire,
> The blood-lust of a thousand years
>   Comes back to fan your hearts to fire!

Are the Aborigines really so enraged against those whom they track (who may, after all, be their own people), or is some of that 'wrath' directed against the work they do, against themselves and the white authorities which employ them? Ogilvie's text opens that ambiguity, only to close it off almost at once.

For there is one task that summons no 'blood-lust' from a past age. The poet claims that 'I have seen your passion sleep,/Your hate and lust and anger die'. This occurs when the black trackers are following 'a gentler trail', rather than one which fugitives have made. He has seen them follow, 'through the scrubland wild':

> In sorrow that you scorned to veil,
> The footprints of a lost bush child.

That is, the Aborigines are given a contemporary, common humanity because of their involvement in the master narrative of the search for 'a lost bush child'. In such an endeavour, they are at once more like 'us' and yet – in their preternatural talents as trackers – most like their essential, Aboriginal selves, hence strikingly different from 'us'. This is the promise of healing between the races in Ogilvie's poem which is radically qualified before, belatedly, it is made.

There are two lost child poems in Barcroft Boake's collection, *Where the Dead Men Lie*, which was published posthumously in 1897, with a memoir by A. G. Stephens. 'The Babes in the Bush' appeared for the first time; 'At Devlin's Siding' had been published in the *Bulletin* on 17 December 1892, signed by misprint 'Barcroft H. Boake, N.S.Wales'. The melancholic author had hanged himself with the lash of his stockwhip, in some measure because of his recent disappointment in love, in scrub at Long Bay, Middle Harbour, early in May that year.

The first of the poems, while conventionally titled, reworks stock elements of the lost child material. Two lively, mischievous, ragged brothers – Tip and Tuck – are delighted to be out of school, and on their long walk home. Though the setting has been denominated as 'the bush', they pass by abandoned mine workings, torn earth, 'great heaps of tailings', stacks of quartz, 'mysterious caverns that yawn'. It is a frightening spot, 'This desolate place of the dead', yet Tip decides to seek out a bird's nest. All at once he falls into a shaft. His brother peers anxiously over the rim but can see nothing. He wonders:

> Would it hurt *him* if he fell?
> Who could tell
> The depth of that horrible well?

The verse form that Boake adopts, with its triple rhymes and interspersed short lines, creates an edginess that sets this poem apart from maudlin performances on similar events. The fallen child's cries lead Tuck to lower himself over the side of the pit and then almost insensibly to let go, and join his brother. Here Boake's control of the sentimental slackens: 'And I trow/That angels' hands caught him below'.

As night comes down, the two boys clasp one another at the bottom of the shaft. Above, a search is conducted without result:

> There are lights 'mid the thistles, and cries of despair:
> A rifle cracks loudly, and bonfires glare …

Below, 'hidden deep', the 'two pretty babes smile in their sleep'. The conceit that they will pass, as if in sleep, to death is routinely enlisted, but with what degree of emotional investment from the author we cannot know. Prematurely interred, these children's bodies have most likely already been lost for ever. Their 'resting' places will remain unknown. Attuned as he is to this painful intensification of parental bereavement, Boake had another, differently slanted account to give of the loss of children, and one which looks towards twentieth-century narratives wherein the roles of mothers and fathers in such losses are paramount.

The title of the second poem of Boake's to be concerned with lost children was first printed as 'Deserted: As Seen at Devlin's Siding'. The manuscript had used only the last three words. The dramatic situation described in the poem involves a desertion, or – more specifically – a mother's abandonment of her infant. The beginning is interrogative:

> What made the porter stare so hard? What made the porter stare
> And eye the tall young woman and the bundle that she bore?

And why does she 'flush, and strive to hide her face' as the train from which she has alighted leaves the platform? She is, of course, guilty of a crime well known to fiction, for instance from the time of Hetty Sorel's abandonment of her baby in George Eliot's *Adam Bede* (1858). But Boake's insistent question, posed in various forms in the first twelve of the thirteen couplets cum stanzas which comprise the poem, concerns the mother's motive rather than the act itself. The questions press relentlessly in on her: what makes her look stealthily up and down the line before giving her breast to the infant 'to still its puny whine?' Why were the saw-millers absent that day?: 'They might have turned a woman from a woeful deed'. And nature was indifferent: 'why was the place so lone/That nothing but the soldier-birds might hear a baby moan?'

Nothing, human or otherwise, that might have interfered prevents the imminent death of the infant, which the mother now removes from her breast. To blame for this domestic tragedy is the unnamed man 'who made of her a harlot'. Remembering her fall, the woman reacts melodramatically. She moans, grinds her teeth and curses. The account of the actions that follow is more disturbing because it is more deliberate and restrained. She falls on her knees and '[scrapes] a cradle in the sand'. Shuddering at 'the buzz of eager flies', the mother binds a handkerchief across the eyes of her sleeping infant. At the moment when she is about to abandon the child, she is still solicitous for it, twining 'fragrant fronds of pine' to shield the baby from 'the burning sun'.

There will be no reprieve for it, either providential or of any other kind. The woman 'strides the platform', trying hard not to think 'That somewhere in the scrub a babe is calling her for drink'. The languid breezes sighing through the pine trees set up a refrain 'that seems to mock her with a baby's cry'. While Boake now exclaims 'Seek not to know!' he has invited us precisely to consider the consequences – not for the child: they are simple – but for the person who abandons it. The ending of the poem is harsh. The woman goes back 'to face the world again'. For her there is no release in pious words, or the comfort of an understanding community with which she can grieve, or even yet in death. This child has been 'lost' through human agency, whether its mother or father is ultimately, or are equally to blame. We are moving beyond the legendary domain in which lost children figure so prominently and where their losses can be accommodated, if with pain, as a familiar tragedy. Instead, we are coming to a starker place where an accounting is made for each loss and blame falls – not indifferently on the Australian bush – but on the people who wish themselves free of their children, and of the burdens of a succeeding generation.

Mrs Praed and the Punishment of Mrs Tregaskiss

Probably in 1891 (the title page of the book has no date) *Over the Sea. Stories of Two Worlds*, a collection of tales edited by Arthur Patchett Martin, was published in London. Taken to Australia as an infant, Martin had edited the *Melbourne Review* from 1876 until his return to Britain in 1882. The contributors he assembled were both English- and Australian-born, although some of the latter, notably Mrs Campbell Praed, had left their native country many years before. In her case it had been in 1875. Patchett Martin's wife Anne, 'Tasma' (Mrs Jessie Couvreur), Hume Nesbit, Mrs M. Senior Clark and the Countess De La Ware were also represented by stories whose settings alternated between England and Australia, as if to create what might now be called a cultural dialogue, but was then rather intended to reaffirm and strengthen the bonds between those whom Martin, in his opening 'Ballade', called 'the Children of Two Worlds'.

The most shocking and accomplished story in the collection comes first. This is Praed's 'The Sea-Birds' Message'. It tells of two abused children, who live by a great lake in inland Australia. That impossibility indicates how the landscape of the tale will be at once naturalistic and symbolic. In her novel *Fugitive Anne* (1903), which was deeply indebted to Rider Haggard's *She* (1887), Praed created a lost race, the Aca, who had long lived undisturbed and unsuspected in the fertile heart that Praed made up for Australia. 'The Sea-Birds' Message' offers no such promise of wonder or riches, instead bleakly insisting on disappointment and loss.

The children in the story are Jane Galvin, 'an odd imaginative child' and her brother Dick, who unfortunately 'had a tendency to water on the brain'. His consequent clumsiness enrages Polly Galvin, the children's stepmother, who misses few chances physically to ill treat him. The kindly father, Joe Galvin, is a stockman, hence away from home for long periods and unaware of his second wife's regime. The absent father is a stock figure of the lost child narrative, often for realistic reasons. It is an ineffectual mother who is usually left at home, rather than a malignant one as in this case. Jane dreams of escape. The seagulls, which must have journeyed far to reach the lake, remind her of the wild swans in a Hans Andersen story. This is how Jane morbidly imagines their intentions:

> she had a notion that they wanted to take her and little Dick to the opposite shore, and that there she would find Death's Garden, where God the Great Gardener gathers His flower-angels, and that there her own mother who was dead would come and meet them, and would take little Dick in her arms, and would lead Jane by the hand – and so they would wander about together in the beautiful garden, and there would be no more harsh words or cruel blows.

Death is conceived as a gentle prospect, allowing a family reunion, so it is unsurprising when, after more brutality from their stepmother, the children take flight, and seek that shore. They take refuge at first on a floating islet which, during a storm that night, is detached from the bank and drifts with them far out into the middle of the lake.

By the time that Joe Galvin finds the children to be missing, it may already be too late to save them. It is not until the next night that he rides up to the station where he is employed, 'and wild with grief and excitement implores the men there that a search party might be got together to hunt for the two children, lost in the bush'. Before joining it, Joe has time to strike his wife, whom he rightly blames for the disappearance of Dick and Jane. Despite the inclusion of 'four bush-trackers' (which seems to be Praed's code for Aborigines), this search party seems more frantic than purposeful, '[rushing] wildly in some direction where they fancied a child's cry came, only to find that it was the cry of a curlew or some other night bird'. Nature's mournful mockery of their endeavours ends when the searchers spot a circling eaglehawk. Galvin is smitten with fear, so he sends the owner of the station forward to find what is there.

Australian readers had long been prepared for the elements of the death scene. It appears at first that the two children 'had stopped to rest and were only sleeping'. The black-and-white illustration of the bushman peering at the two prostrate children closely recalls William Strutt's

'Found', the painting of the Duff children which he had exhibited at the Royal Academy in London. Here the outcome is tragically different:

> Dickie was clasped tight in Janie's arms, and Janie lay, her head upon a stone, her face turned upturned with a smile upon her small swollen lips. When he went closer he saw that they were dead.

But the question of who or what is to blame has been complicated. If their wicked stepmother's cruelties drove the girl and boy away from home, yet Janie at least had formulated a longing for death, thus for reunion with her lost, natural mother. Perhaps she feels guilty at having died first. Praed hints further, in 'The Sea-Birds' Message', at the resolute abandonment of an intolerable Australian existence. The child heeds the siren song of the birds and the terrible fate to which it leads, rather than enduring any longer her life outback. The story is a grim introduction to readers at 'Home' of the fate of European fairytale material in an Australian setting. Or rather Praed's implacably pessimistic version of the lost child story reinforces impressions that British audiences might already have formed from stories in a similar vein, for example in the separate publication there by Macmillan in 1871 of the lost child episode from Kingsley's *The Recollections of Geoffry Hamlyn*. Intended for a juvenile audience, it was simply called *The Lost Child*.

In lamentable circumstances, Praed herself lost all four of her adult children. Maud, born deaf, became insane and from 1900 until her death in 1941 was confined to an asylum in Bournemouth. Injured in a car accident in California, Humphrey developed brain fever and died. Geoffrey, described in Colin Roderick's book on Praed, In *Mortal Bondage* (1948), as 'the black sheep of the family ... a man more after Campbell's [his father's] heart' than his mother's, had left home to fight in the Boer War. After service in the Great War he retired on a major's pension to shoot big game in South Africa. In September 1925 he failed to kill a rhinoceros which then gored him to death. Praed's third son Bulkley – finding that he had cancer – killed himself with a shotgun in June 1932.

Praed may have seen a pattern in this grisly coincidence of ill-fortune, or at least would not have been surprised by it. A reincarnationist (like Haggard) she 'firmly believed that in this life she was paying the penalty for her inhumanity in the Roman life of Valeria'. Crazy as this conviction may seem to us now, it imbued Praed's fiction, notably in another work of the 1890s, her oppressive study of maternal guilt, *Mrs Tregaskiss* (1895). The novel was published in the year that Praed returned from a lengthy visit to Australia, her first since having left two decades before.

We are at once introduced to an unhappily married woman, Clare Tregaskiss, who is nursing a new baby, a second daughter. Two sons of hers have already died in infancy, or – as their father has it – 'the two other poor little chaps came to nothing'. The setting of *Mrs Tregaskiss*, as in most of Praed's fictions of Australia, is the version of Queensland which she styles Leichardt's [sic] Land. In a topical reference to the early years of the 1890s, both a shearers' strike and a drought are impending. Having been forced to leave England, and expediently to marry because of the disgrace about to fall upon her peculating father, the colony's Agent General in London, Mrs Tregaskiss now believes that she belongs to 'no country, unless it be the kingdom of sorrow'. Although she breast-feeds her infant, she was 'not of the type which bounteously nourishes her young'. Her plight elicits one sympathetic response. Doctor Geneste, who – besides his medical practice has been a renowned explorer (he 'opened up a bit of Northern country' and unlike Leichhardt returned to tell of it) – is now a squatter at Darra-Darra. He limps from an Aboriginal spear wound. His mask-like features may shield 'a nervous temperament afraid of self-betrayal'. While tempted by a beautiful and available young girl, who to his unreconstructed gaze 'suggested only what was limpid, sweet, pastoral and altogether feminine', it is Mrs Tregaskiss who entrances Geneste, and whom he will seek to win from her insensitive and hard-drinking husband Keith.

In an eccentric passage, Dr Geneste muses on Mrs Tregaskiss. The insistence of the novel's title on her marital status suggests a kind of imprisonment. Another of Praed's novels is called *The Bond of Wedlock* (1887). Both may have been informed by the long estrangement from her husband, which ended in separation after they had moved to Britain. Geneste judges that not only is there suffering in the smile of another unhappy wife, Mrs Tregaskiss, but that it registers 'a remoteness even from the natural maternal instinct'. Thus he is allowed to guess accurately at the failure as a mother for which bitterly, and in private, she blames herself. Being a doctor helps, one supposes:

> I would make that out from the way in which she handled the baby. But how painstakingly she did it! Maternity with this woman is a duty, not a passion. But that's a modern characteristic. There's nothing of the human mammal about the complex woman of today.

Mrs Tregaskiss, who has left behind the bohemian society in which she rejoiced in London (albeit that she characterises it for her boorish husband as 'long-haired South Kensington painters and the ladies in queer dresses with notions'), is unlikely to be contented with any of the terms of Geneste's description. She has sought a world that is less complex; has tried earnestly to be a mother – all without fulfilment. Instead she feels 'a weary distaste for the whole business of multiplying her kind', and in that response she anticipates the behaviour of unwilling mothers in the fiction of the next century. For Clare's recalcitrant disposition, Praed will see her punished, though surely not without a discernible element of self-flagellation. For example, Clare – like the author – believes that she is paying for the sins of a previous life, 'expiating the vices of a too voluptuous or too ambitious past'.

One of Clare's confidantes is the very rich, apparently misogynistic landowner Cyrus Chance, who tells her directly that it was a mistake to have had another baby: 'What's the good of making another leg-rope to keep you bailed up in your pen here?' is his winning form of words. Of all people, this crusty bachelor now extols the virtues of breastfeeding: 'the mother's milk is soothing to heart wounds'. In Praed's trademark manner, such asseverations of familial conservatism consort in the novel with an apparently heedless iconoclasm. Clare will be severely tempted by the prospect of an adulterous escape from marriage. Her suitor, Geneste, has a ripe amorous history, having availed himself of the moral laxity that the tropics endorses, to take as a sexual companion 'a graceful South Sea Island girl, for whom, till she was killed tragically by a shark while bathing, he had entertained an animal and half contemptuous affection'. No feminist sentiment, nor sanguine reckoning of the way of the world, ever tempts Praed for long from depicting the sorry lot of women, especially if they have been cursed with spirit and imagination.

One of Clare's sternest critics (herself apart) is her eldest child Ning, who tells her mother that she has noted how she is never happy when her husband is at home: 'Ning departed, her solemn gaze haunting her mother after she had disappeared, like an accusing ghost'. The child has intuited what Clare confides to her friend Gladys Hilditch, who has turned up unexpectedly from Britain:

> I haven't cared for Keith – or for the children altogether, because – oh, poor little innocent things, that I had no right to bring into the world! – because they were his.

This admission binds and torments Clare, filling her with 'superstitious dread' that if she allows her relationship with Geneste to develop, 'the expiatory penalty she had half invoked upon her child would be duly dealt forth'. Geneste encourages her to think of the girls as her husband's rather than her own. Like Chance, he describes them as imprisoning – 'Your children are your fetters'. It is Clare who will have to pay the price of breaking them.

On all sides Clare is assailed by conflicting counsel and reproving examples. A neighbour of the Tregaskisses, the dying Mrs Carmody, who admits that once she nearly went off with another man, tells Clare that at least she can take comfort from having looked after her children as best she was able. In fact it was after the death of one of her babies in infancy that Mrs Carmody began fatally to pine. She desires to be buried by the creek near that child's grave. Meanwhile – because Praed always and generously runs any number of heterogeneous plot lines at once – Geneste has been off routing the striking shearers. His activities are sinisterly described as 'a piece of tracking said to be unequalled in the Australian record of criminal hunts'. Those public affairs satisfactorily settled, Geneste is able to invite Clare to a picnic at Lake Eungella. Ning insists that they go. Clare agrees, 'with a guilty joy'. Before she sets off, Keith strikes Clare, accusing his wife of 'poisoning the Pickanniny's mind against her father!'

Ning has been delivered to one of those places that have long tempted Australian children: she was 'firmly persuaded that along the shores of Lake Eungella lay all the wonderful countries of story-land'. She wants her mother to come exploring with her (a prospect never before ventilated in Australian lost child stories) but Clare distractedly sends her daughter away, then feels relieved to have done so. She is glad because the choice between family and lover is clarified in Ning's absence. While Clare tells Geneste that she would leave with him 'If it were not for the children – the poor little children!' she has decided to go. Recalling 'her revolt at different times against the beings she had brought into the world', Clare is prepared to abandon them because of 'those very traits and resemblances which declared that they were not wholly of her'. Agreeing to abandon her children, Clare realises the consequences, more exactly than she can know: 'I will not hear Ning say her prayers tonight. Tomorrow she will have no mother'. Although she has never pretended to be a good parent, Clare tells the censorious (and childless) Gladys that 'I have always been dreadfully sorry for the poor little children'.

It is, inevitably, too late, at least for one of them. Clare will be shockingly punished for a desire that has no time to become a deed. Sleepless that night, she hears a native bear 'which has a cry like a child'. Come morning, with Ning's disappearance discovered, Clare at once knows her fate: 'God has punished me. He has killed Ning!' No gesture is made towards a benign deity. That would interfere with Clare's self-mortification. Nor is Praed finished with her yet. The mother hopes that at least the dead girl's body might be recovered 'so that the dingoes and wild birds may not hurt it', but this wish is also in vain. Geneste finds Ning's corpse and supposes that she may have died of a snake-bite, which would be an unprecedented end in the Australian literature of lost children. What is left of Ning is so horrible to contemplate, that Geneste buries the remains at once. Thus Clare's punishment is completed by a vengeful God (or author surrogate): 'It is not only that he has killed Ning, but he has given her to be devoured by the wild beasts, so that there is nothing of her I can keep, even in memory'. Praed is still not done with the hounding of Mrs Tregaskiss. Clare and Keith are unhappily reconciled. The mother is more solicitous than ever for the welfare of her remaining daughter. In a final, brutal irony, the miserly Cyrus Chance leaves her a bequest of £20 000 that had been meant for Ning. He insists that she accept the money, 'not as a gift from me, but as your rightful inheritance from your dead child', as though money makes up for the loss, and might help to erase the memory of it, and the natural order was so inverted that parents inherited from their children.

Mrs Tregaskiss is one of the strangest and sourest of all treatments of the lost child in Australia. Its heroine is persecuted, by herself and almost all others, from the first pages of the book. In a loveless marriage with children for whom she feels more duty than maternal affection, she is tempted to foresake her family. Clare Tregaskiss's disproportionate punishment is to lose her child and therefore to stay in her marriage. This confused, powerful, nearly sadistic novel sheets home the blame for the loss of Ning to her mother, notwithstanding the truancies of Keith Tregaskiss. More important, the mother accepts, even welcomes that blame. Praed's novel is ostensibly a cruel tract or a parable of the evils of contemplating adultery. In the context of the literature of lost children, it goes further than any previous work in Australia in suggesting that the children of unfit parents (specifically mothers) are better lost forever, better dead.

Henry Lawson and 'The Babies in the Bush'

On 27 January 1894, the acting editor of *New Australia*, the journal of the New Australia Co-operative Settlement Association, explained that she was in the chair: 'Owing to the fact that secretary Head was called away to Victoria by a telegram conveying the terrible news that his youngest child was lost in the Gippsland bush'. Therefore, 'the journal had come out without him'. The man in question was Walter Head; the lost child his four-year-old son, Rowland; the editor, *pro tem*, signed herself as M.J.C., short for Mary Jane Cameron. At the end of 1894 she would embark for Paraguay on the *Ruapehu* to join other followers of the socialist and utopian journalist William Lane's New Australia movement in the settlement at Cosme. Mary Jane Cameron is best known to

Australian literary history as Dame Mary Gilmore. Among those who travelled east to found New Australia was another of Head's sons, this one named Walter for his father, who left for Paraguay on the *Royal Tar* and never returned to Australia.

Thus, in a less drastic sense than his brother, he too was lost to his family. Young Wally Head, who was ten when the ship sailed, had been placed in the care of David Stevenson, an organiser for the Shearers' Union and cousin of the Scottish author Robert Louis Stevenson. Eventually the adult Wally left Paraguay and went into business in San Francisco. Anne Whitehead, in her account of 'the Australian Tribe of Paraguay', *Paradise Mislaid* (1997), relates that Wally Head was unwittingly responsible for the death of William Lane's son, Charlie, only a week after the latter's arrival at Cosme. In a game of cricket a ball bowled by Wally struck Charlie on the chest and he died soon afterwards. Thus eight-year-old Charlie Lane became the first child to be lost in New Australia.

Cameron had concluded her editorial comment on Walter Head's sorry condition by remarking that:

> There is no need for me to use fine words to assure the sympathy of those who read these words, for every one with the heart of a man or the love of a woman will feel for the father down South seeking what he almost dreads to find.

The concluding observation is conventional and well-meant. At the same time it has an ambiguous, nearly sinister ring. Is Head bound to find a corpse? Is it worse to have his fears realised than to live in delusory hope? What will be the condition of the body? Or is the child's survival what, perhaps, secretly, he dreads? In the event the child, who had gone missing towards the end of the previous year, was never found. He was given up as irredeemably lost.

Walter Head was born in Mulgrave, Victoria in 1861. Then it was a bush hamlet, now it is part of Melbourne's south-easterly suburban sprawl. He was the eldest of twelve children of a Methodist storekeeper and his wife. After his marriage to Caroline Riley in 1883 (a union which yielded seven children), he left home to travel through the Riverina in search of work as a shearer. Occasionally Walter Head turned to verse, writing as 'John Drayman'. His more steady occupations were as a journalist and a union organiser. The coincidence of skills was useful for the labour movement. In 1891, while Secretary of the Wagga Wagga branch of the Amalgamated Shearers' Union, Head – with Arthur Rae – helped to found and edit the *Hummer*. When, in September 1892, that paper amalgamated with the Queensland *Worker*, Head shifted to Sydney.

From November he was also employed as editor of *New Australia*, at the same time as he acted as secretary, treasurer and trustee of the New Australia Co-operative Settlement Association. Just after his resignation as editor in November 1893, because of his family's imminent departure for Paraguay, Head's son Rowland became lost, and presumably perished, in the Gippsland bush. The boy had been in Victoria with his mother, visiting relatives before the family left for overseas. Thereafter Walter Head's personal and business affairs unravelled. He was suspected of embezzling New Australia funds. At worst, he may have mismanaged them. His marriage ended. Late in 1894 he set off for New Zealand, which turned out to be a station on the way to Launceston. By 1895 Head had reconstituted himself as Walter Ashe Woods and was editor of the *Tasmanian Democrat*. The next year, as Walter Allan Ashe Woods (another name given, perhaps, to betoken a retrieval of respectability, or at least its semblance) he was in Hobart working for the *Clipper*. By 1903 he was its editor and part-owner, from that forum predicting the 'glorious sunrise of socialism'. Woods convened the Workers' Political League, forerunner of the Tasmanian Labor Party, and was elected to the state House of Assembly in 1906. He was returned six times. There was an interregnum when, unsuccessfully, he contested a Senate seat in 1917. Woods died in 1939. By then a son from his second marriage in 1910 (two years after his estranged first wife's death) was a Tasmanian Rhodes Scholar, one of whose given names was Head.

This is a tale of two careers, or two lives, fissured by the loss of Head's/Woods's son, and by the wranglings within the New Australia movement. It is almost as if the disappearance of Rowland, and the consequent collapse of Walter Head's marriage, permitted the latter's social and political rehabilitation. He went on to live an exemplary life for nearly half a century in Tasmania as a socialist, parliamentarian, journalist and father of a second family. There was to be no such second chance for his namesake, the Walter Head who figures in a short story by an old friend and sometime creditor, Henry Lawson, called 'The Babies in the Bush'.

The short story of 'The Babies in the Bush' was not Lawson's first work to go by that name. He had been well acquainted with Head in Sydney and had hoped to succeed him as editor of the *Worker* but was disappointed. He was also a friend of Mary Cameron, in conversation with whom he had entertained the notion of sailing for Paraguay as well. On 8 December 1900, about seven years after the child, Rowland Head, went missing in Gippsland, Henry Lawson's poem, 'The Babies in the Bush', was published in the *Bulletin*. Colin Roderick guesses that it had been composed some time earlier in that year. There is no specific reference to the Head tragedy, as there soon would be in the short story. Despite what one supposes to be the particularity of Lawson's source, the poem is generalised to seem as if it is speaking of an habitual occurrence in the bush. Categories are conflated. The realistic circumstance of the lost child is enfolded within fairytale. The terrors of loss are sentimentally softened. With its refrain that promises the translation of 'Bush-lost babies' to some kind of pleasant after-world, the poem is concerned to offer what it knows to be a false consolation.

Like so many children soon-to-be-lost before them, the babies in the poem go off to pick flowers. When mentioned again, the inevitability that they will be lost has been established. Separating the first and second stanzas is a refrain that identifies 'a spirit the bell-birds know'. That spirit is capricious: 'either' it chooses to guide 'the feet of the lost aright' (presumably to safety, restored to their families), 'or' (and for no given reason) it does not. In the latter case it carries them (body and soul?) 'up through the starry night/Where the bush-lost babies go'. That is, the poem imagines a transcendent, rather than a mundanely horrible or obscure fate for strayed children. There is a faery home in the heavens, peopled with lost babies, rather like James Barrie's community of lost boys in Never Land in *Peter Pan* (1904) (a play performed with great success in Australia in the early years of the century). The lostness of Lawson's children, it must be said, is decidedly antipodean in cause and kind. They are 'bush-lost'.

The poem's second stanza contends that while 'we' (that is, adults) 'wander away as our fortune needs', the children in question have no such command of their fates: 'what is the spirit that always leads/The toddlers' feet from home?' To pose a question now from outside the poem: is the malign spirit within the Australian bush that encourages the errancy of children the same one which conducts them, once they are dead, when this familiar narrative has run its course, into the 'starry night'? No answer is given, but the third stanza modulates back into a realist mode. The searchers are pictured consoling themselves with yarns of lost children who have been found. The narratives do not work: the search fails. No trace of the 'babies' is detected, 'never a sign of a baby's foot'. The fourth stanza cuts to a domestic tableau. The waiting mother's 'wild fixed look of a life's despair' defines her mental and emotional condition now, and presumably in time to come.

She is comforted 'with a husband's love', in this fashion: the 'strong man' turns his wife's face 'to the stars above' and proclaims 'Our bush-lost babies are there'. Accepting this fiction, 'she sings' (for how terribly long?) 'of a fairy bright/Of a spirit the bell-birds know'. The beneficent, other-worldly presence is at once European and Australian, fairy and spirit of the bush. Its agency is to direct the feet of those who are lost to 'a land of light/Where the bush-lost babies go'. The destination is neither exactly nor explicitly heaven, but a refuge in the southern skies for those who have succumbed to the especial danger that awaits antipodean children: that of being lost, and perishing in the Australian bush.

Lawson returned to 'The Babies in the Bush' in the story of that name which formed part of the collection *Joe Wilson and His Mates*, published in Edinburgh in 1901, in Australia the following year. Some of his best work is there: the four linked Joe Wilson stories and the comic piece 'The Loaded Dog'. Included also is a substantial story, 'The Babies in the Bush', which is an ampler, more concrete, altogether darker version of the material which had been treated in the poem. The epigraph to the story returns us to the poem and to its consolatory intention: 'tell her a tale of the fairies bright – /That only the Bushmen know'. The woman mentioned is evidently the mother of a, or any lost child. It is unclear why Bushmen would collude in this kindly-meant deception. In conclusion, the verse epigraph reiterates the notion of fairies guiding lost Australian children into the stars, to the realm where 'the Bush-lost babies go'.

The story proper begins in descriptive terms that are general. At first it seems that the character of the boss drover has been shaped indifferently by the exigencies of his environment:

> He was one of those men who seldom smile. There are many in the Australian Bush, where drift wrecks and failures of all stations and professions (and of none), and from all the world.

Yet Lawson's account of this man soon becomes particular. 'He' is Walter Head. Strangely, inexplicably, Lawson has used the name of his friend to tell of another bereaved parent, another devastated spectator in a story of lost children. Why he did so may never be clear, although the Walter Head who edited *New Australia* was by now gone forever. The man once of that name was well established under another in Hobart. Was Lawson's choice of name a way of prolonging Head's sorrows, or intended in respectful memory of what he and his family had suffered?

The boss is characterised as an admirer of the melancholy, rather than the rousing verse of Adam Lindsay Gordon. This is the basis of the friendship which he strikes up with the narrator, while they are droving cattle from Queensland to the railhead at Bathurst. The latter is 'an Australian Bushman', who confides that 'I went by the name of "Jack Ellis"'. Gordon, he informs those who might be unaware, was 'the English [sic]-Australian poet who shot himself'. A famous suicide shadows the rest of a tale in which that option to end pain has not been taken up by either the boss or his wife.

The first story that Jack Ellis hears by way of explanation of the gloomy reserve of the boss, a man 'quietened down by some heavy trouble', marks him as a typical victim of outback life in Australia: 'He had been a well-to-do squatter on the Lachlan river-side, in New South Wales, and had been ruined by drought, they said'. Not so: the real, more particular and terrible story will emerge later. At the stage when we meet him, the boss is working for the once penniless man to whom long before he had given a job. 'It's the way of Australia', he ruefully notes. He lives in Bathurst with his wife, and takes Jack to the house once the drive has ended. There is a caution: 'Mrs Head had a great trouble at one time. We – we lost our two children'. It is his hope that his wife gains some comfort from confiding her story to strangers.

When her monologue begins that is how things appear for a while, until the rising note of hysteria overpowers her control of the tale. At first she explains to Jack: 'These town people don't understand. I like to talk to a Bushman. You know we lost our children out on the station. The fairies took them'. Imploringly she asks, 'You surely know about the Bush fairies, Mr Ellis?' He is quick to agree. In the story's reworking of the poem, Mrs Head's mania because of loss generates what had earlier been a sentimental gesture of consolation. It is a frightful obsession in the story:

> at first nothing would drive it out of my head that the children had wandered about until they perished of hunger and thirst in the Bush. As if the Bush Fairies would let them do that.

Steadily, dementedly, she seeks to create a happy alternative to the tragic familiarities of the story of children lost in the bush.

The Head children were named for their parents – Walter and Maggie. That is, they were meant to bear their parents' names and all else that they had inherited from them into the next generation. Those given names were emblematic of a hope of the future that events would soon dash. The loss is accordingly more terrible, not least as we learn of how the father contributed to it. Maggie shows Jack Ellis portraits of her boy and girl, taken when they were two, and six months old respectively. They would be lost three years later. Young Walter's portrait moves her to exclaim 'see, he's got one hand and one little foot forward, and an eager look in his eye'. It is as if, indeed, this exemplary young Australian had a future to anticipate.

The mother's over-rehearsed narrative is a monologue except when she solicits collaboration from two of her listeners, Walter, and Andy, who had worked on their station and is with them still. When the children went missing, Walter 'was away in Sydney on business, and we couldn't find his address'. The children, like so many in fact and fiction before them, had wandered innocently away into the bush to gather flowers, straw hats in their hands 'In case a bad wind blowed' (this line of Maggie's comes from the poem). Mrs Head is sometimes troubled as to why they strayed: 'Do you think the Bush Fairies would entice children away, Mr Ellis?' The boss interrupts crisply and on cue, in consonance with her cracked logic: of course the fairies took the children, 'They had to: the children were lost'.

In his analysis of 'The Babies in the Bush' in *The Receding Wave* (1972), Brian Matthews sees the story as merging the two themes – 'romantic obsession with madness'. He does not mention Lawson's source in the Walter Head story, which makes it easier for him to offer the surprising assertion that 'the events and characters of this story need not be set in the bush'. All he concedes is that 'the bush provides a backdrop – a place for the children to be lost'. In fact the story that Maggie tells is related in a provincial city, Bathurst, where the bush is a distant place of horrors, abandoned, but omnipresent. The burden of the story as a whole cannot be translated away from the bush. This is one of the keenest, most self-conscious and revisionist of all treatments of the lost child material. It deconstructs the sentimental embellishments of the poem. More directly than in any previous handling of the topos of the lost child, Lawson shifts the focus to an analysis of the cause of the event, to the question of who is responsible for the loss. Matthews discerns some of this:

> While the ostensible cause of Maggie's condition is the loss of her children, the accusatory inflection of some of her questions seems to shift the blame insensibly, so that part of her plight may well result from the fleeting intuition of Walter's guilt.

The nature and extent of that 'guilt', its personal and its symbolic dimensions, are explored harrowingly in the remainder of the story.

Before then there is a long, exemplary passage which begins when Jack says to himself 'There was no need to tell me about the lost children. I could see it all'. He imagines a particular search for the Head girl and boy in a manner that suggests how it would have been first optimistically, then forlornly typical of many such searches. There is no more arresting vignette of the search component of the lost child narrative than this. It deserves quotation in full. Standing alone, as it were, this passage indicates how far from incidental is the bush setting of this story of 'The Babies in the Bush':

> I could see it all. She and the half-caste rushing towards where the children were seen last, with Old Peter after them. The hurried search in the nearer scrub. The mother calling all the time for Maggie and Wally, and growing

wilder as the minutes flew past. Old Peter's ride to the musterers' camp. Horsemen seeming to turn up in no time and from nowhere, as they do in a case like this, and no matter how lonely the district. Bushmen galloping through the scrub in all directions. The hurried search the first day, and the mother mad with anxiety as the night came on. Her long, hopeless, wild-eyed watch through the night; starting up at every sound of a horse's hoof, and reading the worst in one glance at the rider's face. The systematic work of the search-parties next day and the days following. How those days do fly past. The women from the next run or selection, and some from the town, driving ten or twenty miles, perhaps, to stay with and try to comfort the mother. ('Put the horse to the cart, Jim: I must go to that poor woman!') Comforting her with improbable stories of children who had been lost for days, and were none the worse for it when they were found. The mounted policemen out with the black trackers. Search-parties cooeeing to each other about the Bush, and lighting signal-fires. The reckless break-neck rides for news or more help. And the Boss himself, wild-eyed and haggard, riding about the Bush with Andy and one or two others perhaps, and searching hopelessly, days after the rest had given up all hope of finding the children alive. All this passed before me as Mrs Head talked, her voice sounding the while as if she were in another room; and when I roused myself to listen, she was on to the fairies again.

The 'hurried search in the nearer scrub' that might have found the children if they had not then strayed far is unsuccessful. The community rallies at once, whether horsemen on the search or another wife off to give succour. 'Improbable stories' of rescues are offered as well – but in this (story) context they are only 'stories', wishful fabrications. The 'real' story of the loss of the Head children is one that Jack does not need to hear, for in a crucial sense this 'Australian bushman' knows it already. While he has not listened to Mrs Head's account, he has missed nothing.

Late in the piece, Maggie adverts to affliction by Voices which have told her 'to kill myself; they told me it was all my own fault – that I killed the children'. It was not, of course, her fault, but by transference her husband must be tormented by the accusation. Nor were the black trackers incompetent. An untimely thunderstorm obliterated the tracks of the children. How they were eventually found is disclosed by Andy, in the second of the vital micro-narratives within the story. The bodies were discovered, like those of many strayed children, 'not so very far from home'. They may have wandered a long way, but in a circle. That they were found, Andy insists, was a blessing:

> when the bodies aren't found, the parents never quite lose the idea that the little ones are wandering about the Bush tonight (it might be years after) and perishing from hunger, thirst or cold. That mad idea haunts 'em all their lives.

In truth, the Heads are haunted notwithstanding. Or rather, it is as if they are already ghosts. In Andy's sympathetic perception, at least of the husband's plight: 'It's the worst trouble that can happen to a man. It's like living with the dead. It's – it's like a man living with his dead wife'.

Sacrificing everything to find a cure for his wife's madness, Head took her to specialists in England and Germany, in the vain hope that Europe might hold the solution to so indelibly Australian a malady. The station had to be sold up. The children, first buried by the Lachlan, were exhumed because 'the Boss got a horror of having them buried in the Bush'. Their remains were removed to Waverley in Sydney (where a quarter of a century later Lawson was to be buried). Head bought the ground, Andy explains 'and room for himself and Maggie when they go out. It's all the ground he owns in wide Australia, and once he had thousands of acres'.

As Andy and Jack go down to take the train to Sydney with the cattle, the boss confides in the latter the nature of his culpability in the loss of his children. He was not in Sydney on business, as he had told his wife, but 'on a howling spree', 'beastly drunk in an out-of-the-way shanty in the bush'. The boss is fallible as Joe Wilson was, liable to disintegration both by such external temptations as drink and by weakness of character. There is no Mary to redeem him, however, no child-bride who (like her namesake Mary Mahony in Henry Handel Richardson's novel, *The Fortunes of Richard Mahony*, 1930, and Joe Wilson's Mary in Lawson's stories) assumes the role of mother as well as wife to her erring, infantile husband. In contrast, Walter Head must manage for himself and his wife. The additional, terrible detail that he has to remember is of how 'the old brute' who ran the shanty never told him of the hunt for the children, thinking the story just a trick to get his customer home. Worse yet than that, Walter Head is persuaded that he could have found the lost ones, being an abler bushman than any who searched. Andy's coda is hardly necessary: 'that's the thing that's been killing him ever since, and it happened over ten years ago'.

The strained sentimental tone of the poem 'The Babies in the Bush' is almost extravagantly dashed by the prose piece of the same name. In the story, lost children make grieving parents mad, as in Maggie's case (or worse, mad spasmodically, aware of her loss at times) or bereft and guilt-stricken in Walter's. The delinquency of the latter did not directly cause the children to stray nor, most likely, did it doom them. Neither thing matters. Walter Head sees himself as guilty. He will not blame a hostile environment to assuage his pains; will not make Australia, or the bush, the culprit. Instead his slow, melancholy self-destruction, his dwelling on how he has squandered his children's future, presages the transformation of treatments of the lost child in twentieth-century Australian literature. That business of children lost deliberately by the parental generation, whether they were aborted, abandoned, murdered, or never conceived, is in its own ways more terrible than the accident that Walter Head lets slowly exact its mortal toll on him.

Joseph Furphy's 'perfect Young-Australian'

Learning that the *Bulletin* would not publish his novel *Such is Life* unless it was significantly shortened, Joseph Furphy travelled to Sydney at Easter 1901 to discuss the matter with the editor, J. F. Archibald. Agreeing to the cuts required, Furphy returned to Victoria and began work at once. The original second and fifth chapters were removed. Ultimately they constituted the bulk, respectively, of two other works: *The Buln-buln and the Brolga* (1948) and *Rigby's Romance* (1946), both published long after Furphy's death. The two substituted chapters were written quickly and finished by June that year. They relate Collins's acquaintance with the incompetent, kindly, autodidact Irish stockman Rory O'Halloran, and Rory's daughter, Mary. In *The Order of Things* (1990), his biography of Furphy, John Barnes argues that the revised material obliquely reflects Furphy's own unhappy marriage, in its treatment of Rory's soured relations with his wife. As well it embodies – through Collins's encomium to youthful Australia in the person of Mary – some of the author's optimism (which he felt too few fellow writers shared) about the very recently federated Commonwealth of Australia. Yet that was an essentially qualified optimism: Mary O'Halloran would become one of the first fictional lost children of the new century.

In the second chapter of *Such is Life* (as it appeared on publication of the novel in 1903), Tom Collins falls in with the boundary rider Rory O'Halloran, a Catholic Irishman now better known by the sardonic nickname Daniel O'Connell, whom he had first met thirteen years before. Rory directs Collins to his homestead, promising to join him there before sunset. The welcome – or want of it – that he receives from Rory's estranged and embittered Protestant wife, gives even the obtuse Collins an intimation of marital discontent. Introduced to the child, Mary, Collins is informed by the mother that 'She's got no name'. That is, the child is unbaptised because of the sectarian disagreements of her parents.

After discerning 'the strong racial index of her pure Irish face', and digressing about the nature and effects of her Celtic inheritance, Collins decides that 'Mary O'Halloran was perfect Young-Australian'. That is, blood apart, 'she was the very creature of the phenomena which had environed her own dawning intelligence'. This daughter of the coming race in Australia is the product of her natural surroundings. Collins elaborates, rhapsodically:

> She was a child of the wilderness, a dryad among her kindred trees. The long-descended poetry of her nature made the bush vocal with the pure gladness of life; endowed each tree with sympathy, respondent to her own fellowship.

A Biblical allusion seems apt for her relation to the young country of Australia: 'To her it was a new world, and she saw that it was good'.

The child is exceedingly attached to her father. When Collins wakes at sunrise the next morning, he finds them already together by the fire. As they leave, Rory mentions having found a swag on one of his fences a week to ten days before, so that Collins is prompted to recall the apparently sleeping sundowner whom he had seen and avoided on his way to the O'Hallorans'. Hurriedly he goes back to the spot and finds a corpse, not a sleeping man: 'Evidently he had not died of thirst alone, but of mere physical exhaustion, sealed by the final collapse of hope'. The causes of death are therefore of the spirit as well as of the body, or so Collins judges. He adds, without then reckoning how far he might be responsible, 'such is life, and such is death'. Letters in the pockets identify the dead man as George Murdoch, from Malmsbury. They 'all were signed by his loving wife'.

Thus Murdoch is buried under his own name, rather than none, or one assumed – as had been the case with the young drowned man, 'James Tyson', in Lawson's story 'The Union Buries Its Dead' (1893). Murdoch is, however, a generic figure as well. His fate, as here pictured, recalls the 'Lost in the Bush' engraving in the *Illustrated Melbourne Post* for 25 October 1865 – 'the sinking of the lost traveller, overpowered by thirst and fatigue'. This common, 'lamentable' end may have quietly agitated young Mary's mind, becoming for her an image of the possible fate of her father as he pursues his lonely rounds in search of stock. Or so Collins will have occasion to surmise, a short time later, in January of the next year.

In his introduction to *The 1890s* (1996), Ken Stewart interrogated the language of 'youth' in colonial and turn-of-the-century Australia. In that discourse, radical and conservative, by and about men and women, bush and city, 'Australia was young'. Moreover it was young

> as a person is young: the anthropomorphic metaphor established associations of human vitality, immaturity and of an awaited future, and at the same time erased the indigenous peoples.

This is the rhetorical context in which Collins spoke of Mary as 'Young-Australian', the type of a new people. With that example in mind, Stewart was prompted to ask:

Is the death of the child Mary O'Halloran in Joseph Furphy's *Such is Life* an exclusively personal disaster, or is it an 'Australian' tragedy, a 'nationalistic' statement concerning young Australia?

If it is, who or what is to blame? And what are the actual and the symbolic consequences of the loss? Was Furphy intent, as Stewart claims Lawson was, on deconstructing 'an official national rhetoric' – here of the promise of young Australia, by enfolding it within the dolefully familiar narrative framework of a child lost in the bush?

Collins hears of Mary's death while camped in Trinidad Paddock in January 1884, with groups of bullock drivers, tank sinkers and fencing contractors, who have been lured there by the cunning Chinese boundary rider, Paul Sam Young. The bushmen while away part of the night telling yarns, as had another group in the first chapter of the novel. In his study of Furphy, *The Life and Opinions of Tom Collins* (1991), Julian Croft notes that all five stories

> involve a loss, though the resolution of each rings the changes with elegant variations on the ways in which that loss is either permanent or temporary, and whether an explanation or resolution to the conflict is known or unknown. Mistaken identity, losing one's bearings, and deceptive surroundings (human or otherwise) are the staples of life in Furphy's novels.

The first story is an ironic prelude to what follows. This is Thompson's tale of how he lost his dog, Monkey. He is interrupted ('speak o' the divil') by the arrival of Barefoot Bob, of whom he has just been speaking. In turn, Bob tells a tale of the avaricious squatter McGregor. When he leaves, for 'a place where there's no admittance for swearers', Thompson begins another story, of the loss of Mary O'Halloran, in the search for whom both he and Bob had recently been involved.

Croft remarks, somewhat captiously, that 'the great virtue of the next story is not so much its content, which is one of the great clichés of Australian literature, but in the way in which it is told'. Thompson had been in the hut at Kulkaroo when he learned, from Webster, the station owner, of a 'Child lost in the scrub on Goolumbulla. Dan O'Connell's little girl – five or six years old. Anybody know where there's any blackfellows?' While the trackers thought indispensable for such emergencies are searched for ('Did anybody know where to find a blackfellow now that he was wanted?' – the question has a mordant historical irony), Thompson reveals what he knows of the reasons for Mary's disappearance. Her father had been away mustering ewes. By the second day of his absence, the little girl was 'not fretful, but dreaming, and asking her mother strange questions'. Their source, it seems, is that fondness for her father, now that he is absent, made 'this affair of the man perishing in the scrub work on her mind'. On the third morning, the mother found that Mary was gone. Evidently the young Australian had set off to give succour to the adult bush worker.

Bob tracks her tirelessly, after a while with the aid of 'an old grey-haired lubra, blind of one eye' who follows the trail like a bloodhound. When three days have already passed, a faint but unmistakable cry of 'Dad-de-e-e' is heard: 'There wasn't a trace of terror in the tone; it was just the voice of a worn-out child, deliberately calling with all her might'. Though the child had been tantalisingly near, she is found dead the next morning. After the stock, hopeful misapprehension – 'Asleep?' – Mary is revealed to have fallen down a bilby hole. Exhausted, her face sank in the loose mould of earth, 'and she had died without a struggle'. Like so many lost children before her, Mary appears to have passed peacefully away, but this is no measure of consolation for her father. He cries – like a wounded animal, like a child – knowing that he has heard his daughter's voice less than an hour before, but will never hear it again. The Catholic priest in Hay, the distant town to which the body is taken, refuses to read the service over the unbaptised child, but the jackeroo Ward, who is an English Catholic, does so.

The bushmen do not long dwell in silence on this intolerable, but not uncommon loss. One of them, Saunders, has found fault with 'singin''-out after lost kids' in the way that the searchers for Mary had done. Interrupting, he tells a lost child story with a happy ending, as near to comic as such things can be. Henry Bracy, Tom Bracy's child, goes missing. He is found at last, 30 feet up a hollow log. The cowering child, hearing his name called, had kept silent:

> Hen-ree! Hen-ree! Boomin' and bellerin' back an' forrid across the bend in the dark; an' he thought the boody-man, an' the bunyip, an' the banshee, an' (sheol) knows what all, was after him.

The legends with which parents had long sought to deter their children from straying into the bush (as in Marcus Clarke's story 'Pretty Dick') were, in this instance, the cause by which the child almost perished. The unusual pendant to the story – rare indeed for this genre – is that Saunders has information about the later life of this found child. Most of them, like the real life figure of Alfred Boulter, disappear ever after from public attention. Henry Bracy – seven in 1871, 'a year after the big flood' – would now be nineteen or twenty, we hear, and went droving sheep three years ago, thus becoming part of the rural community to which he had nearly been lost.

The final story of a lost child is introduced in a manner to suggest that it will top the others. Stevenson tells a tale which dates back to his childhood, when his family was living on the Upper Campaspe near the families of Thompson and Collins. 'In a voice that brought constraint on us all', he begins:

> Bad enough to lose a youngster for a day or two, and find him alive and well; worse, beyond comparison, when he's found dead; but the most fearful thing of all is for a youngster to be lost in the bush, and never found, alive or dead.

Worse still, this is the story of his own younger brother Eddie, for whose loss he has since blamed himself. Eddie was lost the day after Stevenson had come back from three months in Kyneton. Cross with the little boy, Stevenson hit him while they were gathering gum. The child started home on his own and was never seen again. He gave his older brother one last reproachful look which – when Stevenson thinks of it – 'makes me thankful to remember that every day brings me nearer to the end'.

The search began that same afternoon. The father, friends and the government all offered rewards. With a pardonable asperity, Stevenson comments that 'between genuine sympathy and the chance of making £500, the bush was fairly alive with people; and everyone within thirty miles was keeping a look-out'. But it was of no use. The search was dropped. Only the grieving father persevered. At least Walter Head, in Lawson's story 'The Babies in the Bush', had the desolating satisfaction of finding the bodies of his two children. There is no such relief for Stevenson's father, whose neglected property 'went to wreck' and who took to drink, 'and you can hardly call him responsible for the rest'.

There is more: Stevenson's story multiplies the shocking consequences of the loss of the child. He is, of course, as the compelled narrator, one of its secondary casualties. On the anniversary of Eddie's disappearance, his mother took laudanum. The property was soon sold up to pay the mortgagee – a Wesleyan minister. The three remaining children were farmed out to uncles. About four years after Eddie went missing, his ruined father was found dead one morning in the stables of a pub. Collins soon sermonises on the meanings of these tales, but what did Furphy intend by their conjunction? The immediate effect is to prevent a simple, symbolic understanding of the significance of Mary's death. That had, indeed, already seemed a tragedy without meaning. Only in terms of the Young Australia rhetoric which Collins had imposed on Mary could her life be over-interpreted, for example as an indictment of sectarian bitterness, translated from the old world to Australia. Croft runs this line, perhaps with a mischievous exaggeration, to highlight both a possibility within the text and the temptation to exaggerate it. Mary, he says, is presented as torn between 'a seductive patriarchy and a punitive matriarchy, Roman Catholicism and Protestantism'. Tom's depiction of the child 'touches not only the sectarian and gender division within society, but the delusions of white responses to the Australian landscape'.

The two subsequent tales, however, advise the attentive reader that the lost child is – not so much a symbol of the national future in jeopardy – but an example of a recurrent hazard of bush life, to be regarded stoically, rather than polemically. Croft writes acutely of the pessimistic burden of these lost child stories:

> A pessimism that expresses itself in the folk-belief that in the centre of white Australian society lies a vacuum which with regularity but unpredictability takes its tithe of the lives of the young. The vacuum is just that – an absence; it is not malign, nor vengeful, nor understandable, but merely a vacuum into which children disappear. 'Lost in the bush' is the trope which may be seen in countless stories, poems, and pictures, and the 'bush' whatever that might be, is the power which consumes the future generation.

This speaks of the *how*, and assumes that the question *why* need not be posed. It has already been argued above that the bush is not usually the active agent, but the indifferent setting of these tragedies. In the reckonings taken in Furphy's novel, the loss of children is the result of misadventure, or heedless actions whose consequences are out of all proportion to them. Parents are not to blame for these losses, though they become their belated victims. Any understanding reached, so far as this occurred, is nihilistic. Furphy, after all, had been involved in the search for the three lost Daylesford boys in 1867, which ended with the discovery of their mutilated remains. He had no reason to take a sanguine, or consoling view of the phenomenon. The mythologising of Mary is Collins's work, not his.

When the other bushmen go to sleep, Collins remains wakeful, thinking of the lost child whom he had known. His sentiments are mawkishly expressed:

> Dear innocent, angel-faced Mary! Perishing alone in the bush! Nature's precious link between a squalid Past and a nobler Future, broken, snatched away for her allotted space in the long chain of the ages! Heiress of infinite hope, and dowered with the latent fitness to fulfil her part, now so suddenly fallen by the wayside! That quaint dialect silent so soon!

In Australian literature, at least, no-one has spoken about a lost child like that before. Furphy lets the extravagant rhetoric mock itself, but not at the expense of letting us forget the episodes of lost children which have just been narrated. If the meaning of these stories is to be comprehended, Collins's language will be obfuscatory, rather than helpful. It is Tom's 'musings [that] turn to the sentimental and the bathetic', in

Croft's phrase, but this hardly means – as he goes on to say – 'that Furphy lost control of the tone of the novel at this point, and wrote into it the bare, naked feelings of his experience of the deaths of his own, young children'. That is straying from the context. It is Tom, not the author, who wants to turn Mary's death into an exemplary cliché, in the same manner as he had earlier exalted her promise as a national type.

Nevertheless, in speaking of the bush as 'that power which consumes the next generation', Croft has highlighted two core questions about lost child narratives. Who or what is to blame for the losses? What is their symbolic and psychological (which is to say their national), as well as their literal meaning? The bush will cease to be the setting, let alone the culprit in most of the literary treatments of the lost child topos from the middle of this century. It will rather be a human desire to abandon or to prevent the coming of 'the next generation' which will be central to these cheerless versions of an old story.

Part II

In the Twentieth Century
THE CHILD ABANDONED

When, near the end of the colonial period, eleven-year-old Clara Crosbie disappeared in the bush outside Lilydale, black trackers were called upon to find her. The skills of other trackers had been employed five years before during the last hunt for the Kelly gang. On that previous occasion, their efforts were not needed. This time they were to no avail. The child was found by chance, in time. Lilydale is now an outer eastern suburb of Melbourne, overlaid by the Melways grid. These days, psychics and psychologists, social workers and police would probably have been involved in a search whose participants would most likely fear in advance that it was doomed. For – more than a century after Clara Crosbie was lost and found – the figure of the lost child still haunts the Australian imagination. Many novels, stories, plays and films since the 1950s are preoccupied with terrible transformations of that figure – abandoned, abused, aborted, abducted or murdered. This is tragic material for writers as seemingly unengaged with, or unimpressed by each other's work as Patrick White and Frank Moorhouse, Kate Grenville and Tom Keneally, Ray Lawler and Carmel Bird. The lost child is also the subject of films that have come from books: *Walkabout, Fortress, Manganinnie, Evil Angels, Picnic at Hanging Rock.*

Veritable children, lost forever, were the victims of notorious crimes and misadventures in post-war Australia. In 1960 the Sydney schoolboy Graeme Thorne became the first Australian to be kidnapped for ransom. He was murdered soon afterwards. The three Beaumont children vanished from Glenelg Beach in Adelaide on Australia Day 1966 and – wild rumours aside – have not been seen since. Seven young women were abducted and killed in South Australia between December 1976 and February of the following year. Most of the bodies were buried near Truro, north-east of Adelaide. Azaria Chamberlain perished, by human or animal agency, at Ayers Rock in August 1980. Besides these actual tragedies, the metaphor of the 'lost child' has been applied to many real events in Australia, in ways that are at some times troublingly loose, at others sadly apposite. To speak of the Aboriginal 'stolen generation' for instance, is to draw on the potency of that metaphor of the lost child in ways that are politically charged. The phrase summons up the suffering in thousands of childhoods lost when boys and girls were removed, by government authority, from their natural parents and fostered into the households of European Australians. The ensuing study of the many and disconcerting manifestations of the 'lost child' in the later twentieth century suggests that these represent as intense an anxiety as they had in colonial Australia.

To move from the first to the second part of this book, from 'Discovering the Lost Child' to 'The Child Abandoned', involves not only an elision in time, but also something of a paradigm shift. The first part, 'Discovering the Lost Child', was concerned with the second half of the nineteenth century, in which many Australians uneasily assayed their place in this country. The title referred, as well, both to literal searches for and metaphorical uses of the figure of the lost child. 'The Child Abandoned' brings us to a moral terrain that has been radically transformed. Put starkly, the movement is of this kind: twentieth-century lost child stories are about the rending of communities, rather than the uniting of them. They tell of institutional brutality and of individual perversity, moreover of the suspicions that these engender about a society in which the abuse and loss of children can seem inevitable, if regrettable, and worthy of note mostly for the peculiar horrors that some of the stories reveal. They describe younger generations 'stolen', slain, abandoned, ill-treated, or deliberately not conceived. In the second half of the twentieth century in Australia, the figure of the lost child is not a revenant from, or an orphan of the colonial past, but someone (or many) vividly and disquietingly presented, perhaps in an anatomy of this society (in fact or fiction or film), or in the probing of the destructive psychological maladies of individuals.

In the long gap of time between Joseph Furphy's cluster of stories in *Such is Life* and the Thorne kidnapping, the figure of the lost child did not altogether disappear from the national life or literature, but its importance seems diminished, its occurrences both less typical and less spectacular. As argued above, in this period – the first half of the twentieth century – Australian fiction is extensively occupied with revisionist imaginings of the taking of the land by Europeans. These are stories which have less to do with the vulnerability of children in the inhospitable outback, than with ultimately successful pioneering endeavours. Both in fact, and in literature, the lost child re-emerges in the second half of this century, as the focus of further, if more obscure anxieties. It was as if some Australians seemed to question not so much whether they belonged in this country, but whether their children should, or were to be, part of its time to come. Implicitly as well as aloud, they asked if succeeding generations of Australians should be brought into being at all. At large, this impulse resembles a cultural death wish. In the individual cases brought forward in this section of the book, children suffer from the terrible attentions both of predators and of institutions. Many of them do not survive, but we who do ought to be moved to wonder at the well-springs of this Australian anxiety, and at how to reckon with and respond to its consequences.

Some old-fashioned versions of the lost child material have been benignly revived in the modern period. The story of 'The Little Boy Lost', Stephen Wall of Tamworth, became the consoling stuff of country-and-western music. Not only was Stephen found alive after losing his way in the bush, but he earned a place in modern ballad of the sort usually reserved for those who had perished. Johnny Ashcroft and Tommy Withers guaranteed the boy a part in the grand narrative of lost children in Australia, however anachronistic his ordeal might have appeared in the 1960s, when he went missing.

The impression of anachronism – the sense that the old lost child stories had been superseded by ones much worse – is exemplified by Judith Wright's poem 'The Precipice', which was first published in *Meanjin* in 1953. According to Veronica Brady's biography *South of My Days* (1998) the poem was based on an actual, if inexplicable event. A woman took a bus to Mount Tamborine in southern Queensland with her children, and then a taxi to the National Park. She walked with them along a path through the rainforest. Coming to the cliff at the end of the path, she jumped, with the children in her arms. Brady feels able to find two causes, if drastically different in scale: 'Her husband had returned from the war an emotional and physical wreck, and she could not endure any more his violence or the threat of a holocaust'. The poem is not so reductive, beginning as it does:

> At last it came into her mind, the answer.
> She dressed the children, went out and hailed the driver.
> There she sat holding them; looking through the window;
> behaving like any woman, but she was no longer living.

If the woman's anxiety is explained in part – 'To blame her would mean little; she had her logic,/the contained argument of the bomb' – this does not impress us as sufficient. A deeper, more personal pessimism has driven her to the cliff's edge: 'she took the children in her arms because she loved them/and jumped'.

Violence against children is here (and in other cases to be reviewed below) the consequence of a desperate love. Often, in examples that are too plentifully available to us, violence is rather the result of systematic, premeditated or habitual cruelty. The four sections of 'The Child Abandoned' are divided generically, as were the sub-sections of 'Discovering the Lost Child', but again with the caution that these different forms of narrative deeply influence one another. This second part of the book treats of the lost child in the latter part of the twentieth century, first 'In The Theatre', specifically in the plays of Ray Lawler and Patrick White, and then 'In Fiction'. Next are considered 'Book Into Film', that is novels and other kinds of narrative which have been given cinematic treatments. Finally 'True Stories' are analysed – a small, if often frightful sampling of the manifold ways in which modern Australia has seen the loss of children. In terms of the historical traverse which it has made, the book rightly ends with a brief consideration of one of the most terrible of those true stories: that of the Aboriginal 'stolen generation'.

No attempt is made to find an answer for an abuse of the young that, relatively recently, has become more perverse, sometimes organised and certainly more widespread than anything that colonial Australia had to show. For all the diverse witness, whether anguished, or puzzled, or affecting detachment, of White and Bird, Ian Moffitt and Jennifer Maiden, Nicolas Roeg and Fred Schepisi, no conspiracy theory emerges in this book. Discernible, however, is a deep ambivalence about the next generation in Australia, as indeed there has been about the last few of them, but there is no thorough-going plot to destroy it. Some of the puerile would disagree. In *Gangland. Cultural Elites and the New Generationalism* (1997), Mark Davis asserted that 'youth and their preoccupations are being discredited, even demonised in the media'. For Davis, events such as the controversies over Helen Demidenko's *The Hand That Signed the Paper* (1994) or Helen Garner's *The First Stone* (1995) have 'obliquely or indirectly ... involved an attack on youth'. The problem, for Davis, is that 'a certain cultural establishment' hangs on to its power. Davis's complaint is not at all endorsed by what follows in 'The Child Abandoned', which traces not a trivial and dubiously reasoned argument about the cultural exclusion of the not so young, but the destruction of the lives of children. It was a cynical and humorous and appalling old man, Shakespeare's Falstaff, who in *1 Henry IV* declared that 'They hate us youth'. Falstaff had the benefit not only of the wisdom of his years, but of a miraculously resilient and supple will that he deployed to extend his childhood. So many Australian children, real and imagined, those whose stories are rehearsed and pondered here, had no such opportunity. The evidence of the true stories and of much imaginative writing and film from the second half of this century is that – more direly than Chatwin's Arkady had suspected – Australia is 'the country of lost children'.

In The Theatre

Colonial Australia saw the lost child presented on the stage in ways that were comic, saccharine and reassuring, rather than tragic or admonitory. The cavortings of pantomime, in Australian versions of the 'babes in the wood', rendered the bush an altogether less terrible prospect than many actual lost children had faced. One who survived such an ordeal, Clara Crosbie, found herself transposed to the Sydney waxworks at the end of 1885, there to stand for a season as a living embodiment of a child's indomitability. When, in the second half of this century, lost children reappeared in the theatre, it was usually by report rather than in person. If they were already lost when the plays began, they figured disturbingly by their absence. It was the nature of their lost condition to be either children who never were, or who were already, and early dead. These are the silent sufferers whom Ray Lawler and Patrick White depict in a number of their plays: the children never born to Roo and Olive, Ern and Nora, besides others who have perished more terribly and capriciously, in manners that allow little consolation, either symbolic or sentimental.

Ray Lawler: Bubba and the Baby Dolls

One of the most striking and complex variations on the theme of the lost child, although it has rarely been discussed in those terms, is Lawler's play *Summer of the Seventeenth Doll*, which was first performed in 1955 and published two years later. In the play, a couple faces the consequences of – among other choices – the decision not to have children of their own. We witness the results of their attempt, playful but ultimately desperate, to find symbolic and actual surrogates for the children whom, perhaps, they feared to have, and for the domestic future, the married life that for so long they declined to contemplate.

Melodrama is the mode deployed for many of the versions of the lost child material in Australia in the second half of the twentieth century, whether in fiction or in drama. Now melodrama, Eric Bentley suggestively affirmed in *The Life of the Drama* (1965), 'is the Naturalism of the dream life'. He wanted to establish a regard for the serious purposes to which dramatists put melodrama, for he saw it as 'drama in its elemental form, more natural than Naturalism'. Thus, 'the dramatic sense is the melodramatic sense'. Yet Bentley tended to ignore the ways in which naturalism and melodrama can and do cohabit, within the theatre, as within the family. In the potent case of Henrik Ibsen, this was not only a matter of what he had assimilated from the *pièces bien faites* of the French dramatist Eugene Scribe, but of his intuition into how the naturalistic surfaces of his dramas – the clothes, furniture and other physical possessions, as well as the formerly reassuring social and cultural assumptions of his characters – are so perilously maintained, are so vulnerable to loss through the eruption of melodramatic plot into the hitherto serenely plotless lives of these characters.

Often this occurs through the disclosure of a guilty secret from the past, such as Nora's in Ibsen's *The Doll's House* (1879), or that of the 'pillar of the community' (the title of another Ibsen play of 1877). The nature of Patrick White's insistence on the pasts of his dramatic characters – and the lack of, or sparing of the consequences of the revelation of those pasts – is an index of the extent to which he helped to naturalise melodrama in the Australian theatre in the second half of the twentieth century. No longer a European or American mode, and nineteenth-century in origin, though dressed in contemporary and local costume, modern Australian melodrama (in theatre and in fiction) dramatised central enmities, anxieties and inadequacies that writers perceived in Australian life.

Not the least problem of describing Ibsen or Anton Chekhov as naturalistic playwrights (or, in Australian literary history, Lawler and Alan Seymour) is their frequent employment of the central situation of melodrama. This is the threat of loss, of dispossession, which is often represented through a jeopardised stage property – Ibsen's 'wild duck', or the kewpie dolls that Olive harbours in Lawler's play *Summer of the Seventeenth Doll*. Such objects transform themselves from details of the naturalistic setting of the play into a symbol of the insubstantiality of that setting. Which is to say that the objects are appropriated for, and by melodrama.

In *Summer of the Seventeenth Doll*, Lawler's central stage symbol – the collection of 'sixteen kewpie dolls, wearing tinsel head-dresses and elaborately fuzzy skirts, attached to thin black canes shaped like walking sticks' – constitutes an unlikely and unpretentious dramatic property, particularly when so much weight of significance is placed on the dolls by other characters in the play. This is much of the point. The relationship within the Carlton terrace house has become so durable and contented that a simple, sentimental object such as the kewpie doll is adequate to register the remembered happiness of Olive, Roo, Barney, their next door neighbour young Bubba Ryan and the now departed Nancy. Beginning as a joke between Roo and Barney, the Queensland cane-cutters who spend five months each year with two Melbourne barmaids, Olive and Nancy, the dolls have come to represent how the lay-off arrangement has lasted so long. The dolls are also a symbol of time arrested, of a denial that anything between these people has changed. In particular, this is an idyll that children of their own have never been allowed to interrupt.

Of course this desire for a life untrammelled by time is self-deluded. *Summer of the Seventeenth Doll* dramatises the wasting of romantic illusions and the inchoate frustrations of its characters. In some respects, the real climax of the lives of Roo, Barney and Olive has already passed, without being fully heeded by them, before the play begins. Nancy is gone, abandoning them to marry a man called Harry who works in a bookshop. Pearl, the barmaid who is her unhappy replacement, brings an alien voice and sterile moralising into the house. Roo has been physically bested by the younger cane-cutter Dowd, while Barney's favours are now regularly rejected by women. Lawler has learned from Chekhov how to position his characters in situations where they are already doomed without admitting this to themselves, situations, moreover, that are climactic not only for them, but for the social group to which they belong.

There have been some over-schematic attempts to parallel the ageing of Australia with that of Roo and Barney, to represent their kind of rural work as about to be superseded by mechanised and less individualistic kinds of labour. Thus in *After 'The Doll'* (1979), Peter Fitzpatrick wrote that 'the review of seventeen summers is also in some ways a valediction to an old order'. But the play is more complex and poignant. Roo cannot accommodate to the waning of his physical powers and the compromise which he makes in taking a city job in a paint factory. Still in his work clothes he is confronted in the Carlton house by Dowd, a version of his younger self. Roo especially loathes the way in which he will be replaced (and in another sense duplicated) by a man from the younger generation. Vainly, and in a yet more desperate compromise about his work, Roo heads outback again with Barney at the end of the play. He has temporarily pretended that their 'mateship' has not been another of the losses to be reckoned. Mateship may be a vanishing element of the national life that can only deceptively be renewed, or an insistence upon it may be an admission of how much else these 'mates' have already lost.

Ibsen's naturalistic plays are imbued with a strong sense of determinism. Both the characters' heredity and their social circumstances make likely the fates that they have to endure. In Lawler's play, Emma is the croaking, gnomic voice of such determinism, especially in the last act, where she enlightens Roo about how he has aged without wanting to acknowledge this. The characters have increasing difficulty in believing the story of the sixteen successful summers: 'There's not one thing I've found here that's been anything like what you told me', Pearl complains to Olive, shortly before she abandons the house in the final act. Those sixteen previous summers have amounted to a miraculous resistance of probability, and of how the circumstances of separation and reunion would predictably and much sooner have soured. As Emma also points out, the wonder is that this idyll, both domestic in setting and anti-domestic in its refusal to admit children (Bubba excepted), has lasted so long, not that it has come to an end.

The recognition that there is an end is accompanied by Olive's destruction of the dolls. The symbolic procedure involved would be crude (the dolls represent romantic illusion; that they are smashed so easily reveals the fragility of illusions: one recalls Tennessee Williams's play *The Glass Menagerie*, 1944), if we were not given an intimation of how much self-destruction is involved in their damage. And there is a further and more important symbolic aspect of the dolls as stage properties. Cradling a doll, Olive holds a surrogate for the children whom she has never had. After Olive has received the seventeenth and last doll from Roo, we read in one of Lawler's frequent and over-explicit stage directions that 'She holds the doll almost as if it were a baby'. The grasping of the doll is a gesture that starkly emphasises not only Olive's childlessness, but how childlike she has remained. As Roo says to her on their last morning: 'Y'know, a man's a fool to treat you as a woman. You're nothin' but a little girl about twelve years old'. The plays of Lawler and White have in common the theme of childlessness, of what does not get born in Australia. Maybe the absence of children is the instinctive way of some, but not all of the characters, of removing one prospect of future loss by the present deprivation of themselves. Perhaps what is also expressed is the fear of one generation of its supersession by the next (as is the case with Roo and Dowd) and one that might be more 'grown-up' than it is.

Barney, of course, has children, as he owns up to Pearl: 'Yes, kids I got all right. In three states'. Or, as he states the case a touch resentfully, and in resistance to the comforts of cliché: 'I haven't got a family, what I got is kids'. There are, for instance, the two eldest boys, Lennie and Arthur (the latter named for his father, but known – like his father – by a nickname, Chippa in his case), for whom Pearl starts knitting jumpers.

Barney is affectionate to his children at a distance. If he has deserted their mothers, he has always paid them maintenance. His kids are kept far from him, so that they cannot interfere with his footloose life, or with what is in truth a protracted adolescence.

One of the salient features of *Summer of the Seventeenth Doll* is not just the valiant, naïve attempt by the characters to live, as it were, outside time, but the desire of some of them to remain lost in childhood, no matter that they are nearing middle age. This is particularly the case with Olive, of whom Lawler instructs us early that 'Despite a surface cynicism and thirty-seven years of age, there was something curiously unfinished about OLIVE, an eagerness that properly belongs to extreme youth'. The attempt to keep Kathie Ryan as an infant, as Bubba, is an exercise in infantilisation that has failed without Roo, Barney and Olive being aware. Bubba is the child surrogate for the childless couple of Roo and Olive, kept for their comfort – as they think – perpetually in a state before adulthood. It is a bleak and predictable irony that young Kathie, as Roo finally admits, has 'outgrown the lot of us', and that she contemplates a future with Dowd.

At the conclusion of *Summer of the Seventeenth Doll*, Roo tells Olive a truth that her romantic valuation of life will not allow her to concede: 'This is the dust we're in and we're gunna walk through it for the rest of our lives'. Thus he discloses the melodramatic 'secret' which Olive has never been prepared to confront. The radical anti-climax of marriage, the decline from poetic tinsel to dusty prose, the dissolution of the myth of Roo's prowess and privileged occupation, and his willingness to submit to domesticity (to turn Olive, perhaps, from lover to mother) – all that he now offers Olive is anathema to her. She rejects him and his marriage proposal. Preferring a melodramatic fate for herself, desiring vengeance through taking the victim's part, she sends Roo off aimlessly wandering with Barney. Such is the bleak irresolution of *Summer of the Seventeenth Doll*.

Now destroyed, the dolls stand blatantly, and poignantly, for the avoidance of a conventional family life between the principal characters. Most obviously they represent children who were 'lost' because they were never desired. That is, the dolls in a sense stand for a fear of the future, of an interruption to the blissful stasis that Roo and Olive have confected and reaffirmed every summer for so long. Significantly the dolls do not change with each year, despite Olive's wistful claim when she holds the seventeenth doll 'as if it were a baby', that 'Other times they've been pretty, but this one's beautiful'. Bubba is a tacit reproof to the choices which Roo and Olive have made. She has refused to remain a child. At the same time, she is incidental to the strange longing of Roo and Olive to be without children, yet to remain as children. That is the mythic core of *Summer of the Seventeenth Doll*, and the basis of its reflection on all the stories of lost children, in such different modes, which had been told and performed for a century in Australia before Lawler achieved fame.

'They wasn't in our line': The Lost Children of Patrick White

In Patrick White's novel *The Vivisector* (1970), the child Hurtle Duffield is lost to his family through being sold. The rich Courtney family want a son. The Duffields, who are poor, sympathise to a point and can oblige. They have, as Mrs Duffield complains, 'seven kiddies'. The Courtneys are burdened with Rhoda, 'that little girl … with the funny back'. At least she, Mrs Duffield supposes, will 'never suffer this part', that is the sating of a man's pleasure, and its consequences. Grumbling at her lot, Hurtle's mother balances 'money' against 'blood', before deciding, and then saying distinctly that 'I would give away any of my children, provided the opportunities was there. Blood is all very well. Money counts. I would give – I would give Hurtle'. And she does. Mr Duffield fears social and moral censure: the criticism of a father who cannot provide for his children, and the doubt as to whether such a course would be 'ethical'. But the child is sold. Hurtle's mother takes that practical view that 'we did it for the best'. Her husband lacerates himself in a manner that most likely will never end, whatever forms it takes: 'We sold 'im like a horse!'

White's earlier fictional treatment of a lost child had been ostensibly more conventional. In his revision of the Australian saga novel in *The Tree of Man* (1955), a lost child episode takes its place together with those other predictable national disasters of the pioneering life – fire, flood and drought. The incident in question, involving an unnamed, unclaimed lost child, follows the disastrous flood near Stan and Amy Parker's place, in the region that thereafter will be known by 'the official voice' as Durilgai.

On the night when people stranded by the flood, or who have come to look at it out of curiosity, decide to head home, somebody asks 'Whose little boy are you?' There is a child, crying in the dark. The butcher's wife avers that the 'kiddy's been crying all day'. He will not answer questions as to where or to whom he belongs. 'He only looks. An cries'. This woman's decision, which she has not yet acted upon, is to go to the police and 'give him in charge, as a lost child, of course, nothing nasty. People, you know, can't stand it'. While not amplifying on what test of 'people's' nerves is involved in and by the lost child, the butcher's wife is especially disconcerted by those who ask her to do something about it, as if the boy were hers, or her responsibility.

It is 'a lost child, of course', a familiar casualty of such a disaster as the flood. More disturbing for the butcher's wife, and perhaps for the other onlookers, is that the child – although found – remains profoundly lost. Rescued from the flood he might have been, but he is estranged from the well-intentioned folk around him. Amy Parker intervenes: 'She had to get over the side of the dray, as if some purpose were forming in the darkness. She had to touch the child'. To her question about his name the child is silent. His face 'was fully closed … She held in her hands the body of a caught bird'. For a second time she asks for a name, but 'the child eluded her, except for what she was holding of his bones'.

The childless Amy decides to turn the lost boy first into a person and later perhaps into her son: 'we'll have to find you a name', she declares and then informs Stan that 'we're taking the kid along with us'. As people around them talk about the objects which have changed hands in the flood – pots and pans, cheeses and rope, a world gazetteer, 'even a hip bath' (which the Parkers take as well) – an anonymous voice observes that 'Parkers got a bran new kid free for nothing'. The 'kidnappers' Stan and Amy drive home together with the mute child. The man's sympathies are personal rather than paternal: 'Stan Parker sat with his own awkward, uncommunicative childhood all along the inevitable road. He could feel the resentment of the strange boy pressed against his side'. An unusual future is being planned for this lost child. Not returned to his own family, he is on the verge of being adopted by strangers, without consideration of legal process, and as a surrogate for the child whom they have been unable to conceive.

The Parkers have also appropriated the bath, and that is what they talk about instead of the child. For his part, the boy 'sheltered behind their words, against the stars'. But he speaks at last when food is in prospect, remembering having eaten pork once, with crackling on it. Almost at once, the lost child stops talking about his past. He 'closed again. Deliberately. It was as if he had determined to originate on that night, outside the butcher's shop at Willunya'. Not that he will for long fulfil the role that Amy Parker intends for him. As she thinks of it: 'She would imprison the child in her home by force of love'.

But in the morning he has gone. In White's subtle variation of the nineteenth-century topos of the lost child, the boy whom the floods have thrown up chooses to be lost once more; he refuses the domesticity promised by the Parkers. Stan rationalises. The child did not want them: 'He didn't belong to us'. They decide that, Amy's hopes aside, it is 'all right'. They will cope with their childless condition, for 'Their lives had grown together'. As time passes, the Parkers will have two children, Ray and Thelma, both of whom will deeply wound and disappoint their parents. Although the incident of the twice lost child will be remembered in the district, 'nobody heard of the lost boy that the Parkers found at Willunya in the floods'. He has been re-absorbed into the country, has become part of the skein of folk memory. In the formal terms of this novel, he found himself depicted out of his time. The boy is a nineteenth-century figure given a cameo appearance in a novel of the mid twentieth century, in that skewed and revitalised saga novel that is *The Tree of Man*.

In his drama, as in his fiction, White has been a traducer of forms, a mixer of literary modes. Any attempts to explain his plays through concentration on naturalism and its formal rejection within them, ignores the two naturalisations that White essays: of Australian vernaculars into a language of poetic drama, and of Australian life into melodrama. This is the literary mode whose actions are performed with extravagant language and gesture, and whose central, abysmal theme is dispossession, the loss of property, chastity, reputation, life. This White sees as best fitting a nation bereft of history and unsure of its moral or practical tenure of its country in the future, a nation for long dominated by perceptions of internal and external threats. Or, as his polemical play *Big Toys* (1978) would argue, a nation that was indifferent to the dangers which White believed passionately were posed by the mining of uranium.

White wrote *The Ham Funeral* in London during 1947–8, but it was not performed until 1961, in Adelaide. White insisted that it was 'not a naturalistic play. The chief problem was how to project a highly introspective character on the stage without impeding dramatic progress'. His expressionistic devices included the use of an anima figure, who explains to the young man (what the three levels of the set have already indicated to the audience) that as a writer he will 'wrestle with the figures in the basement ... passion and compassion locked together'. In his prologue, the young man, who may be in part an ironic portrait of the author during his London sojourn in the 1930s and 1940s, admits that 'Once I almost wrote a play, in which the situations were too subtle to express'.

Of course White has written that play for him. Its obsession is already with language, in particular with the advent of poetry into the speech of ordinary people, the horrors of silence and of its interruption, the contortions of speech and the struggle to overcome impediments to speaking. The landlady interprets a damp patch on her wall this way:

> 'Ole continents to them that knows. Africa couldn't be darker to me. Once I almost screamed. Then I wondered if anyone would hear me. Other people are deaf, you know.

There is some trace here of the divided impulses within Dickens's characters between sociability and solipsism, between the urge to bridge physical separateness through speech and the solace and relative safety of self-communion. But there is also an altogether different note, and one that comes to be distinctive of White, when at last the landlord, shockingly, speaks: 'You ask me the story of me youth. You'd ask in the same breath for a basinful of blood'. As though the effort of this utterance is fatal, the landlord dies soon afterwards. Following the ham funeral, his widow reflects:

> Dry! No doubt ... (*drinks*) ... about that. Couldn't get me words out without a little bit of assistance. Death's a dry business ... Nothing drier ... (*tortured*) ... 'xceptin' love.

This is the general human sorrow which White will naturalise as an Australian problem with an idiom of its own. That was one of his main literary objectives of the mid 1950s to the early 1960s, the period when he naturalised himself again, by rehabituating himself to Australia. This was the time when he wrote the novels *Voss*, *The Tree of Man* and *Riders in the Chariot*, as well as three more plays of which the first, *A Season at Sarsaparilla*, 'A Charade of Suburbia', had its premiere – again in Adelaide – in 1962.

In that play in particular, a motif introduced in *The Ham Funeral* is again of importance. In various guises this is the figure of the lost child. During a rancorous exchange in the first play, the landlady declares 'I 'ad a child. It died. That's all I admit'. Her husband's response is to offer a bitter epithet for the child: 'The little, blue-faced, wizened pimp'. The child, 'the little bastard', which presumably died soon after its birth, is apparently the product and perhaps the price of one of the adulteries to which the landlady confesses. The adultress of *A Season at Sarsaparilla* is cursed (and punished) by childlessness. This is Nora Boyle, wife of Ern, the kind and easily cuckolded sanitary man. When Rowley 'Digger' Masson, a mate of Ern's from the time of the war in the Western Desert turns up unexpectedly, and is invited to stay, he tactlessly tells his host that 'You ought 'uv had a few kids, Ern. Five. Or seven. Seven's lucky ain't it?' Making things more uncomfortable, Rowley then asks Nora why they have had no children, and is told '(*grimly, quietly*) We tried. But they wasn't in our line'.

The action of *A Season at Sarsaparilla* is focussed by White's treatment of attitudes towards the practice of marriage in post-war Australia, particularly towards child bearing and rearing. By the end of the play, Mavis Knott has subsided complacently into motherhood. 'She'll settle down to it like shelling peas', as the childless Nora prophesies resentfully. In turn, Nora has survived another spasm of adultery, this time and predictably with the family friend and intruder Rowley Masson. Reconciled, temporarily, with Ern, Nora muses of a time in 1948 when she had thought herself pregnant: 'I thought I'd copped it at last. I was carrying you! YOU ... But it was only another false dawn ...'. This recollection is oddly expressed. It is as if the child she wanted truly to bear was her husband, and that this explains her capricious and treacherous mothering of him, and attempt to infantilise him, as their marriage runs its course.

Next door to the Boyles live the Pogsons. He is a 'business executive'. In his domestic life Clive Pogson is content, in general, to allow his wife, Girlie Pogson, to dream of her lost childhood, the pastoral gentility of Rosedale where 'nobody used words ... Nobody was in business then, everybody was on the land ...'. Her present responsibility is to mould their two daughters, Judy and Joyleen (Pippy) for their inevitable marriages. 'What more can anyone expect?' he says once, in unison with Girlie. Of the female characters in the play only Julia Sheen, who becomes pregnant to an older, married man, the unctuous Mr Erbage, and then kills herself, suffers irreparably. But her death is soon forgotten, in order that the proprieties and priorities of Sarsaparilla can be maintained. Another of White's sententious young men, Roy Child, remarks with tiresome over-explicitness: 'So they die. So they are born. And are the sins of the watchers forgiven, in the backyards, at dusk?'

It is Roy (whose surname indicates fatefully his problems of becoming an adult) who has failed to give assistance to Julia Sheen. She confided to him euphemistically but directly that 'I'm in a spot of trouble'. His lame response was to ask 'what about the child?', to which she bleakly returned 'He won't be the first child who hasn't had to suffer'. All Roy can manage in reply is to call out as Julia leaves 'If you're going short in any way ...'. But her retort '(brutally)' is 'One thing I'll never do is go short'. What she does is to kill herself and the unborn child by crashing her car. He (or she) thus becomes another child who has not had to suffer, while Julia suffers no longer either. It is only left for the sanctimonious Erbage to bring Roy the news that 'the young lady's ... passed on'. He has heard that she was pregnant but will accept no culpability – 'it don't seem fair if a little bit of pleasure goes wrong'.

In the next of White's plays to be performed, *A Cheery Soul* (1963), the theme of the lost child is scrutinised in a different mood. Instead of the desolate story of the death of the pregnant Julia, if not from spite at least from despair, in a suicide that was treated with indifference by those whom it was most meant to move, we have macabre comedy. Feeling herself to be selfish in the good fortune that she enjoys, Mrs Custance persuades her husband that they ought to give a home to Miss Docker, the indomitable and appalling 'cheery soul' of the play's title. White gives us a brief exchange between husband and wife: Mrs Custance exclaims 'It would have been different if we'd had some kids. I wonder if people ever think we couldn't be bothered? That'd be awful!' Awful and unjust, for – as Mr Custance dryly responds – 'Want us to go round with a placard: VICTIMS OF THE ABSENT-MINDED SURGEON?' But Mrs Custance is not one to draw attention to herself by making a fuss: 'Ah, Ted! We've been through all that before. It wasn't his fault. I was on the wrong trolley'. How is one to gauge the tone of this exchange? The lost prospect of children has been over time transformed into a comfortable, almost comic experience shared in private by this long married couple. Instead of the children whom they might have had, the Custances are about to let Miss Docker into their house. She will prove to be every bit as capricious and demanding as a child might have been, although the Custances escape with less damage from her than the Reverend and Mrs Wakeman later in the play.

In the plays that White wrote in the late 1970s and early 1980s, after a break of nearly two decades, he was by turns polemical and self-parodic. In *Big Toys* (1978) he assembled his smallest cast: the childless Bosanquets, lawyer Ritchie and his decorative wife Mag, who has recently joined the Labor Party for diversion, and the trade union leader Terry Legge. The latter will be compromised by Bosanquet in the corruption trial of Sir Douglas Stannard in which they are ranged on opposite sides. Compromise is the variously-faceted main theme of *Big Toys*. By others it may sometimes be regarded as betrayal. Usually it can be styled by oneself as the necessary accommodation to difficult circumstances. In the stridently topical conclusion of the play, White uses Terry Legge to trumpet against compromise in the matter of the 'biggest, gaudiest toy that ever escaped from a child's hand' – uranium.

Terry is another victim of a White melodrama, dispossessed of his self-respect ('It's bitter if you begin to feel you're not what you thought you were'), not by any villainous intriguer, rather by political exertions and later by moral compromises on his own behalf. The melodramatic action is internalised in *Big Toys*. Ritchie is no moustache-twirling rogue. His wife and accomplice is engineered by the dramatist into an improbable state of metaphysical remorse. The material objects of stock melodramatic plotting have no value here – neither jewels, nor chastity. The power over others that might secure them is the end itself for the Bosanquets. Rejecting the material blandishment of a Ferrari, Terry may have failed to realise how surely that power has yet been exercised over him.

The subtitle of *Signal Driver*, which was first performed in Adelaide on 5 March 1982, is 'A Morality Play for the Times'. This implies a misleading propinquity with *Big Toys*. Centrally and more emphatically than in any of his other plays, White's business in *Signal Driver* is with the trajectory of an Australian marriage. Theo and Ivy Vokes endure six decades of married life, in spite of his desire to escape from her, and of her adultery. In the three acts of the play, we see them successively in the 1920s, the 1950s and the 1980s. At the end of the first act, which is set in a bus shelter on the outskirts of the city, 'the Vokes plod through the dark and eventually exit in what they presume to be the right direction'.

The unillusioned, yet ultimately respectful view of marriage in the play is announced by one of the two 'timeless supernatural BEINGS ... presented as a pair of super deros', who oversee and comment on the action (and on a famous Irish playwright: 'Makes yer fuckun tired waitin' for somethun to happen'). The Second Being declares: 'Hang out the fairy lights. Marriages and history wouldn't look too bright without 'em'. White conceives of Australian marriage, at least in *Signal Driver*, but arguably in a more general fashion, as the association between two people who survive the threats to them, not because of heroic rescues or exposures of villainy, but by a native, dogged capacity to endure what befalls them. Dispossession – as forfeiture of social independence and moral selfhood – is essential to White's melodramatic characterisation of the Vokes. If such losses are not precisely made good in the play, other compensations, semblances of substance, are contrived and agreed upon between husband and wife.

In Act One, Ivy announces one kind of loss (and one that is emblematic of White's drama): 'the child we've never had; that would have made our marriage binding'. Then she adds 'Only children – and death – make a marriage real'. Theo is not a sympathetic listener: '(*hardening*)' she tells him of her conviction that 'Children are what I see as spirit – if grown from love'. Now while this may be the wistful viewpoint of one who believes herself incapable of having children (from want of 'love' perhaps), Theo's intemperate response suggests a deep antipathy to the thought of bringing a next generation into being:

> Children can and do grow into monsters and set about devouring the world. All monsters started as children, planted lovingly in hungry wombs.

Her only reaction to this acrid outburst is to say 'ours would be different'.

By Act Two, 30 years later, the Vokes are in a position to judge. Like the Parkers, this couple's long wait for children is eventually rewarded. Ivy makes the best of what they have: 'I only wanted a couple. With more you can't give them the attention children need'. But the children have been a source of disappointment and sadness. Nancy is married to Erroll

Bonser, 'the worst kind of business con', while Tom is lost to them as well, having committed suicide by a drug overdose. Theo dolefully summarises: 'the poor bugger Tommo dead, and Nancy as good as in her prestige straight-jacket'. Always capable of finding consolation by euphemism, Ivy declares that 'the replacements may have looked in – our little grandchildren'.

In the final act of *Signal Driver*, Ivy muses on 'the milky faces of little children', but this is not an innocent remembrance. The children are 'dead or multiplying'. She dreams of a girl, Lurline, who might have been her granddaughter: 'I dreamed I stabbed ... mutilated ... I burned her in the backyard'. This dream is as real to Ivy as 'the rooms in huge unoccupied houses, full of torn-up letters ... and the little milky faces of children waiting to have their revenge'. It seems that the children have secured or intuited knowledge of their parents' darkest secret – that they want them dead, or would rather they had never been born. The nightmare floats free from the play, takes on an independent life, much as did the Custances' exchange from *A Cheery Soul*. Each of these visions of lost children is likely to haunt and disconcert playgoers and readers; each is an emblem for the riven world, with its often fatal antagonisms between parents and children, that White apprehends. Whether his attitude toward them is mocking or sorrowing, is left tantalisingly unresolved.

Netherwood, which was first performed on 11 June 1983, recapitulates in parody the plays by White that went before it; becomes a bizarre summary and valuation of the dramatist's career as well as a riposte to his critics. The setting of *Netherwood*, 'a large, dilapidated Australian country house (perhaps in the Bowral, Moss Vale, Robertson area). The period is vaguely 1970s', suggests, in spite of the historical moment, White's schooldays at Tudor House, near Moss Vale, in the 1920s. One element of the play's manic parody and of its melodramatic texture is the recall and exorcism of authority figures who menace the inmates of institutions – whether schools, or liberally-run asylums (as here).

Everywhere recalled are characters from White's earlier plays. Unwittingly echoing the 'cheery soul', Miss Docker, the ex-boxer Harry Britt proclaims himself 'a norphan'. Alice Best, who with her husband Royce manages Netherwood, is earnestly and futilely charitable in the manner of Mrs Custance: 'we're here to offer our services. I want us to have this large family of ... people the world sees as hopeless'. But White's extreme inquiries into definitions of the self through self-abasement (conducted, in his novels, from the time of Theodora Goodman in *The Aunt's Story*, 1948) emerges parodically when Alice declares her motives: 'to cook simpler meals for our simpler fellows. To wash excremental sheets. Service is a kind of sacrament'. The slatternly Mog, who works at Netherwood as a maid, is allowed to enunciate what had perhaps congealed as White's theory of communication between humans: 'Words knot themselves too easily, when they don't turn to broken glass. Postcards, if you're lucky, and the memory of silences in backyards'.

Master themes of his previous plays recur. Alice, predictably, is childless. So is Harry: 'Myra didn't want any'. And so is Mog, but for the extravagant reason that she suffocated her infant in a plastic bag. The central stage property in *Netherwood* is 'a raised baby's chair of the commonest kind, with a tray for feeding'. Mog obsessively touches the chair, as if it is a correlative for, and reminder of the child whom she killed. The chair has a history. It belonged to the Du Faurs, the previous owners of the property. They sold up in grief when their child was lost. It is remembered by their neighbours, the Stubbs, simply as 'the kiddy that fell in the dam'.

When Mog enters the house for the first time in the play she is carrying a pullet whose neck she has just wrung, cradling it in her hands. She tells Alice that the fowl is 'a little reminder'. Alice is puzzled, but Mog is willing to explain: 'The kid I had … Plastic bag'. Its father was Father …, an unnamed Catholic priest. Here, as before, White's treatment of lost child material teeters uneasily on the edge of black and tasteless joking. How sincere is Mog's sorrow? How much of what has happened does she understand? As she sits down to write the story of her life (a project that is never concluded) Mog reveals that 'I was the middle one of seven kids. My mother didn't want me'. This is enough for Alice to tell Mog that she had not had a child because 'I was afraid'. As surrogates, she has gathered together the inmates of Netherwood. In one of the scenes of play-acting within the play, Royce and Harry themselves become like children. But Alice will not prove to be the most protective of mothers for them, or the others.

White sustains an interest in Mog's lost child for far longer than in similar circumstances in his previous plays. She tells Harry that 'I prayed that it would go away, but it didn't'. When Royce unblocks the sink, she asks 'And what did you find? Not a baby, I hope?' On another occasion, after approaching the baby chair, Mog bows her head, weeps softly, touches the chair and wonders 'What would he have become if he had grown? A man – or a monster, or a man?' And then, in grief, Mog prays:

> O Lord God of men and crims, I still see the little wizened face looking at me through the plastic window. Didn't have time to speak to me. Perhaps wouldn't have in life.

Her words, 'wizened' and 'monster' in particular, echo *The Ham Funeral* and *Signal Driver*, thus spanning the period in which all of White's plays before this one had been written.

The action of *Netherwood* is extravagantly melodramatic. The folk in the home are threatened with dispossession. They might lose their dwelling place, their illusions of self, even their lives. Preying upon them are three types of intruder: the psychiatrist Rolf Eberhard, who has informally treated Royce and Alice Best and who now returns to disturb them afresh; the police officers, who join in the murderous shoot-out with which the play concludes, and Mr and Mrs Stubbs, who live on the neighbouring property and are now filled with a righteous sense of the proper and traditional uses of land that they feel is being ill-treated: 'Isn't it our country? Wasn't meant to be loonyland'. In Mr Stubbs, White parodies the stoic bushman of legend (and of Australian dramatic history) by having him parade the battle honours of rural work – scars from digging fence poles, a foot trampled by a steer and 'me groin that the *barbed* wire savaged'.

During the extirpation of Netherwood, the Stubbs, Mog, Harry and a police constable are shot and killed. The target of parody here may be the violence employed to precipitate climaxes in earlier Australian plays. This involves characters such as Roo and Barney in *Summer of the Seventeenth Doll*, Alf Cook in Seymour's *The One Day of the Year* (1960, 1962) and Norm, in Alex Buzo's *Norm and Ahmed* (1968, 1969). The police sergeant summarises: 'Comical bastards, us humans. Seems like we sorter choose ter shoot it out … to find out who's the bigger dill'. Those last words may be White's invitation to his critics to prove themselves, through their interpretations, to be the biggest dills. *Netherwood* has exaggerated into parody the themes and character types of his previous plays almost – it might appear – as an annulment of what had gone before, thus acting perhaps as an incitement to himself or to other Australian dramatists, to begin anew, to reject the tempting because tried forms and formulae.

One situation that he neither neglects, nor fails to exploit – in complicated, perverse and contradictory ways – is that of the unwanted child. The boys and girls of White's dramas are lucky to survive their parents. Neglected, aborted or murdered as they so often are, these children are emblems of those adult fears of the self and the future that the plays vividly dramatise, if also with a frustrating offhandedness. White's motives remain obscure. Either there is nothing more harrowing than the loss of children, or that loss is a thing of little importance. White's plays explore, or casually remark too many kinds of loss to allow for secure judgment about his stance. Thus the plight of his lost children remains a crux in his work, but as a signal ambivalence.

In Fiction

Among the 'images of society and nature' which Brian Kiernan found and analysed in seven modern Australian novels in his book of that name (1971), the lost child had no place. Yet for more than 40 years, from Patrick White in *The Tree of Man* (1955) to Carmel Bird in *Red Shoes* (1998), writers of fiction in Australia have not regarded the lost child merely as a cultural artefact of the last century, subject of a set of stories exemplary of the hardships of pioneering in the bush. They have seen this figure as representative of some of the worst exigencies of the present time. The heterogeneous group of authors who are considered here – some of them famous names, others who deserve to be better and more seriously known – all treat of contemporary predicaments of the lost child in Australia. The exception is an historical novel, David Malouf's *Remembering Babylon* (1993). Its benign and salving conclusion, its paradoxical hopes for the future of lost children, may only be possible because the novel is set in the last century and not in this.

For the circumstances in which Australian children are lost in the latter decades of the twentieth century have sharply changed from the colonial period. If men and women of those earlier societies had been unconvinced of their rights of tenure in Australia (when they thought of the issue), many members of later adult generations – according to the imaginative witness of this fiction – wished to be free or rid of their children. Selfish this sentiment often was, and on occasions covert and celebrated, cruel in issue beyond belief, yet its desired outcome was clear: to be relieved of the burdens of children, thence to disclaim responsibility for the future. In the phrase of Thomas Keneally's Sal Fitzgerald in *Passenger* (1979), this may signify 'Our dread of the coming society'.

The fiction of eight authors is discussed here: by Keneally, Frank Moorhouse, Leone Sperling, Beverley Farmer, Ian Moffitt, Jennifer Maiden, Bird and Malouf. Treatments of the lost child by Gabrielle Lord and White fall more conveniently into other sections of 'The Child Abandoned': 'Book into Film' and 'In the Theatre' respectively. And numerous other writers might have been included. Stephen Crisp, protagonist of Robert Drewe's first novel, *The Savage Crows* (1976) loses one child to abortion (because its mother rightly senses Crisp's indifference) and another when his ex-wife and her lover move to England. In Kate Grenville's *Dreamhouse* (1986), the beautiful Louise Dufrey is unluckily impregnated by her husband Reynold, whose preferences are in fact for his own sex. But she does not bring the child to term. Louise miscarries. The loss of the child then becomes the means of Louise's liberation from a bad marriage.

Both Drewe and Grenville deploy lost child episodes as part of their anatomies of contemporary Australia. In Drewe's novel, for instance, a heedless hedonism contributes to the abortion and also blights the life of a small girl. They are common casualties not only of adult selfishness, but of an unarticulated nihilism. That sentiment is discovered by all of the authors who are discussed below. Often its manifestations for the fate of children are terrible. These writers of fiction are, or were, working coincidentally, but not in concert. One could mention other names and titles as well, to emphasise how notable, if unexpected, is this conjunction of interest in the figure and the history of the lost child. For example, Margaret Scott's historical novel, *The Baby-Farmer* (1990), might be thought in part to deal with contemporary anxieties by analogy. It treats of a systematic abuse of children in Victorian Britain, where unwanted babies were farmed out in the knowledge that frequently this would lead to their deaths. Bird's *Red Shoes* imagines the same practice in a modern Australian setting.

In Jack Hibberd's tragi-comic novel, *Memoirs of an Old Bastard* (1989), in which every sadness is met by jest, an ageing, epicurean millionaire is in search of the child whom he abandoned when she was four at the Good Shepherd Convent in Collingwood. Years later he learns from the nuns that his daughter has been abducted. The fate that then and therefore awaited her in Melbourne, 'catamite and nymphet capital of the world' he too readily guesses. The girl's foredooming name is Perdita – the little lost one. It is a name that she shares with a famous young lost woman, the heroine of Shakespeare's late romance *The Winter's Tale*. The father of the modern day Perdita muses that 'Children once died naturally, in the arms of their mothers, from the plague'. Now their urban fates are likely to be dire and without parental consolation.

A later novel of Hibberd's, concerning a daughter, abandoned as a child, who now searches for her father, was called *Perdita* (1992). In Carolin Window's *Dim* (1996), a child born with nine lives risks losing all of them because of the predatoriness of adults. The grown-up brother and sister, Kit and Viv Estevan, in Alan Gould's novel *The Tazyrik Year* (1998) are aptly styled 'lost children', for they have retreated ferociously from the present into a world of play which ignores the passing of time.

All these writers are informally collaborating – if not on a secret history, in the sense of a record being kept but officially hidden from view – then on a miscellaneous, often horrified inventory of myriad, intolerable, singular acts of cruelty towards children. To read of the rage of parents against their sons and daughters, born and unborn, in the work of Keneally, Sperling, Farmer and Bird, is to discern a generational and psychological crisis so acute that even they will not tease out all of its implications for contemporary Australian society. To read of the fates of the despairing, youthful urban tribes in the novels of Moffitt, Maiden and Lord, is to believe that – more fully than ever in the previous century – this is truly 'the country of lost children'.

'Our dread of the coming society': Thomas Keneally's Fiction

The ghosts of lost children throng the fiction of Thomas Keneally. There is the child which Ann Rush conceives in *Bring Larks and Heroes* (1967), despite the superstitious protection of the St Megan's cord, but which, because she is hanged, she never lives to bear. In *The Survivor* (1969), Ella Ramsey is delivered of a stillborn child. Thereafter she refuses to consider adoption for 'her pride and shame were as basic as those of a tribal woman cursed with a dead womb'. Keneally has also depicted, in *A Family Madness* (1985), the deaths of the Kabbel children in a suicide pact and the accidental murder of Kate Kozinski's son and daughter in *Woman of the Inner Sea* (1992). The importance of lost children in Keneally's fiction was elaborated in my *Australian Melodramas* (1995):

> Besides these losses, Keneally writes – from the point of view of the foetus – of threats to abort it in *Passenger*; depicts Jimmie Blacksmith's premature rejoicing in the birth of a child whom he did not father; imagines the central blankness in the lives of numbers of childless couples. Subtly and variously, he has meditated on the significance of the lost, dead, imperilled child in Australian culture, and on the importance of that figure to literary melodrama. Unsure of how to identify its villains; uneasy in acclaiming its heroes and heroines (or crediting either their virtues or their potency); desiring the happy ending that the genre promises, but uncertain as to whether that promise will be made good, Australian melodrama in this century nevertheless has its unequivocal aspects. The terror of deprivation of material substance, and of national and personal identity is at its heart. The loss, or at least the absence of children is its secret, shocking emblem.

For a key element of the plot of *A Family Madness*, Keneally drew on a true story of the loss of children. His author's note, at the end of the book, informs us that:

> In a suburb of Sydney, Australia, in July 1984, a family of five willingly ended their lives. Their consent to their own destruction had its roots in events which occurred during World War Two, in voices heard and insupportable fears endured in that era.

From this basis, he develops one of his richest anatomies of the sorrows and strangeness of contemporary life in Australia.

The Penrith Rugby League five-eight Terry Delaney works part-time as a security guard for a firm owned by Belorussian migrant Rudi Kabbel and his family. He falls in love and begins an affair with Danielle, Rudi's daughter. In consequence he alienates himself from his wife and hopes to marry Danielle, who falls pregnant to him. When Delaney hears that news:

> Everything he'd thought solid – marriage, two runs in first grade – had run to water. His fatherhood dominated all. And there was this added in: Danielle would not protect herself from the other Kabbels; but she *would* protect a child.

He is too sanguine. Believing in the imminent end of the world (Rudi's son Warwick speaks of an apocalyptic tidal wave, the *tsunami* – 'everyone knows. There'll be one in the end'), the Kabbels sell their business and seem to have 'vanished from the earth', Danielle included. She gives birth to a child in the fitting room at Fossey's, but although this enables him to track the family down, Delaney will never see the baby girl, his daughter. The unnamed child becomes one of five victims in the 'family madness' of the novel's title, perishing along with her mother, Rudi Kabbel and his two sons. The ending is shocking if not unexpected. Keneally writes not only of the 'madness' of this particular family, but of a kind of nihilism that is also native to Australia. The tragedy, that is, does not seem to be only an alien, European, migrant event, whatever its origins in the older Kabbels' experiences during the war. A fear of the future that is drastically and terribly resolved by the death of a family does not seem incongruous in the Australia that Keneally imagines.

In *Woman of the Inner Sea*, another of Keneally's ambitious, eccentric and compassionate anatomies of Australia, Kate Kozinski – who is holed up in a pub in the western New South Wales town of Myambagh – shows her friend Jelly a photograph of her two children, Siobhan and Bernard. While Jelly is seeking the right mode of response – 'inquisitive, respectful, ready with the apt word of praise' – Kate bluntly tells him: 'I've lost them'. Jelly asks at once whether the father had taken them away and she replies that indeed he had: 'He argued he was a fitter person. His mother argued that too'. She is playing with words, perhaps reticently or from a self-protective reflex. In fact her children are dead: asphyxiated in a fire at her Palm Beach home, while she was in the city dining with her father. Now, in hiding outback, Kate finds that 'grief had seized up her womb'. Her periods have stopped. No longer does she 'go through the phases of desire'. Driven to the fire by her father, Kate sees only 'the black hole where the children had vanished'. Her estranged husband berates her: 'Why weren't they at the dance class?' 'Where were you?' 'Why weren't you with the children?' The charges he makes will seem to Kate to be altogether just: 'He was quite right saying she should have been there'.

Which is to say, she would have died along with her children. Except that such was not Paul Kozinski's intention. The arson – for so it will turn out to be – was intended to kill Kate, whom he had expected to be at home, and not the children, whom he thought would be at the dance class. At last Kate will understand, after many months of suffering, that the loss of the boy and girl was not her fault:

> She had not thrown her children away, as the old version of the story told her. The point of the question, *Why weren't you there?* had been reversed. She had not thrown the children away. They had been snatched.

Understanding that, Kate loses 'the gravity of blame'. The malevolence of their father, not a mother's delinquency, has caused the loss of the children.

In seeking to murder his wife, Paul Kozinski has killed his son and daughter. The intention was to make it easier for him to marry his mistress, Perdita Krinkovich, whose given name is – like the lost daughter in Hibberd's *Memoirs of an Old Bastard* – that of the heroine of *The Winter's Tale*. Bumping into Perdita in a department store, Kate is enraged to find that she is pregnant, and reckons the knowledge this way: 'That is my child, she thought, she has captured my child'. Although not for long: on the evening that Paul Kozinski is arrested for bribing a cabinet minister, tax offences and sundry and predictably connected matters, Perdita miscarries. Another child is lost. Kozinski goes to gaol and eventually Perdita succumbs to a banker, Paul Ferris, 'pleasant and untormented, he has earned his money in accredited ways, and no curse of lost children lies over him'. That curse can never be lifted from Kate, whose children have died instead of her, victims of resentment and sexual caprice. Their father, it appears, valued them only for the name that he had given them, and raged not at their loss, but at the disappointment of his schemes to free himself of a wife.

When, in the summer of 1956, seven years before the action of *The Survivor* begins, Ella Ramsey becomes pregnant, she soon begins 'to bleed dangerously, as often as once a week'. While the rate of her bleeding increases, the embryo continues to grow. 'Fearing a monster', her husband 'began to insinuate the idea of abortion'. Ella refuses. After long believing herself to be sterile, such talk seems to her like betrayal, however much her husband has her health in mind. But the child within her womb is doomed: 'In the seventh month, in a vast baby-farm of a hospital', it dies and is 'released by Caesarean section'. Another story of a woman who refused an abortion, polemical rather than sad in its tone, is central to Keneally's novel *Passenger* (1979). To state the case that way is, however, grossly to simplify one of the most prodigally plotted of all his novels. Yet of the many stories that are started in *Passenger*, that of the young and beautiful mother-to-be, Sal Fitzgerald, is paramount.

The novel is narrated by her sentient foetus, who remains the reader's droll, if often anxious guide to the adulteries of Sal's husband Brian, the succour which she receives from the mysterious American called the Gnome, her escape to Australia from Britain and his own birth. Going to Australia with the Gnome, who has helped her to break out of an asylum to which Brian had had her committed, Sal is following the path of his Fitzgerald ancestors. One in particular has so exercised her that he is to become the subject of her second novel. This Fitzgerald (who would receive 500 lashes once in New South Wales for claiming to have seen evidence of homosexuality among kangaroos) was involved in the 1798 Irish Rebellion. Captured, and sentenced to transportation for life, Fitzgerald was put in the hold of the prison ship *Minerva*, where he waited for six months before it sailed for Australia. As Sal explains to the lascivious gynaecologist, Dr Ford: 'The Irish convicts were full of a vague, demoralising dread. The way we are. That's what the book will be. An essay on dread. Our dread of the coming society'. Her historical inquiry explains itself by its relevance to the present, but who does Sal mean by 'our'? It is as if she has anticipated the kind of selfishness that her husband will show in his demands that she have an abortion, then dignified it with a metaphysical dimension. And yet Keneally, one suspects, subscribes to such metaphysics. Those, like Brian Fitzgerald, who can imagine nothing beyond their own needs (however elegantly, or with apparent disinterest, these might be described by them) can argue by reflex for abortion. A next generation is no concern of theirs. The demands that it might make upon them are almost at all costs to be avoided.

Now in one of its many aspects, *Passenger* might be thought to be an anti-abortion tract. Keneally cunningly lets the foetus address the reader on that matter; speak to those who have no doubt labelled me in moral, political and other terms – you have called me an anti-abortionist, an enemy of Zero Population Growth ... a sentimental pleader of the rights of foetuses. None of that am I. Let others make their own plans. I am a pleader for *myself*. I want no sharp knives for me.

This may be disingenuous. If the unborn could speak (and only in this fiction of Keneally's is that possible) they are indeed unlikely to welcome the prospect of abortion. That disclaimer done with, Keneally sets the many plot strands of *Passenger* into reckless motion. Some of them bear on the novel's essential theme: how can children be protected from adults? The Fitzgeralds' landlady, Clytie, is having tea with Sal when they are accosted by Clytie's 'dotty' cousin Elspeth, who asks the mother-to-be whether she has seen the article on the Virgin Birth in the latest issue of the *Month*. Besides this crazed non sequitur, Elspeth is also free with the opinion that Sal will return to the Catholic church, for 'who else will protect your baby at this stage in history?' Later Clytie's companion George will reminisce to Brian about an earlier and perilous stage in history, the time of his service as an army doctor in Yugoslavia in 1944. Then he performed his first abortion, pretending that it was an appendix operation, to protect a pregnant partisan woman from being shot. This was 'an abortion of convenience'. The child was his. Such stories throw into relief incidentally – although one cannot feel accidentally – what will become of Sal's desperate attempt to save her baby son.

Her saviour, the Gnome, is himself an abandoned child. As he explains to Sal, he is an orphan, 'They tell me that my mother gave birth to me at a table in a diner called Caruso's in Pittsfield, Mass'. The Gnome is obsessed with the belief that he has never been 'adequately introduced to the world'. Thus he forms the weird belief (but one altogether plausible to him) that when Sal is delivered of her baby, so will he also be delivered: 'I'll be after forty years a child of this earth'. That is the sort of dreaming which makes it easier for Brian to damn Sal with guilt by association and to have her committed. On assignment in Israel, to cover the Yom Kippur War, he has fallen in love with an Australian journalist, Annie Newman. He lies to her: 'I have no children' and then proceeds to try to ensure that this remains the case.

Confronting Sal on his homecoming, he tells her crudely that she, or they if she prefers, 'ought to get the thing terminated'. Not only does he want the marriage cancelled, 'I want the fruits cancelled. Having a brat ... it'll start Annie off on a basis of guilt over you, over the brat'. And then: 'Get rid of the foetus ... It hasn't got a future'. 'It' is a 'thing' without a name, an impediment to the carnal, child-free future that Brian Fitzgerald, having mapped it in his head, now seeks to impose on his wife. Abetted by Sal's rage at what he desires, Brian is able to have her taken into custody. She is incarcerated in a ward for women who – as one of the inmates explains to her –

> all feel aggression ... Against their own children. They said they were only putting people in who had aggression problems towards their children. It's an experiment, to let us talk it out. Pooling our guilt. Why did they put you in here, when you haven't got a child?

The notion of therapeutic self-help among would-be infanticides has its piquancy, if not for Sal, to whom it is 'that dormitory of child-killers'.

But, with the Gnome's help, she gets away. Her son is born in Australia, if not without further difficulties. For all that has imperilled it, this precious child has not been lost. *Passenger* is, no doubt, special pleading by Keneally for the unborn, but he feels their plight keenly, less for doctrinaire reasons, than for his apprehension of all the suffering to which children are put in the world that he translates into his fiction. The power of that dark sentiment, 'our dread of the coming society' (which would, in a different mode, agitate the Kabbels in *A Family Madness*) is one which his fiction both reveals, and confronts. And not his alone: if it is depicted by very different fictional means, and in a spirit that is more pessimistic, that same 'dread' preoccupies numbers of the characters in the fiction of Frank Moorhouse.

'Keeping control of the young': Frank Moorhouse and the Lost Child

Frank Moorhouse may at times have posed as a *flâneur*, but he is unjestingly in earnest concerning his craft. The settings of his short stories are often exotic, but much of his fiction has a strong regional tinge. Thus he fervidly claims a Balmain grandmother, and in his writing makes frequent, if ambivalent returns to his childhood territory of the south coast of New South Wales. As Christopher Brennan was dogged with the notion that his work was a *livre composé*, so may Moorhouse be. However fragmented or discontinuous internally, each of his books builds upon, tenuously or tenaciously connects with and draws sustenance from its predecessors. Moorhouse is the lachrymosely joking chronicler of loss in contemporary Australian society, and he also represents the difficulty of belonging, of finding lodgment here. Cosmopolitan Moorhouse has yet made a central item of his work the revision of one of the oldest and most tenacious of Australian cultural (and originally rural) motifs – that of the lost child. In his treatment of this subject, Moorhouse writes in some measure as a cultural diagnostician, one who confronts the social consequences of libertarianism in Australia since the 1960s. At the same time he reveals the naïve yet self-protective orphan in Australian culture which perhaps he feels himself to be.

Of *Forty-Seventeen* (1988), the collection of Moorhouse stories with a title like a skewed tennis score, the judges for the *Age* Book of the Year Award said that it was 'full of the stains of real feelings'. Of Moorhouse, who won the award, that he can 'still be very smart, witty, cute ... but also that he is a writer who can take intractable, ephemeral material, without a standard plot, concentrating on the fragmentary nature of life ... and yet leave at the end a lingering sense of human warmth and frailty'. This commendation implied that Moorhouse had graduated from the merely 'smart, witty, cute' (for example as the Australian author whose career began in *Man* magazine and who subsequently sold stories to *Squire* and *Playboy*, the chronicler of the bathos of 'days of wine and rage' in Balmain), to a humanistic, serious address to contemporary life. Thus the judges (Tony Lintermans, Mudrooroo Narogin, Jocelynne Scutt and the *Age* Literary Editor Rod Usher) turned Moorhouse's career into a laudable progress, rather than seeing in it the stealthy building of an oeuvre, by accretion, recycling, cannibalising of his own, earlier work. For *Forty-Seventeen* had a long preparation, one that is acknowledged implicitly in its treatment of his old theme of lost children (lost in the senses of unwanted and abandoned, rather than physically strayed), as well as by Moorhouse's familiar and often irritating tactic of using old stories again, and in the belief that they are the only signposts in which he can trust in his journey of discovery of modern Australia.

Moorhouse's first collection of stories, *Futility and Other Animals* (1969) concluded with 'The Third Story of Nature' in which a young woman called Cindy confronts her mother. Cindy would have a fictional after-life in several more volumes, as an exemplary member of the 'modern, urban tribe' of which Moorhouse writes. In *The Everlasting Secret Family* (1980), for instance, she appears as a university lecturer in history. For the moment though she is a participant in one of those chilly domestic scenes, compounded of stubbornness and lack of charity, that Moorhouse has been writing eloquently for many years. Pregnant, unmarried and in Sydney, Cindy (in whose name that of the city sounds as well as a travesty of a fairytale heroine) refuses to go home to the reproving solicitude of her parents. She thinks to herself:

> Her baby would be born into a time when grand-daughters would not understand their grandmothers. Perhaps we were creating an orphan generation – no parents and no God.

This story ends in bitter argument, its residue 'the hopelessly shattered links between the three generations'.

This is a prospect to which Moorhouse returns in 'Milton Rebutted – Intellectual Tricks and Accusations' – second last of the *Tales of Mystery and Romance* (1977). There the narrator, a divorced man, a specialist in putting himself at social hazard, whom we are enticed to regard as another of Moorhouse's many surrogates, muses that 'Each radical generation places the older generation on trial simply by progressing the issues. They create ideological offences which indict the generation older than they'. That last named victim generation – constituted by the parents of the people whom Moorhouse usually describes (that is, the generation of his own parents) – is the subject of his third book, *The Electrical Experience* (1974).

There Moorhouse gives the pre-history of Terri McDowell (born early in 1939 in a bad bushfire season, in a country town on the south coast of New South Wales; compare Moorhouse, born 21 December 1938 at Nowra). Terri had been a significant character in his previous book, *The Americans, Baby* (1972). In *The Electrical Experience*, Moorhouse offers an account of the life and values of Terri's father, the soft drink manufacturer and Rotarian, T. George McDowell. It will be a matter of bewilderment to T. George that his daughter 'nurtured in the good fellowship and the ethics of this home', could have become things he scarcely wishes to name. For McDowell (in some ways an antipodean Babbitt), Moorhouse contrives an idiom that insists upon its authenticity: 'I do not care for words in top hats', McDowell says. 'I believe in shirt-sleeve words. I believe in getting the job done. We're like that on the coast'. Accepting a further civic responsibility, as District Scout Master, McDowell recalls his discovery – during a trip to the United States for a Rotary Convention in 1923 – that a whole generation can be 'lost', of how it is possible for 'control to slip and for civilisation to be without a generation to take over'. Thus he offers as 'the supreme challenge' to his audience – ' "holding" the next generation. Keeping control of the young'. Gertrude Stein, who popularised the phrase, 'the lost generation', which she claimed to have heard from a motor mechanic in Paris in the 1920s, would not have been so sanguine about this prospect.

For the last story of *The Electrical Experience*, 'Filming the Hatted Australian', McDowell is off-stage. With the pathos that is an important part of his range, Moorhouse has shown George's breakdown in the previous story. It has come because he feels his generation, business and values to be overwhelmed, lost in their turn. Next Moorhouse shows the kind of development which contributed to McDowell's collapse. His daughter, Terri, has employment with a film crew that enjoys a government grant to portray 'an Australian, vintage 1910'. That is, they are being paid to prey upon the past, on the world and time of their parents. They are licensed to accuse that generation of self-righteousness, hypocrisy concerning sex, lack of self-examination and – centrally – to say 'you buggered up your kids'. Moorhouse's satire is most often gentle and unemphatic. It may be that usually he does not feel sufficiently far from his satirical targets. But here he surely asks how often one can assume the moral right to assault the sustaining clichés and verities of an older generation, while savouring one's own?

Failure to ensure the passing on of those truths would probably be McDowell's explanation of how the generation of his daughter (and Moorhouse) came to be lost. The rootlessness of Sean, the protagonist of *Forty-Seventeen*, contrasts with the insistence of McDowell on the roots that he has put down and the responsibilities which he has assumed in one community. Yet, in different terms, each might lament that (as McDowell puts it) 'I sold my works and days'. The unanchored, bereft, unaccommodated state of the main character of *Forty-Seventeen* is expressed in inanition ('on some days it was only a tepid curiosity and a tired-hearted buccaneering which carried him on') but more positively in his whimsical questing for origins. He seeks them not in his parents' lives, not in the house where his father's voice relentlessly hectors him 'Plan the work; work the plan', and where he is blamed by his family 'for making a joke outside the comfortable boundaries of their shared love'.

This was the unforgiving territory, recalled by an abandoned or disowned child, of one of Moorhouse's apparently most heartfelt pieces, the section of *Room Service* (1985) which he called 'Oral History of a Childhood'. The assumption of Sean in *Forty-Seventeen* is that ties between the most recent generation of parents and children have been regrettably but irreparably severed. Younger, the protagonist might have felt this as liberating. Now it is a cause for muted lament. Hence he goes further back, searching 'for psychic traces of his great-grandmother in the depressed, run-down, turn-of-the-century resort district around Katoomba'. This desire for a richer provenance than the parental generation seems to have provided is so familiar in contemporary Australian fiction, and as an impulse towards autobiographical writing, that it can receive less than its due notice. It is a desire which occasions the quest for an ancestor's 'psychic traces' whose telling is intermittently undertaken in *Forty-Seventeen*.

If this is a way in which Moorhouse shows himself in sympathy with some important strands in recent Australian writing, for instance the upsurge in works of autobiography in the 1960s which was coincident with the start of his own career, he has in the main carefully understated his considerable acquaintance with Australian literature. Critics have sought, and been encouraged by the author to make trans-Pacific comparisons instead. They had seen an affinity with Henry Lawson in Moorhouse's reluctance to write a novel, a notion that he confounded at length with his tale of the League of Nations, *Grand Days* (1993), in which McDowell makes an appearance and Edith Campbell Berry, who dies after being shot in Lebanon in an incident in *Forty-Seventeen*, is the heroine. Without due care, critics have accepted Moorhouse's explanations of his 'discontinuous narratives', perceiving there a debt to Lawson's Joe Wilson sequence. However comparisons with American authors – Ernest Hemingway and Donald Barthelme among them – have more often been made. Moorhouse may have welcomed this placement of himself on the edges of Australian literary history, almost as if he were an orphan.

That Hemingway's influence sounds in the weighting of Moorhouse's sentences is undeniable. Moorhouse once spoke to me of his admiration for the mass of such a simple Hemingway sentence as 'The boat came on across the bay'. Other influences are thematic: seriousness concerning vows, about doing things right with words and with the hands, an urge to the definition of feelings, a connoisseurship of the secular world. Consider the fussiness about manners of Edith Berry in *Grand Days*, with her talk of the Way of Circumspection and the Way of Compassionate Confession. At other times, however, Moorhouse treats these matters wryly. The passage in 'A Portrait of a Whore', one of the stories in *Forty-Seventeen*, reads like an unobtrusive parody of Hemingway's 'The Snows of Kilimanjaro':

> He'd talked with Carter, Brezhnev. He'd published important papers. He'd stayed in the finest hotels in the greatest of cities. He'd been drunk with ambassadors, heads of state. He'd been part of historic occasions. But he had not become a writer.

The burden of *The Americans, Baby* was an exploration of the costs and ambiguities of Australian cultural dependence (and not only for writers) on the United States. It was in part a definition of the national enemy. Yet it was also a sympathetic treatment of the pervasive American misreading of Australian culture. Moorhouse's allegiances are not easily tagged.

What of his own readings of Australian culture? Revising and following Lawson, Russell Drysdale's painting and the revisionary fiction of Murray Bail, Moorhouse's celebrated story 'The Drover's Wife' presented one of the sacred figures of Australian literature for ribald reinterpretation. The impoverished Italian student, Franco Casamaggiore, argues at an international conference that the 'wife' is in fact a sheep, familiar love object of lonely bush workers. Frank Moorhouse is, however, altogether more respectful concerning another item of the national literary and artistic tradition. The figure of the lost child is not the inside joke, but the secret theme of Moorhouse's writing. Persistently he has been an accountant of social and emotional loss. The loss of children signifies the loss of the future. This is the complement in his fiction of those broken links with previous Australian generations of which he has also written.

Moorhouse's lost children are not rural waifs, like those depicted by Kingsley, Clarke, Furphy and Lawson, boys and girls who perish – on a simple reading – because of the harshness of the Australian bush or the delinquency of their parents. They are in no danger of rescue by a loquacious, moralising kangaroo like Ethel Pedley's Dot. No 'bush fairies' will sing them to their rest as in Lawson's poem 'The Babies in the Bush'. Moorhouse's lost ones are the urban children who might have been. Introducing *Futility and Other Animals,* Moorhouse argued that 'the central dilemma is that of giving birth, of creating new life'. The comment was under-explained. Did it refer to his writing, or to the characters of whom he wrote? The dilemma is not resolved in these tales of children miscarried, aborted, not yet born, idly dreamed of, never to be. In the opening story, Anne has just miscarried. In the next, Moorhouse introduced an academic called Anderson Fith. A tireless avoider of fatherhood, Fith leaves his wife because she wanted to be a mother, and then will not move in with his mistress when she refuses to abandon her children. Later he persuades a lover (Anne again, pregnant by someone else) to have her child adopted so that its presence will not interfere with his sabbatical leave. Subsequently Fith breaks off an affair that has just resumed when his lover mentions children. These contorted efforts to avoid begetting are comic without being uproariously funny. Fith is the first detailed portrait by Moorhouse of a character in flight from the future, of one able – by his efforts of ego – to feel both persecuted and self-righteous in his evasions of paternity.

Futility and Other Animals provides some of the pre-history of *Forty-Seventeen*. In 'Rambling Boy' (a story that Moorhouse uses again in the later volume, recycling his work as persistently and assiduously as McDowell did his soft drink bottles), there is the first mention of Sean and of Chris, the abandoned daughter whom he has never known. Terri McDowell makes her first entry too, in the poignantly titled 'I Saw a Child for the Three of Us', where she makes love with a homosexual called Bernard in the wistful half-hope that she might provide the two of them, and his lover Mervyn, with a child. But a child in what capacity? It will not be as an heir, nor as a successor. The volume ends with Cindy pregnant. Her unborn child is already unwanted by Cindy's parents because of its provenance. Hence Cindy's expression of her fear that she is part of the making of an 'orphan generation – no parents and no God', one, that might be to say, which is composed of lost children.

Relating the misadventures of the Associate Professor Milton and of the hapless hero (the Sean of *Forty-Seventeen*) in *Tales of Mystery and Romance*, Moorhouse wrote comically of autogenesis, of failed, self-deceiving efforts to give oneself a new life, rather than of creating it for others. Sean and Milton have had a clumsy homosexual affair. This is another of the modes of denial of the future that Moorhouse probes. Later Milton, who for the time being is a cynical proponent of Zen, pompously announces 'we are all into a different trip now', a 'new Life Style' (if not truly a new life). In several of the *Tales of Mystery and Romance*, Sean has a reunion with Robyn, his ex-wife, in Portugal. Concerning their daughter, she takes the route of sentimental comfort: 'Chris is me', 'I am a combination of myself and my children'. But in response to that he lectures her: 'Children were once an economic necessity and then a religious obligation – now nothing more than a suburban convention'. Robyn prefers not to talk in those terms, rather she tells him pityingly of how much he has missed. To the extent that the connection can be made, part of this attitude is explained in the story 'The Loss of a Friend by Cablegram'. Its narrator, Sean again, thinks of how his parents deny the worth of their child by delivering opinions in such a way as to suggest that 'anything I had to say would be of no value. This was the dead baby buried there in every conversation'.

It is a child's feeling of worthlessness, its dread of being unheeded that is here bitingly brought back to mind by this shocking image. The rest of the passage indicates how – of all the variously lost children in his fiction – the shape-shifting, name-changing Moorhouse male protagonist is the veritable lost child. This protagonist, for instance incarnated as Sean, a man in early middle age in *Forty-Seventeen*, is mischievous, selfish, bound by arcane rules and vows, grieving for an obscure cause, possessed of a consciousness that is acutely vulnerable to impression and to harm. Besides this, he has the unhappy complement of an unforgiving memory, is undirected in his social life and is not able consistently to laugh away feelings of persecution.

Moorhouse has sustained not only the *faux naif* persona which is the prime vehicle of his comic writing (the jokester who is fair game for bell-captains all around the world, the peripatetic Francois Blaise) but a genuinely naïve one. The fractured world that his characters perceive about them, with its avenues to past and future closed off, is seen as if with the eyes of a child, one who is lost but shrewd, wary but able or willing to avoid putting the self at risk. Moorhouse's 'discontinuous narrative', the practice which he named as long ago as *Futility and Other Animals*, is not only the issue of his belief that there is no sure point of moral reference, no guarantee of progress, no stable centre of the self. The technique also expresses the cannier, practical intuition that there are no secure places for the threatened and vulnerable ones whose spokesman, by default, Moorhouse is. The lost child-adult at the centre of his fiction (in *Forty-Seventeen* this is Sean, complemented by the figures of his daughter and of his teenage lover) savours present moments, but is thwarted in his hopes of a comforting regression to the past or of securing any prospects in the future. The family past to which the child might wish to return is coldly denied it by the disappointed generation of its parents. The next generation (Moorhouse's own and that of his surrogates) which might by procreation bring the future to be, has failed, declined or forgotten to do so.

In Moorhouse's fiction, the Romantic heritage has narrowed to the figure of the abandoned child-adult, still possessed of moral perceptiveness, of acute sensory capacities, but bereft of a future. This is the way in which he symbolises the uprooting of the urban tribe. By analogy, it is also a colonial dilemma which is rehearsed here, one that implies the desertion of the colony of Australia by an imperial, British parent, which bequeaths memories and outworn institutions, but neither a lien on the future nor a guarantee of it.

Leone Sperling's *Mother's Day*

While Moorhouse depicted the desire to abandon, or not to conceive a future generation of Australian children, writers as otherwise diverse in style and preoccupation as Leone Sperling, Beverley Farmer, Ian Moffitt, Jennifer Maiden, Gabrielle Lord and Carmel Bird have been drawn to write of sharp and shocking instances of particular abuse. Collectively, though, their work in this vein imagines a wasteland across which children are hunted, or in which they have been cast aside by predatory or indifferent adults. After her first novel, *Coins for the Ferryman* (1981), and the two novellas, 'Thanatos' and 'Narcissus' which were published as *Mother's Day* in 1984 and the three linked novellas, *Oasis* (1990), there has been silence from Leone Sperling. Hers is another example of an all too typical career trajectory for an Australian writer: an unusual talent is suddenly revealed and as quickly vanishes from view. Yet Sperling's first two works, and *Mother's Day* in particular, deserve renewed examination. 'Thanatos' and 'Narcissus' are two of the most shocking of modern Australian treatments of the lost child theme, not least for the cool explicitness with which they depict the circumstances of baby killing and allow the reader to infer the motives for it.

'Thanatos' – a title blunt enough in itself – opens with a brief explanation that Sperling calls 'Hate'. She reveals that 'This is the story of a mother and a daughter who hated each other with great passion'. It may be that they were unaware of the hatred that infused their mutual dependency. The catalyst that would violently clarify it was the arrival of an intruder in their lives – a man who 'fed their fire and touched off their tragedy until it had no choice but to hurl itself to its determined end'. Before this occurs, we are introduced to Eve (whose name is that of the first mother) and the baby whom she names Ruth, in the mistaken hope 'that this daughter would dwell in harmony with her mother forever'. Eve 'was a hermit'. If in the past she had certainly known 'passion and despair, heartbreak and happiness, pain and joy', Eve had decided 'that the world of men and women was not for her'. Thus she has retreated into herself, into an hermetic, post-sexual world where she and her daughter will be inviolate. Or so she believes.

Next we encounter the disturbed child called Jonathan. To his mother he is simply 'the dirty little rotten bastard'. A masturbatory frolic with the clothes and in the bed of a 24-year-old woman sees the teenaged Jonathan sent to reform school. As a young adult he enjoys sneaking into female public toilets where he masturbates while watching and in particular listening to women pee. Though it is as yet unknown to any of them, he is on course for the home of Eve and Ruth. Arriving to paint the house, he will stay on as a boarder.

The literary mode in which Sperling is working has elements of melodrama. Jonathan is a villainous intruder, bent on the possession and dispossession of the two women. He will however find himself entangled and implicated in their lives to an extent that he had not foreseen. From another angle, in the clarity and concentration of its action, in the cue of its beginning ('This is the story ...'), 'Thanatos' looks like a modern or even an ur-grunge fairytale for three characters. Yet its form is more exactly understood in terms of the comments by the American poet, Howard Nemerov, on the novella form. In his essay 'Composition and Fate in the Short Novel', Nemerov wrote that there is 'one theme which is pervasive to the point of obsession' in the novella:

> The theme is broadly speaking that of *identity*, and the action deriving from it may be generalised as follows: the mutual attachment or dependency between A and B has a mortal strength; its dissolution requires a crisis fatal to one or the other party; but this dissolution is represented as salvation.

The pattern of 'action' that Nemerov describes eerily fits the events of Sperling's story, but if that last word of his is appropriate for the conclusion of 'Thanatos', then it denotes a deeply ambiguous 'salvation', one that is achieved through irreparable loss.

Before that occurs, Jonathan has infiltrated the house. After a 'clear-sighted' reckoning of his circumstances, he decides that he will seduce the daughter before the mother. Lucky Ruth, then, for she has her hymen ruptured and – improbably – enjoys her first climax at the same time. Eve follows: 'She is undone in an instant'. Her many years of abstinence from sex abruptly end. She lets herself be taken every night, complies with all Jonathan's sexual demands, but 'steps outside her body ... abandons her body and leaves it on the bed – unpatrolled, unsupervised, unleashed'. Meanwhile, and only for a time, Ruth's 'ignorance and innocence combine to swathe her in the delusion of being loved'. By the time that Ruth wakes up to the situation, Jonathan's attitude towards her mother is beyond his control, he 'constantly swings between obsession and desire', rather to the former when he learns that she is pregnant to him. For, to his surprise, he is filled conventionally 'with pride and joy'. The only problem is that Eve tells him that this baby (as Ruth presumably had once been regarded) is hers alone, and that he should leave.

He does not, and the next phase in the fatal entanglement of the three of them sees lover, daughter and mother together in Eve's bed, in a 'triple fusion'. In particular, Eve and Jonathan make love to Ruth. Perversely, but without hesitation, the mother repossesses her child. Yet it is Eve who breaks this circle, withdrawing to focus on the impending baby, sending Jonathan back to work and Ruth to school. Having – as it were – lost her childhood a second time, Ruth feels 'Hatred of Eve. To be rejected; to be dismissed; to be torn away from the heat of love. Intolerable. Unbearable'.

The climax of this story involves, in Nemerov's terms, the dissolution of a mutual attachment of 'mortal strength' by a fatal crisis. It comes just before Eve gives birth again. Before leaving for hospital, she takes a bath. As Ruth watches, we recall the earlier scene in which Eve washed and massaged her daughter in the bath. But Ruth, 'fired with the power of angels and the strength of gods', grabs a carving knife, pushes her mother's head under water, plunges the knife into Eve's throat, face, breast, heart. The baby is still moving in Eve's stomach so Ruth – to complete the work of extinction that she has begun – slits her mother open and delivers the child. The infant, which would have been her half-brother, she drowns. At that point, because he can hardly be excluded from the bloody end of the story, Jonathan comes in, sees the carnage and bashes himself insensible against the side of the bath. Ruth then washes, dresses and walks out of the house.

The title of the story has told us bluntly and with deceptive brevity that it would be about death. Eve's sexual refashioning of Ruth into a dependent child again, and then the rejection of her, leads to the violent severing of their bonds. 'Thanatos' is not, however, a case of fratricide and matricide born chiefly of Ruth's envy of the child about to be born and resentment of her displacement in, and from her mother. It is

Ruth's own lost childhood, briefly glimpsed, recaptured and then irrevocably foregone, that impels her.

Sperling was not done with stories of 'Mother's Day'. The mordant title under which the two novellas are collected mocks the cloying, artificial celebration of maternal virtues each May. From 'Thanatos' we move to 'Narcissus', from death to self-love. The second story begins with a prologue to the main events. Once concluded, it is never adverted to again. The extent to which it may explain the tragedy that occurs a generation later is never reductively emphasised, but the memory of its horror necessarily lingers. The prologue introduces a young wife, Margaret. She is nineteen and has spent but fifteen days of 'marital bliss' with her husband, Joe, before he goes off to war. Their baby daughter is born, with difficulty, in December 1941.

For Margaret was 'not ready to be a mother'. She tries physically to prevent the baby from being born, as if the desire not to have children could still, just at the moment of labour, be realised:

> She tightened herself up and resisted what was happening in her womb. Consequently the baby tore the unyielding flesh and Margaret had to be anaesthetised at the moment of birth and extensively stitched up together again. They stitched up the sides of her vagina and they even had to stitch up a tear in her bowel. She was not permitted to get up for a week and she was definitely not allowed to shit. When they brought Margaret the baby, she didn't believe it was hers. Her body had been outraged and so she turned her face to the wall.

It is the nurses who name the child Judith. Neither mother nor baby ever smiles at one another. Their truce lasts four and a half years, until a war-damaged and at first unrecognisable Joe comes home.

His desperate and – as he guesses – final wish is for Margaret to conceive again. Thus he intends to will his body 'to remain alive until after the birth of his child'. A son is born, but Margaret's 'maternal instincts', which Joe fondly hoped would awaken, do not stir. When the baby is six months old, Margaret takes it outside, pours petrol over the two of them and sets them alight. Joe tries unavailingly to smother the flames so that 'all three were engulfed, consumed and destroyed by Margaret's blinding need'. What was that 'need'? Is it to be banally understood as the frustrated desire for a life unencumbered by children? Or is it a darker intuition into her own loathing of the maternal role imposed on and expected of her? Sperling leaves these, and other questions, unanswered. By implication, there can be neither a full nor a satisfactory resolution of them.

Judith goes to foster parents; excels at Sydney University and is arrestingly beautiful. Moreover 'She moved forward as if she had no past'. The memories of her childhood have determinedly been lost. Once again, Sperling constructs the novella with the clean narrative line, the treacherous simplicity of a fairytale. At university in the early 1960s, Judith meets the tall, handsome Jewish law student Rheuben. He makes love to her, but she never reaches orgasm. Her urgent need is instead for 'constant words, assurances and reassurances'. Sinisterly, 'everything went according to plan' for them – they marry, Judith learns to cook and entertain in a home at St Ives, Rheuben succeeds at the bar. Yet he is not happy in his marriage, not least because there is no conventional reproach that he can make to his wife. There were

> actions of love, gestures of love, proof of love and yet they did not add up to love. Rheuben felt unloved. His worship of Judith, his adoration of her body had failed to awaken any sensual response in her.

But, as the author explains, Judith 'was not hiding her inner self from him. The thing she was hiding was her own hollowness'.

What she unexpectedly discovers is the depth and intensity of her narcissism, 'a self-love of ... frightening intensity', which at once explains to Judith why men desire her and especially the strength of Rheuben's love. Looking in a mirror Judith masturbates and comes at last. In its hectic pacing and excessive supply of detail, it is another violent episode, congruent with the description of the murders at the end of 'Thanatos'. Judith comes violently: 'she let her hands fly with new-found strength from clitoris to cunt almost plunging her fist into herself and screaming out loud at the moment of shattering climax'. She is still unable to reach orgasm with her husband, but accedes readily enough to the next stage in the tidy plan of their married life, which is to have the first of two children.

Judith prepares, single-mindedly, for the birth of a girl. Presumably she intends to bring an image of herself into being. But she gives birth 'to a red-faced, ugly, squawking, screaming male child'. Like her mother, Judith declares that the baby is not hers. At home the baby behaves like one, screaming, vomiting, '[covering] itself with shit'. He is far from being the object of Judith's pre-natal desire: 'a beautiful and perfectly well-behaved replica of herself'. At this point Sperling hints, perhaps unnecessarily, at the cause of Judith's rage: 'Instinct, primal and raw, banned for a lifetime, was now unleashed in Judith. She did not know how it could end. She did not know where to turn'. As psychiatrist and poet Craig Powell has pointed out (in an analogous context): 'in the ordinary course of events, a woman harbouring an unconscious primitive rage toward her mother is in danger of re-enacting the injury with her own child'. 'Narcissus' ends as 'Thanatos' had, in the bath. Judith drowns the 'angry' baby. Freed of the child, she can now smile at 'her mirrored image' and seeing in it, behind her, the reflection of the bed, anticipate her intense and solitary pleasure.

Is this the 'mother's day' that women secretly desire? Do they long for their self-love to be undistracted and untrammelled by children? Each of Sperling's novellas readily encourages psychological explanations for the behaviour of those who kill children (and others), but each also resists them. Offered rather, irreducible and inexplicable, stark in outline and terrible in incident, are stories of the fatal relations of parents and children, intimations of why children are lost and of the consequences for those whose wishes are granted.

Home Time with Beverley Farmer

Beverley Farmer's stories about the killing of children, 'Marina' and 'Fire and Flood', were first collected in *Home Time* (1985). Each of them has a programmatic feel, as though their somewhat mechanical narrative structures were the necessary means to negotiate the terrible material with which the stories deal. The circumstances of the loss of children in each are markedly different. In 'Marina', a Greek migrant woman bashes her child's head against a wall until it dies, while in 'Fire and Flood' a man loses both his step-son and his wife in the separate accidents that are indicated by the title of the story. Farmer explores *how* those deaths came about. The *why* of them remains problematic, although there is some sense in each case that the victims' fates was a given, an inevitability. The unnamed narrator of 'Fire and Flood' can only surmise that 'We are set in motion by a malevolent hand, unable to know in what our actions are rooted or what fruit they will bear'.

'Marina' sympathetically evokes the cultural and emotional isolation of a young wife and mother, without ever insisting that there is a sufficient connection between Marina's sufferings and her final actions. Her tribulations are oppressive. Husband Michali, who strayed with Marina during his first marriage, is now – she supposes – dallying contemptuously with another. There is no support for Marina within her family: 'My own mother hates me', she wails. A desperate attempt to ring her mother-in-law in her village in Greece is unsuccessful. Marina's child, cause of a large portion of her despair and helplessness, is first glimpsed disquietingly at the story's opening. The baby's 'puffy head was haloed. Hairs tufted it', while its body is wrapped 'In the shawl that Michali's mother had sent, with the blue bead sewn on it against the evil eye'. This is a world that has turned sinister for Marina: 'a black blowfly' squats by the baby's cheek, the water surrounding a votive candle is 'furred with black insects', and Marina recalls that the priest at her wedding 'sprouted so much black hair that she thought the resonating cave of his mouth must be furred bushy black'.

Marina has maudlin dreams of her own end, when – 'having hurtled from an ivied window' – she will become for others an object of pity, rather than of indifference or scorn: a 'Poor dead lady'. In a reverie, walking along St Kilda beach, she imagines how her child might be lost:

> I am riding pillion on a motor-bike over a bumpy metal bridge, carrying the baby piggy-back. It falls off into the river. I see it lying on its back deep inside the clear water. I plunge my arms in and lift it up, but its head topples off and floats away. What can I do? Mama, tell me.

Despite this plea, there is neither an adviser nor a confidante to whom she can turn. It is at this point of the story that we learn how Joss, Michali's first wife (and mother of his first child, Eleni) had died in a car accident. 'Smart and efficient' she may have been, but Joss 'drove right off an overpass at the end of the West Gate Bridge'. Maybe she was dazzled by the glare of the sun 'on sheets of rainwater mirroring sky and clouds'. Or perhaps she committed suicide, 'crushed at full speed'.

Farmer favours neither conclusion. Nor will she give clues to explain why – so abruptly – we learn of how and when Marina kills her child. The narrative of that event is blunt and horrible. The crying baby is swung against a wall until 'it stopped its noise, hanging from her hands'. Marina cradles the head of the dead child. Now 'with a sweet sting her milk let down' and the breast milk's 'white spray fell quietly in the baby's face'. Readers may find a troubling disjunction between Marina's stresses and the desperate manner in which she resolves them. And that may be part of Farmer's point. The killing of the child is influenced by the mother's loneliness, misery and despair, but it is a grossly disproportionate response. The assertion of Marina's own wants is at the shocking cost of another lost child.

In a squalid flat, by a noisy railway line, a man learns penitently what it is 'to live alone inside a web of black branches'. He has fled to Melbourne from a town along the south coast of Victoria. In agonisingly swift succession, it seems to him, he has lost his step-son Sam – trapped beneath a fallen tree in a bushfire and burned alive – and his wife Joan, who drowned in a flooded river, not far from the site of the earlier tragedy. They are both victims of the natural disasters which were a staple of nineteenth-century Australian literature and of the historical fictions of this century. When it appears that a serious bushfire outside their town no longer poses a risk to them, Joan has allowed her son to be minded by neighbours. But as she confides later to her husband, exaggerating her guilt, 'I couldn't wait to get rid of him'. An idle, momentary and essentially innocent wish has been direly granted. It may be that Joan's subsequent death – like that of Joss in 'Marina' – is also a suicide, although that is a possibility which is neither explicitly suggested, nor refused.

When she drowned, Joan was three months pregnant. In her death, another child is lost. The husband feels of Sam's and Joan's deaths (and of the hostile insinuations about his role in them which afterwards spread in his community) that the tragic two-part episode 'has that touch of the grotesque that makes a legend'. Bereft, grieving, assailed by anonymous letters, he eventually gives up his teaching position and heads into obscurity in Melbourne. Trying to make sense of what happened, he claims that his multiple family tragedy, 'our story', seems 'to make clear that I was instrumental in their deaths'. The narrative has more clearly denied that he had any such culpability. The man's wish to take on guilt for the deaths is psychologically plausible, if pointless, but its significance is more general. In terms of the Australian cultural obsession with the loss of children he is acting as if he had caused the deaths of Sam and the unborn child. That is, he has taken responsibility after the fact of the accidents, as if for a ridding of the world of children that subliminally he may have desired. Maybe they have been lost in his place. These children may have borne what should have been an adult's portion. But his wife is dead too, taking her own child with her. For a story that is so neatly arranged, 'Fire and Flood' is revealingly unable to subdue its many and complex intimations of besetting adult anxieties about children, and their loss.

'Who would bring kids into this world?': Ian Moffitt's *The Colour Man*

The contemporary fate of lost children has long exercised Ian Moffitt. In his thriller, *Death Adder Dreaming* (1988), the hero is an ex-policeman, Rod Grant, whose adoptive father 'brought him home as a baby in his saddlebag in 1948, when Rod was about five'. The Aboriginal boy had been found 'crying beside his dead mother in a wurlee up the scrub'. His father-to-be had heard a noise 'like a dingo pup yelping'. This lost Aboriginal child, found rather than stolen, is fostered by a white policeman and his family. Grant's story is exemplary, but incidental to the action of the novel. In an earlier book of Moffitt's, *The Colour Man* (1983) (published in the United States in 1985 as *Presence of Evil*), the figure of the lost child is omnipresent. The novel is one of the most disturbing and wide-ranging of late twentieth-century fictional treatments of this material.

The setting is the Sydney harbour-side suburb of Danby (that is, Manly) and particularly its hinterland, Black Bay. In the opening of the novel, the middle-aged shopkeeper John Lynch, who has pretended to be fishing, is stopped by two policemen in a patrol car. They tell him of a 'kid in a phone booth down the wharf. Overdose ... cold as a bloody mackerel'. Black Bay gives refuge of sorts to a tribe of lost children, who think of themselves graphically, but hopelessly as the Wrecks. These are their forlorn circumstances: 'the Wrecks occupied one end of the beach: runaway boys and youths, too young for the dole, who lived in shanties and under driftwood and plastic among the rocks'. The youngest among them are Lynch's prey, ripe to be lured to the underground rooms that he uses in the abandoned headland fort cum quarantine station.

If the Wrecks stand for the lost child as a palpable but intractable social problem (much like the children whom George Jeffreys will encounter on the other side of Sydney in Jennifer Maiden's novel *Play With Knives*, 1990, or those in the inner city in Gabrielle Lord's *Whipping Boy*, 1992), Moffitt is also concerned with particular kinds and causes of abuse of the young. Lynch, who begins by shaving boys' heads and putting them in dresses, graduates to murder. Nick Andrews, the 'colour man', or feature journalist of the title, gets too late on his trail. Andrews and his frosty wife, the lawyer Jan, have bought a Danby house that used to belong to Herbert Ludwig, the former, and of course corrupt, New South Wales deputy police commissioner. He is the father of Lynch and of his schizophrenic sister Olive, or Sally Anne, whose own illegitimate daughter, Jenny, died of heart failure at the age of ten after having been abandoned in the house.

This is one of the secrets that Andrews uncovers. He will hear both Lynch and his sister ask, in similar ways, 'who would want to bring kids into this world?' The question is rich coming from Lynch, but apt as well: this is not a world that he has made on his own, this society in which children are assaulted, deserted, turned into occasional fodder for headlines (something of which even Andrews is guilty for his own purposes), vulnerable to sexual interference, destitution and mental cruelty. Lynch, we are hardly surprised to learn, was himself an abused child, belted mercilessly by his father. Moreover he believed in and fantasised about a family connection with an axe murderer, transported from County Cavan in Ireland. On an occasion which Lynch relishes thinking of, the homicidal ancestor slaughtered a family, but gave its little girl ten minutes to say her prayers for having been 'good'.

In the cosmology of *The Colour Man* all fates are entangled. Besides his investigations into who is intruding into his house, Andrews desires some kind of cultural understanding of the horrors which he comes upon. Accordingly, he seeks out the Eurasian Dr Lin, a retired government medical officer who had been in charge of conducting post-mortems at the time when Andrews was covering the coroner's court as a reporter. Outlining what he knows of Lynch and his frightful family, Andrews hopes for an explanation of what he has found, and guessed. Lin's answer is almost too pat, and prompt:

> My dear Andrews, the brutalisation of children is hardly a departure for humanity. Children are irrelevant – they've always been irrelevant. Look at the deaths – it's hardly a new story. I assure you.

Lin blames Christianity: 'All those worthy hypocrites mumbling about the innocence of children, and what do they build their fortunes on? Original sin'.

Whether he turns to Lin, or scrutinises his immediate surroundings, Andrews is confronted with images of lost children. It is as if the moral weather of Australia is fatal to its younger generations. At the Danby waxworks, for instance, are displayed

> bushrangers and soldiers, an opera singer and a jockey, a group of Famous Missing Children in little flowered frocks and bathing suits – one of them carried a wax loaf of bread in tissue paper.

They are not named, but these are likely to be the Beaumont children, who disappeared from the Glenelg Beach in Adelaide on Australia Day 1966. It is a mystery that, unknown to Andrews, Lynch savours. He has a file on the case:

> The old newspaper clippings always gripped him, especially the disappearance of a family of three children in the sixties – he had torn out several stories about that. He leafed through them slowly; he had got to know the children quite well through his reading.

This is a notion that is hideous in its understatement. While he dwells on the details of their young lives, Lynch is essentially coveting the lost children's pain.

Across the street from Lynch's shop is the house that Jan and Nick have bought. As he is pulling ivy off a wall, Andrews uncovers a little rectangular window, through which a small face peers at him. It turns out to be a doll, not a child, but this leads Andrews to discover the attic in which young Jenny died. Moffitt jumps forward in time for a moment:

> Later, remembering the death of Jan's baby, Andrews began to wonder if the cottage itself, and its contents, might have exercised some psychic influence upon her ... For the cottage, with death in its womb, certainly appeared to transform her into its own image.

Andrews will dwell on this, 'probably because he never married again or had children'. 'Jan's baby' is the child of theirs that she aborted, purportedly because she no longer loved him. At the climax of the novel, when her daughter Katie (from her first marriage, to a merchant banker) has gone missing, Jan, who has been brought up a Catholic and now works for a conservative Catholic law firm, will blame herself for this because of the abortion: 'I've sinned ... I've taken a life'.

That decision was a sign that the marriage was dying. What speeds its end is a long anticipated, but unavoided catastrophe. Harried by Andrews's inquiries into his past, Lynch kidnaps Katie and flees with her to the bush region where he grew up. They are heading for the heart of a disastrous bushfire. Before Andrews can effect a rescue, Lynch dynamites Katie and himself. *The Colour Man* has traversed terrible territory. Few other Australian novels so determinedly face the extent and connection of the abuse of children. They are 'lost' because of the 'presence of evil', but also because that evil seems to find fertile ground in Australian society. Horrors rise up from the past: the Irish convict murderer, the kidnapping of the Beaumonts are the dark historical background for an assay of the contemporary scene. There children huddle in beach-side shanties, visible prey. Adults are either helpless to take care of them, or indifferent or – worse – see their plight as sexual opportunity. Lynch's tale is all too fully and persuasively contextualised in Moffitt's novel. For *The Colour Man* is a grim compendium of the ways in which so many children are lost in contemporary Australia, whether they suffer as individuals because of adult evil, or as the neglected, desperate segment of a whole youthful generation.

'I've had my children': Jennifer Maiden's *Play With Knives*

At the end of Jennifer Maiden's first novel, *The Terms* (1982), the town planner and activist Ian Anstey learns of the death of his son, Llew. The news comes in the form of an overseas phone call, from his estranged wife Rae. Before his companion, Chrisogon Lyle, can hand him the phone, Anstey knows instinctively what the news will be. The child has been run over on a pavement by a reckless driver. When Chrisogon ventures that it should have been her who was lost, Anstey – for a moment – agrees. This is the bleak, unresolved ending of a novel which, for most of its action, is topically concerned with the attempt to stop an inner city development in Sydney in the early 1980s. Besides its core of political events, *The Terms* is shadowed by episodes of child abuse. Chrisogon (named by fond parents for her golden hair) lives in a flat next to a migrant couple whom – she deduces 'from habitual blows and resigned screams' – indulge in a 'nocturnal habit of child-thrashing'. In the society depicted in this novel, children are silenced if not silent victims; they are scapegoats for parental frustration and unhappiness. That said, one is still not prepared for the novel of Maiden's that came next, eight years later. And few readers may now know of it, so swiftly have some of the finest Australian novels of the last quarter of a century been forgotten; left to go out of print; been succeeded for short seasons of public attention by modish and trivial fiction.

Play With Knives (1990) is set in the western suburbs of Sydney. Maiden was herself born in Penrith, in 1949, while one of her writer-in-residence stints – which she completed in 1989 – was at the University of Western Sydney. Characters in the novel who care for children professionally believe that many of those in the city's west have effectively been abandoned to their own boredom and despair. The novel's narrator, the probation officer George Jeffreys (who is happy to claim a distant relation to the famous seventeenth-century English hanging judge) is importuned for money at his local pizza parlour by a group of these children: 'they smelled of grog, vomit, sweat and sex'. Literally and morally, they are in limbo.

Jeffreys has by now taken on his hardest case, that of Clare Forster. First he must judge whether she is fit to be paroled and sent out into a community that she has not known since childhood. Then he must monitor her adjustment, if such she can manage. For Clare Forster

> had killed three small children. Two were girls and one was a boy. She paid most attention to him. The other two were witnesses. She smothered them and knifed him. To be fair to her, I'll admit he died the quickest. She carved his throat and the blood ran so fast and so far that by the time she had whittled the stars and flowers into every orifice they were not obscured by liquid at all.

When she killed her step-sisters and step-brother, Clare was nine. She is sixteen when George Jeffreys takes her case. Did Maiden perhaps have in mind the story of Mary Bell, from Newcastle in England, who – in the early 1970s at the age of ten – killed two little boys, Martin Brown and Brian Howe? Or is it an especially Australian psycho-pathology which she investigates?

If she is 'my murderer', an obsessive interest to him, and even at last his lover, Clare never seems to Jeffreys to be a monster. She speaks of the murders with a chilly matter-of-factness less – it appears – from detachment, than from a lack of continuing curiosity about what she has done. As she explains to George: 'It seems – seemed – quite logical to me. Mum had told me not to go to the pictures. She hadn't told me not to kill the children'. In consequence of her crimes, rather than heredity, Clare has aged prematurely. She is 'the white-haired girl' of the novel's long, and ironically titled first chapter. The palms and soles of her feet are wrinkled. And what of those whom she has bereaved? While her mother muddles along, collecting pets that she can never keep alive, Clare's stepfather, George Forster, sank 'into a mechanical depression'. After a slight disagreement with his employer, Forster gassed himself in his garage. Lost also, if it had ever had a chance to be formed, is that moral sense, that reckoning of guilt and the consequences of her actions, which adults wish to find or to implant in Clare. Not least, Maiden implies, this is because of their own tormenting intuitions of a moral emptiness within themselves.

Clare's step-brother was named Anthony. Her mother's child by a different father was Janice. Her other step-sister, George Forster's second child, by a wife now deceased, and Anthony's brother, was called Tess. It is not long before that resonates with George: 'the name "Angel Clare" began searching my mind mockingly'. He cannot, however, imagine that the Forsters were keen readers of the novels of Thomas Hardy. Clare, on the other hand, is schooled in the Brontes, so he tries her with a work by Hardy – *Tess of the D'Urbervilles* (1891). Having related its plot to Clare, dwelling on the last lines about the sport which the President of the Immortals has had with the doomed Tess, George says – not with much critical acumen – 'It's beautifully written but Hardy didn't invent credible plots'. Clare is at once ahead of him: 'Neither does the President of the Immortals'. Maiden invites us to think of another Hardy novel which is not named here – *Jude the Obscure* (1895). Is George too obtuse to see its greater pertinence to Clare's case, or is knowledge of that book something which he chooses to suppress?

In an agonising scene in *Jude the Obscure*, the three small children of Jude Frawley kill themselves. The eldest, 'Father Time', or little Jude, is the son of Arabella Don, Jude's former wife. The other two are the children of Jude and his cousin, Sue Bridehead. The family has recently arrived in Christminster, where they have had difficulty in securing decent lodgings. Speaking carelessly to little Jude, as though he is older than his years, Sue tells him that 'All is trouble, adversity and suffering'. When he wonders whether 'It would be better to be out o' the world than in it', she nearly agrees with him: 'It would almost, dear'. His youthful moral sense is troubled. Why, he asks, 'if children make so much trouble ... do people have 'em?' What agitates him more is that Sue is not his real mother, and therefore need not look after him. He reflects on the land where he grew up with his natural mother: 'I troubled 'em in Australia, and I trouble folk here. I wish I hadn't been born!' Children 'born that are not wanted', little Jude judges, would be better killed directly, 'before their souls come to 'em, and not allowed to grow big and walk about!' The news, which Sue now confides to him, that she is to have another baby, only compounds the boy's despair.

Next morning Sue finds the bodies of the three children, all hanged, a 'triplet of little corpses'. A message, written on a scrap of paper, has been left by little Jude: 'Done because we are too menny'. While Sue's nerves understandably give way, Jude tries stubbornly to find some explanation for the loss of the children. The doctor who attended the suicides tells him that it was in little Jude's nature to die this way:

> The doctor says that there are such boys springing up amongst us – boys of a sort unknown in the last generation – the outcome of new views of life. They seem to see all its terrors before they are old enough to have staying power to resist them. He says it is the beginning of the coming universal wish not to live.

Certainly little Jude, who was mournfully eloquent on his own behalf, if not familiar with this kind of psycho-social prophecy, conceived of himself and of the other two children as a burden of which their parents would like to be rid. They fulfilled the doctor's hypothesis of 'the coming universal wish not to live' among the latest generation. These children are lost by their own, that is, by children's hands. Are they therefore anticipating, or shockingly consummating the desires of their parents? The Hardy episode that George forgets or chooses not to mention to Clare, has more to say of the forlorn and perilous state of children in contemporary Australia than is to be found in all of *Tess of the D'Urbervilles*. This unspoken scene implicitly darkens all that we learn of Clare's killings and – had she been aware of it – might have helped to put the explanation of a motive into a mouth and mind at present indifferent to finding one.

In a radically dissimilar fictional register from Hardy's novel, and especially in its early stages, *Play With Knives* is uncomfortably overstocked with what the doctor, Clem Dixon, calls 'macabre jokes about tortured babies'. Maiden does not spare us examples. 'What's black and furry and knocks on the back door?' 'A baby covered in funnel webs.' George has not heard this one before and suspects that 'it might be an authentic western suburbs version' of the joke. There are more: a riddle about the difference between a truckload of babies and a truckload of ping pong balls; a joke about a nurse dismembering a 'brat' which was 'dead anyhow' and this: 'What's blue and sits quietly in a corner?' 'A baby with a plastic bag.' The adverb has a sinister power which seems beyond a child's invention.

Eventually intersecting with Clare's story is that of a serial killer in the western suburbs, the so-called gladbagger murderer. The adjective comes from the means by which he stores his victim's remains. This is a frightful, but no longer an unfamiliar kind of crime. It does not pose, for George, the same problems as Clare's. In her case, while feeling – he claims – 'all the appropriate moral reactions', he had 'never really been able to imagine the victims – because they were such young victims – as people'. He will have no such problems with one of those whom the gladbagger kills. His sixth victim is George's wife, Heather.

Shortly before her body is discovered, George has a key interview with Clare. For appearance's sake, perhaps, she has acquired a good-natured boyfriend, a tradesman called Greg. When George asks her – affecting to believe that in Clare's life there might be normal outcomes – 'How many children do you and Greg want?' she answers 'I won't marry. And I've had my children'. George finds the second statement to be 'tasteless', but Clare has learned enough of his moves and expectations (and is, indeed, an expert mimic of his speech patterns) to reply promptly 'Catharsis'. But whose and which emotions have been purged? And what are the implications of her first answer? Is Clare suggesting that to murder children is the surest way to bear them or to possess them? In a letter that she writes to George after his wife's death (which, in a postscript, she suspects 'is a love-letter') she says of her crimes that 'what I remember most is feeling that they simply belonged to me, that I had a right to judge them, even if cruelly'. In murdering the children, Clare had played at being a parent, at the same time as she was a child. Invested with the power of life and death in the one guise, she was powerless in the other. To have killed three children, as Clare had done, seems – from her comments – to have had all the essence of the experience of parenthood. That is to say it meant the power to do harm to the young. This intimation, Clare's retrospective interpretation of her actions, is the most truly disturbing of the novel's many-faceted reflections on the figure and fate of the lost child in contemporary Australia.

But these reflections are not yet concluded. Talking about her childhood, Clare reveals it to have been the most desolate of seed-times. As she tells George: 'I can't remember what it felt like, never to have killed anyone'. Not long afterwards, she faces her own death. For Clare meets the gladbagger, a man who has had her death in mind for some time and who now intends that she should be his eighth victim. Maiden has not much distracted us from the central business of the novel, that is the relationship between the probation officer and his charge, by hints as to the murderer's identity. Clare reveals that she had once suspected that it was George. In fact the gladbagger is his trusted family doctor, Clem Dixon, a frequent late night drinking companion when called out to the Jeffreys' house to treat their asthmatic daughter, Sheridan.

In explaining his motives to Clare, the doctor is almost too helpful, too explicit. He tells her archly that 'I'm responsible for my children, little princess. When I give them death, I give them back their innocence'. This exultant expression of the power that he has assumed is in a different key to Clare's description of her emotions when she killed Anthony, Janice and Tess. Nor did she feel that 'innocence' was in question, let alone that to murder was a way of restoring innocence. And when do children lose that quality? Clem continues to explain how his adult victims can also fit the terms of his scheme. The schoolteacher Heather Jeffreys is judged by Dixon to have been 'Fanatically worldly. She was a child who destroyed children by making them compete'. This is a peculiar kind of sophistry. It is as if the doctor seeks excuses for regarding all his victims (including old and middle-aged women) as children, the better to justify what may seem to him to be a crusade, rather than a thesis to be tested. In the world of *Play With Knives*, all are imperilled, whether by those who are homicidal and in positions of trust, such as Doctor Clem Dixon, or by their private demons, as in George Jeffreys' case. But it is the young who are most vulnerable, not least because of the belief of the gladbagger that their sacrifice may afford the kind of redemption for which the parental generation otherwise seeks in vain.

Maiden was sufficiently engrossed with the material of *Play With Knives* to write a sequel. Provisionally titled 'The Blood Judge', it has not yet found a publisher. One excerpted chapter appeared in the magazine *Ulitarra* (No. 8/1995) to tease readers of the earlier book with what more might be. Some developments in the characters' lives were made clear. George Jeffreys has left the probation service. His relationship with Clare continues, though it is not certain what form this takes. Sheridan, Jeffreys's daughter, has a child and Clare is apparently living with another man. In the excerpt, Jeffreys is in Asia, observing a trial. Neither his presence nor the nature of the trial is fully explained. Compelled to continue the story of the survivors of *Play With Knives*, Maiden has teased readers with its rich and dark possibilities. Unhappily they may wait for the full text in vain.

'Infected by Lost Child disease': The Fiction of Carmel Bird

Soon after the opening of Carmel Bird's novel *The Bluebird Café* (1990), we are introduced to the only resident of the ghost town of 'Copperfield on the Welcome River in the far north-west of Tasmania at Cape Grim'. This is Bedrock Mean, who stays there 'mourning for her daughter, hoping that one day Lovelygod will come back'. For on 17 August 1970 (a decade to the day before the disappearance of Azaria Chamberlain), the ten-year-old midget disappeared – if not inexplicably – then in a manner which has generated countless, contradictory theories; led a stream of amateur sleuths to Copperfield and to the writing of a play by the expatriate Tasmanian Virginia O'Day, among many representations of the mystery. Born in Los Angeles, the child was named 'in the fashion of flower children of the sixties, Lovelygod'. But she was naturalised by the place of her disappearance, becoming 'one of those mysterious and tragic Australian children who vanish, leaving no trace'.

In the twenty years since that event, Bedrock Mean has imagined 'many, many strange ways in which she could have gone'. Some of them come from novels, others from non-fiction accounts of lost children. While her husband Carillo's search is 'in the world' (as head of the James Barrie Institute for the Recovery of Lost Children, in Los Angeles), Bedrock's 'is in my mind and spirit, in my heart'. When she reads of lost children, she is 'for a short time excited and elated as if Lovelygod is coming back to me'. While 'the Lost Child of literature in this way consoles and sustains me; the lost children in the newspapers fill me only with dread, and wind me in a tangle of despair'. Reading omnivorously yet without hope of ultimate consolation, Bedrock comes to think of herself as 'infected by Lost Child disease'. But what is the pathology that she has named?

Partly it is a desire to shift the blame for the child's disappearance from unknown, malignant agencies, or simply misfortune, to herself. Superstition is active as well, in the notion that Bedrock's having read lost child stories to her somehow made it more likely that Lovelygod would become one of them. At the same time as she is an abiding source of private grief, this lost child is a commodity, a public property. The theme park operated in Launceston, in northern Tasmania by The Best Family, their 'Disneyland of the Antarctic', includes an Historic Museum Village in which Copperfield is replicated for the delectation of tourists with a desire for Tasmanian Gothic. One of the exhibits is a wax figure of Lovelygod. Its plaque rehearses 'every possible theory' that has been proposed to explain her disappearance. The range of suspicious agents has luridly widened since nineteenth-century narratives of children lost in the Australian bush. Perhaps, visitors can read,

> she was stolen by scientists; she was murdered by her parents; she was taken by a Tasmanian devil; she was kidnapped by circus dealers, by priests, by the owner of a brothel; she wandered into the bush and fell through the floor of the horizontal forest; she was taken by creatures from outer space; she spontaneously combusted; she ran away. Did Lovelygod Mean ever really exist?

Spectators are invited to subscribe their own theories in the book provided. This lost child story has mutated from terrible fact into speculative fiction, save that one or more of the fictions may be truth.

Few contemporary Australian authors have meditated more self-consciously and have more explicitly treated the figure of the Lost Child in historical and modern settings than Bird. Her radio play, *In Her Father's House*, dramatised an episode in the life of the Aboriginal girl, Mathinna, who was briefly adopted in 1841 by the Lieutenant-Governor of Van Diemen's Land. In 1998, Bird edited a collection of narratives of Aboriginal children who had been forcibly removed from their parents, many of them drawn from the official government report, *Bringing Them Home*. This was *The Stolen Children. Their Stories*, in whose introduction Bird declared that:

> No two words strike deeper into the human heart than the words 'stolen children'. Nothing is more valuable to us than our children, nothing so irreplaceable, so precious, so beloved. The history of white Australians is marred by children lost in the bush, children spirited away by unknown agents. The stories of these children have become the stuff of myth, icons of horror, and they ring with the notes of darkest nightmare. How must it be, then, to be such children, stolen children? How must it be to be children who have been snatched away from their mothers and systematically stripped of culture, language, rights and dignity?

The lost children, whether from *The Bluebird Café*, such stories as 'Mr Lightning' and 'One Last Picture of Ruby Rose' in her collection *Automatic Teller* (1996), or in the novel *Red Shoes* (1998), are at risk from adults whose responsibility they are, rather than government policy. They grow up – in so far as they are allowed to – in a world where men and women seem dedicated to the ruin of the youngest generation. The children's bodies and souls are in jeopardy. They are prey not only in life at the hands of serial killers and religious sects, but after their disappearances or deaths as well, when they become fodder for fears merchandised at second hand, at an apparently safe remove from those who have suffered the losses and might be grieving for them. Thus in 'Mr Lightning', photographs of the first girl to be stolen from her home 'went up all over the city, all over the country – on billboards, notice-boards, buses, taxis, bridges, lamp posts, trees'. This lost child, who will never be found, is 'Like a wanted man or a pop star, Alice was everywhere'.

In *Red Shoes* the main character Petra was nearly aborted by her mother with the aid of 'a long steel knitting needle and half a bottle of gin and a hot bath'. As a child she is sexually used by the Reverend Somerset Love. Later she will be involved in what is effectively a baby farm, Sister Winter's Shalimar, where children – surrendered for adoption by their unwed mothers – are taken by the Hill House Brethren. Periodically, the novel surrenders its narrative to other stories in a fashion that is characteristic of Bird's fictions. As Bedrock Mean had pondered the happy endings to the stories of the abandoned Pinocchio and Agnes, daughter of Gudule the Recluse, in Victor Hugo's *The Hunchback of Notre Dame* (1831), so *Red Shoes* is full of interpolations, from fiction, film and history. Often these are stories, obsessively related, of child abuse. In the St Bartholomew's Day Massacre of 1572 in France, a man stabs a baby and throws it in the Seine while 'Children themselves tied belts around the necks of babies and dragged them screaming round the streets like dolls, until they fell silent in death'. The figure of the abused, abandoned, kidnapped, murdered child is sovereign in Bird's fiction, and its presentation the more frightening because effected with such equanimity, with a sense that this is now the normal state of affairs. Bird has dragged the lost child from legend and from newspaper coverage of distant events (the slaying of sixteen schoolchildren at Dunblane in Scotland in 1996 is several times alluded to in *Automatic Teller*) to the centre of our attentions. This tormented figure becomes the terrible, defining circumstance of the present time.

The Lost Child's Unwelcome Return: David Malouf's *Remembering Babylon*

It is not the loss, but the recovery of children that animates some of David Malouf's most arresting prose, this, together with intense sensual recollections of his own childhood, and imaginings of the childhoods of others. Indeed Malouf's work emphasises, if with a certain plangency of tone that qualifies confidence in what is being asserted, all that which connects us with the past, how far from bereft or abandoned in time we ever are or should believe ourselves to be. As Digger Keen, hero of Malouf's novel *The Great World* (1990) states the case:

> Even the least event had lines, all tangled, going back into the past, and beyond that into the unknown past, and others leading out, also tangled, into the future. Every movement was dense with causes, possibilities, consequences; too many, even in the simplest case, to grasp.

This view of one's place in the world is as much terrifying as it is consoling. If all of Malouf's characters are given a sense of their provenance, individual identity at the same time seems to dissolve in historical flux.

His first novel, *Johnno* (1975), begins with the return from Europe of Dante, the narrator, who has been called home to Brisbane because of the death of his father. Sorting out and separating his own and his father's belongings, he comes upon an old school magazine. Cheekily peering out from a group sports photograph in which he did not belong, is Dante's best friend, Johnno. After this shock, Dante realises that 'the book I had always meant to write about Johnno will get written after all'. He will retrieve Johnno from the past, evoking as well the times which they spent together and explaining what kept them apart. The same years and places were also given life again in such poems by Malouf as 'Year of the Foxes' and in his autobiographical work, *12 Edmondstone Street* (1985).

Long before the novel's present time, Johnno had been lost forever. Whether by accident or suicide, he has drowned in the Condamine. When he was a child, Johnno's eccentricities had been tolerated because his father was one of many thousands of Australians who did not come back from the Second World War: 'the reason for Johnno's wildness, it was universally agreed, was that he was a war child'. By an act of will and imagination, in some measure as a gesture of restitution for occasions of bad faith, Dante gives Johnno the fuller life of which circumstances and character had conspired to deprive him.

In *An Imaginary Life* (1978), Malouf's next novel, the poet Ovid is exiled among those whom he regards as barbarians; he is despatched to a bleak, distant reach of the Roman Empire, to Tomis on the Black Sea. There he finds an altogether unanticipated peace, through the encounter with a wild child who miraculously appears to him in fact and then enters his dream, vanishes, only to return the following year. Into the poet's last years, this found child brings an unbidden grace; he is like a healing natural force, and he is there with Ovid at the moment when the poet passes from history and the world, back into his own long lost childhood, as the boy disappears again before his eyes.

As Malouf turned increasingly to 'the matter of Australia' for his fictional subjects, to its involvement in the Great War in *Fly Away Peter* (1982) for instance, to the Second World War and its aftermath in *The Great World*, he came upon – not surprisingly, but in ways that arouse our sense of wonder – the figure of the lost child. More particularly, and unusually, he imagined in *Remembering Babylon* (1993) the perturbation which is caused by the return of one who, once a lost child, had been given up for dead and long forgotten. Marooned as a thirteen-year-old on the north Queensland coast, Gemmy Fairley was found by Aborigines, who took him to live among them. By his focus on an abandoned child, rather than an adult, Malouf is giving a distinctive treatment to a familiar national story, that of the lost white man or woman (William Buckley, say, or Eliza Fraser) nurtured by Aborigines, who is eventually returned to the society whence he or she came, but is never fully accepted there again.

The situation that Malouf constructs is more disquieting. For the lost child, who was a stock figure in many narratives of colonial Australia, apparently has been assimilated into the alien, aboriginal world which so troubled the first generations of settlers within or at the margins of that world. He or she had stood, in profound if occluded ways, for the anxieties and insecurities of adults, of parents. But what if the lost child is found again like Gemmy – not after a desperate search of eight nights and nine days like the Duffs – but years into the future when the child has become an adult? What will non-European, uncivilised, Aboriginal Australia have made of this figure?

When the Aborigines find Gemmy, his flesh is raw and ulcerated by sea water. As the description of him is extended, it is as if Gemmy is magically transformed, but at first he 'had still been half-child, half-sea-calf, his hair swarming with spirits in the shape of tiny phosphorescent crabs, his mouth stopped with coral'. That is, he is found freed from history and the particularity of his origins, in a state of metamorphosis, half a creature of the land, half of the sea; half human, half animal. When the three children from the settlement glimpse Gemmy in the opening scene of the novel, he again seems to be in a state of arrested transition. This account of him is impressionistically rendered:

> In the intense heat that made everything you looked at warp and glare, a fragment of ti-tree swamp, some bit of the land over there that was forbidden to them, had detached itself from the band of grey that made up the far side of the swamp, and in a shape more like a watery, heat-struck mirage than a thing of substance, elongated and airily indistinct, was bowling, leaping, flying towards them.

The sentence unfolds itself in a leisurely fashion until the autochthonous creature is freed from its bonds of earth. Then the pace quickens to a frightening conclusion. A lost child has returned. Lachlan Beattie's first thought is 'A black!' He is wrong, although Gemmy's long and then resumed association with the Aborigines will particularly taint him for some of the white people in this place.

To them, also, he remains in part what he first appeared to be for the children: not a thing of substance, but a mirage. Indeed they would rather not see him. They wish to remove him from their presence altogether, and from the humble history which they are making, whether this means returning him to the natives, or sequestering him with the eccentric Mrs Hutchence on the outskirts of the settlement, or at last – and with comic improbability – using the good offices of the Premier of Queensland to find him a post as Customs Officer at Bowen. To these folk Gemmy is preferable as a mirage, or as another legendary lost child of the past. From the standpoint that regards Gemmy as mirage or legend, the unpalatable past that he summons up, and especially his cohabitation with the blacks, can be regarded as fanciful.

Uncomfortably, though, he has ceased to be the latter and never was the first. As it is, Gemmy's lost years among the Aborigines rekindle in many of the settlers 'a terror you thought you had learned, years back, to treat as childish: the Bogey, the Coal Man, Absolute Dark'. Unwelcome revenant, Gemmy comes to represent atavistic fears that the community thinks to extirpate by assaulting and expelling him. He is elected as the convenient, punishable surrogate for the elusive and menacing Aborigines, not least because the fate of this once lost European child was to have become, to some extent, aboriginal himself.

In his first appearance to the children, which also marks his re-emergence into European sight, Gemmy seems to them – as he had at first to the Aborigines – to be a creature in the process of shape-changing:

> The stick-like legs, all knobbed at the joints, suggested a wounded waterbird, a brolga, or a human that in the manner of the tales they told one another, all spells and curses, had been changed into a bird, but only halfway, and now, neither one thing nor the other, was hopping and flapping towards them out of a world, over there, beyond the no-man's land of the swamp that was the abode of everything savage and fearsome and, since it lay so far beyond experience, not just their own but their parents' too, of nightmare and rumours, superstitions and all that belonged to Absolute Dark.

The incomplete metamorphosis represented here has complex resonances. Provisionally the approaching figure, the child long ago lost, is assimilated into the white children's familiar, cautionary tales ('all spells and curses') as he had many years been into the Aborigines'. To the former, he is rather a figure of the landscape than in it; it is as though he has been magically but dangerously transformed during his lost years into the spirit of that place beyond the borders of settlement. That is, he is a liminal creature, one who properly belongs to the margins, but which trespasses over them now by crossing a borderline from the 'savage and fearsome' world (as the white folks suppose it to be) into another where civilisation is tenuously maintained. Seen ludicrously drawing near, 'hopping and flapping', as if an emissary from a non-human order of beings (or so it falsely seems), Gemmy is also journeying backwards to the children from the fearful, unconscious mind of their community. Seeking solace at last among those he deems dimly to be his own kind, Gemmy has manifested himself as their daemon.

For the time that he lives uneasily among the settlers, they will subdue their terrors by regarding Gemmy more simply as one of themselves unhappily gone native and thus – in senses beyond the metaphorical – more surely lost than ever:

In taking on, by second nature as it were, this new language of looks and facial gestures, he had lost his white man's appearance, especially for white men who could no longer see what his looks intended, and became in their eyes black.

In such moments, the sinuous sentences which Malouf deploys in *Remembering Babylon* may hint at special pleading. The fear among European Australians of the Aborigines, or worse, of becoming like them (as Gemmy is presumed to have done, this being the essence of his lost condition), is depicted as the expression of a 'horror' at the instability of the self in this alien place. That, it could be argued, is the psychological spring of most lost child narratives, as they are retold, perhaps, rather than as they were directly experienced. The smell of 'a half-forgotten swamp world', of atavistic remembering, is part of this 'horror'. Worse, it leads to the abysmal terror whereby 'as you meet her face to face in the sun, you and all you stand for have not yet appeared over the horizon of the world'. A primal fear of Malouf's fiction is being expressed here: that the deep, longed for consolation, however fragile, of links with a known past might be lost.

Before the end of *Remembering Babylon*, Gemmy is lost to the European community in Queensland again. Improbably offered the public service post, he flees rather than accepting it, once again appearing to step off the world (as did the child at the end of *An Imaginary Life*), carrying with him the story of his life that Mr Frazer, diarist and scientific amateur, had written down, but which the rain erases. Vanishing, Gemmy passes for a second time into the comfortable kind of remembrance that is called legend. For Frazer, though, Gemmy the lost child, the hybrid, is a 'forerunner'. Far from indicating the unfitness of Europeans to live in this country, he has been assimilated, because 'no longer a white man, or a European, whatever his birth, but a true child of the place as it will one day be'. Thus Frazer fashions his own story, not only of how the lost child Gemmy was found transformed, but what the inheritance of all who have lived among Aborigines might be. For him, if for no-one else in the novel, this lost child is the most welcome of revenants, the most hopeful of portents for a national future.

Book Into Film

When Australian film-makers took up stories of lost children, they usually adapted them from novels, or derived them from the collective memory that incidents in the nineteenth century had furnished. For instance, more than a century after their ordeal, the story of the Duff children was retold in a film made for schools by the Victorian government. This was *Lost in the Bush*. Directed by Peter Dodds, shot on location outside Horsham in the Wimmera and acted by enthusiastic locals, the film had its premiere in the town on 13 June 1973. In *The New Australian Cinema* (1980, edited by Scott Murray), Susan Dermody judged that its subject was 'a highly recurrent motif of Australian culture, that of "lost in the bush"', while Virginia Duigan called it 'the most realistic' of Australian children's films and 'the most emphatically Australian'. Evidently, for Duigan, this emphasis had more to do with aspects of the characters and landscape than with the central narrative. She singled out

> the children with their broad hats under the burning sun, the white-haired little boy, the leathery honest bush faces of the farmers in the search party. The scrubby bush is also unmistakable, and one regrets that this was chosen rather than Frederick McCubbin's tall timber country.

Its patent silliness aside – for the film was shot on location, where the Duffs were lost, in 'scrubby bush', rather than 200 kilometres to the east, by Mount Macedon, site of McCubbin's two paintings of lost children – Dermody's comment unwittingly reveals how these stories and settings conflate. She seems to have an ideal image of a lost child episode in mind, to set against individual representations. Directors, of course, must make particular selections of place as they shape lost child narratives.

'Dot and the Kangaroo'
Reproduced with kind permission of Yoram Gross Film Studios

Often, as was said, novels are the source of them. Thus Ethel Pedley's tale for children, *Dot and the Kangaroo* (1898) was filmed in 1977 by Yoram Gross, in an entrancing combination of live and animated action. (The piglet star of another film in this idiom, *Babe* (1995), was also a lost child.) Earlier, James Vance Marshall's *Walkabout* (1961) was the basis for the Nicolas Roeg film of that name released ten years later. Joan

Lindsay's *Picnic at Hanging Rock* (1967) was filmed by Peter Weir in 1975; Beth Roberts's 'story of old Tasmania', *Manganinnie* (1979) in the year after its publication. *The Earthling* (1980), directed by Peter Collinson, was not based on a novel. It told of the return of a dying man, Patrick Foley (William Holden) from the United States to Australia and his chance and at first unwelcomed encounter with a violently orphaned child, Shawn Daley (Ricky Schroder) whose parents had been killed in a campervan accident in the outback. *Mad Max: Beyond Thunderdome* (1985) was the third and last instalment in the film series that first brought Mel Gibson fame. One of its key moments is the account of the origins of civilisation by members of a lost juvenile tribe, the self-styled 'Children of the Crack'. While the original incident referred back to the actual kidnapping of primary school children at Faraday in Victoria in 1972, *Fortress* (1986) was directly based on Gabrielle Lord's 1980 novel. *Evil Angels* (1988) (or *A Cry in the Dark* as it was released in the United States) drew not on fiction, but on John Bryson's long and impassioned reconstruction (1985) of the loss of the baby Azaria Chamberlain at Ayers Rock in 1980 and the subsequent trials of her parents. But the cinematic treatment of children lost in the Australian outback had begun long before.

The Back of Beyond

One of the most striking, and earliest, of these films was John Heyer's black-and-white documentary, *The Back of Beyond*. Born in Tasmania in 1916, Heyer worked for Cinesound in the 1940s and then made propaganda films during the Second World War. In 1946, he was appointed to the Australian National Film Board. After two years, he moved to head the Australian branch of the Shell Film Unit. By 1956 he was in London as executive producer of films and television for the parent company. Heyer's most famous achievement remains *The Back of Beyond*, which he filmed within a budget of £12 000. In 1954, the year of its release, the film was seen in non-commercial venues by 750 000 Australians. It also won the Grand Prix for the best documentary at the Venice Film Festival of that year. Heyer had enlisted a strong team of writers. Poet Douglas Stewart was credited with dialogue and narration, together with Heyer, while the script collaborators were another poet, Roland Robinson, and Heyer's wife Janet.

The Back of Beyond sought to capture the desolate essence of life in the semi-mythical region which is designated by its title, by concentrating on a single stretch of country: the 500 kilometre Birdsville Track from Marree in South Australia to its Queensland terminus at Birdsville. This 'lane through the burning centre of Australia' is littered with bleached bones – of dinosaurs, camels, horses and men. Burke and Wills ventured here in search of an inland sea – twelve million years too late. Aborigines are still to be found, but they are judged to be 'part of a dying race'. In the wake of explorers, prospectors and drovers, comes Tom Kruse the carrier. His work, as a deliverer of mail and supplies, provides the focus of the film.

With one companion in the cab and an Aboriginal child hitching a ride, Kruse sets off from Marree, 'the ragged flower of a town', a 'little town of tin'. The truck has been loaded, letters written for Aboriginal women by kindly whites and the weekly run begins, an ordeal of heat and sand. Stark against the bare landscape are human figures: the Afghan camel driver 'who fought the desert by compass and Koran', and whose chant mingles with the harsh cawing of a crow; stockmen with a mob of cattle –'the silence wakes to the crack and cry of drovers'. Dead cattle lie along dry creek beds, but when the Cooper floods, it catches those that have lived through droughts, and 'drowns and hangs them up in the trees to dry'.

There are scenes of Kruse efficiently at work, manoeuvring the truck over sand drifts with strips of tin for the wheels to grip, and passing on Flying Doctor messages to a beleaguered woman who is ailing and alone on a station. Or Kruse seems to be doing this: the participants' voices were dubbed by professional actors when Heyer edited the film. Travelling further down the Birdsville Track Kruse comes to the ruins of buildings. One of these is Father Vogelsang's Lutheran Mission, built 50 years before 'with burning faith. Now a haunt for the wind'. And a haunt for Jack the Dogger, who works as a dingo killer.

Kruse and his companions arrive at Clifton Hills, last of the five stations along the track to Birdsville, where once there had been fifteen. *The Back of Beyond* becomes a threnody for a lost way of life on these cattle stations: now 'all that remains is the music of their names'. The people are gone, but 'their stories live on in the tales and legends of the track'. Heyer now pauses to tell one of them. The documentary mode is suspended, while a story of two lost girls is harrowingly re-enacted and recalled.

While their father is away mustering cattle, two little girls come upon the body of their mother, sprawled in the yard outside the back door. A far distant neighbour's voice can be heard on the wireless, calling in vain for Jessie, the mother, to answer. Unable to work the wireless (improbable as that sounds) the older girl Sally decides to make for the track and then to walk along it to the nearest station, 40 kilometres away. Roberta, the younger, does not know what happened: 'Sally just told her they were going to play travelling and camping'. The girls load the billycart with water, food and their dog, before setting out across 'the

'The Back of Beyond': 'into the ocean of sand they went'
Copyright of John Heyer

steel-shod surface of this desperate region. Even the animals appear to regard it with dismay'.

The part of lost children's stories that is hidden from adult view – their ordeal by heat or cold, hunger and thirst, the terrors which attend the realisation that they cannot find their way – are agonisingly presented. The girl cooees without response. As they trudge over the sand dunes, one of them plays a pipe. When they come back upon their own tracks, Sally bravely decides to keep going so that her sister will not worry. The dog is abandoned. There is no sign of any landmark that might guide them home. Towing the billycart, the girls move through a plain of dried bones, under a pitiless sun. And then they disappear from view. Two days later their father comes searching for them, following their tracks for 45 kilometres until they are lost 'under wind-blown sand. The children had vanished. What became of them isn't known. Into the ocean of sand they went'.

The Back of Beyond returns us to the present, as Tom Kruse negotiates a sandstorm. Scenes follow of Joe the Rainmaker and of an old Aboriginal teaching a black and a white child to read the sand, 'a game that may mean life or death'. It is long ago too late for Sally and Roberta to learn that skill, but Heyer portrays indelibly what they might have suffered. To the post-war generation, the three-quarters of a million Australians who saw the film in its first year, Heyer's may have become the characteristic image of lost children. It does not represent the typical cases of the nineteenth century, when children wandered into bush or scrub, not desert, and strayed from settled areas rather than such a wasteland as that by the Birdsville Track. Yet no other narrative more vividly intimates the 'lostness' of strayed children, in an indifferent landscape, far from the care of parents who – on this occasion – could bear no blame.

Walkabout

Nicolas Roeg's film *Walkabout* with a script by the British playwright Edward Bond was shot in Sydney and outside Alice Springs from August 1969, before it opened in the United States and then Australia (without much success) in 1971. A 'director's cut', with restored scenes and remastered sound track, was released in 1998. The film was based on a novel by James Vance Marshall, published as *The Children* in 1959 and as *Walkabout* two years later. A knockabout character who was twice gaoled by the Hughes government for his opposition to conscription for the Great War and who was a mate of Henry Lawson's, Marshall was apparently not the sole author of *Walkabout*. Somewhat cryptically, *The Oxford Companion to Australian Literature* claims that the book was:

> written by an English author who collaborated with Marshall in that he used, with his consent, his notes on outback life deriving from his period as a sandalwood cutter in the Northern Territory.

It is hard to believe that after such experiences, Marshall was also the source of the pseudo-ethnography that pocks the novel.

Two American children, a girl called Mary and a boy, Peter, who were on their way to Adelaide, are the only survivors of a plane crash on the Sturt Plain in the Northern Territory: 'It was a far cry from here to their comfortable home in Charleston, South Carolina'. At first the desert appears benign to them, 'a flowering wilderness of eucalyptus, lantana, brigalow and iron bark' (whose names they could scarcely have known). Then an apparition appears: 'ebony black and quite naked'. He is at once the occasion for the author's cultural comparisons between the 'coddled', 'psycho-analysed' products of 'the highest strata of humanity's evolution' and a people whose 'way of life … was already old when Tut-ankh-amen started to build his tomb'. To the Aboriginal boy the whites' freakish appearance and clumsy movements suggest that they are 'perhaps the last survivors of some particularly backward tribe'. For her part, Mary recoils in horror from the boy's considerate touch: 'It was terrifying, revolting, obscene. Back in Charleston it would have got the darkie lynched'.

Yet she will learn something about cultural relativities from this experience. In the desert 'most of the old rules and the old values seemed strangely meaningless'. Evidently the missionaries 'hadn't got round to Australia yet. Perhaps that's why it was called the lost continent'. In a missionary spirit, she gives the Aborigine her panties to cover his genitals. 'Decency was restored', but not for long. He snaps the elastic while performing a ritual dance for the children. In its descent towards travesty, *Walkabout* now imagines the Aborigine considering Mary as 'a budding gin'. As well he might, but when – guessing his intentions – she returns an 'appalled' gaze, the boy trembles uncontrollably, superstitiously believing that she has 'seen in his eyes an image: the image of the Spirit of Death'. He now knows that he is doomed, although he still feels obliged to lead the strangers to safety. Dying with a 'forgiving smile', the Aborigine breaks Mary's heart. Authority passes to her brother and she walks naked behind him, having lost her dress, 'torn beyond repair by the claws of a koala'.

Another group of Aborigines points these lost children to safety and *Walkabout* (the novel) concludes before the end of their journey. It is hard to know what gripped Roeg about the book. Certainly significant revisions to its plot were made for his film. Improbabilities remained. The two lost children, with their parents, are first seen in Sydney. A drive for a picnic seems to remove them swiftly into the desert, as though to argue for the actual as well as the symbolic contiguity of city and wilderness in Australia. In the film, the unnamed, and soon to be lost children, are introduced as a girl (Jenny Agutter), who is in the senior years of private schooling, and her younger brother (played by Lucien John, Roeg's son). A glimpse of home life shows a mother preparing food while the father (John Meillon) silently drinks. Roeg cuts to what looks like central Australia. The father, who may be a geologist (his tape recorder plays geological data), has driven his children away into the bush for a picnic. He sits up in his Volkswagen, incongruously clad in suit and tie, while his daughter lays out watermelon, pawpaw, chicken, ham and beer. What occurs next is Roeg's most radical revision of his source.

Rather than being the victims of an accident, the children have been set up for murder. Their father starts shooting with a pistol. Having failed to hit them, he sets fire to the car, thus stranding the children. Then he commits suicide. The man's motive must be inferred. His own mental torments are evidently severe enough for him to believe that this is no world for his children either. As it happens, while not murdering them, he has abandoned them in the wilderness. Lost, the two children set off into drier, red soil country. Fortunately finding a waterhole and fruit, they settle in for their first night. When they are pictured at dawn the next day, the composition of boy and girl entwined in sleep recalls (unwittingly or not) the stock nineteenth-century magazine illustrations of children lost in the bush.

As in the novel, an Aborigine (David Gulpilil) appears. He dances towards them. The boy's unguarded first thought is 'Dad'. The girl crisply demands 'water. I can't make it any simpler than that' and asks 'where is Adelaide?' Without the mediation of language in common, white and black perform for each other. The white boy gradually sheds his clothes, his sister shelters from the sun under a home-made umbrella, while the Aborigine hunts and kills a kangaroo. An aeroplane flies indifferently overhead. The Aborigine paints on the boy and on rocks. Roeg cuts puzzlingly to scientists (presumably not far from the children) about to release balloons in the desert. In a long scene, the girl swims naked in a pool while the Aborigine hunts and fishes. It is an anticipation of a sexual conjunction that will not come about.

Somewhere nearer to settled areas, they come upon an abandoned shack made of corrugated iron. The only sign of its habitation are pictures on the walls inside. The boy finds a road, but the Aborigine draws him away from it. Lying down among the bones of animals, he paints himself white and performs a courting dance for the girl. Terrified, and attracted, she repulses him. By next morning she has herself and her brother back in their carefully preserved school uniforms. During the night, the Aborigine has hanged himself in grief and disappointment. With preternatural calm, the girl asks her brother whether he has eaten his breakfast, and they set off along the road to safety. The girl's only audible reflection on the Aborigine's death is the chilling line: 'I suppose he thought he was doing the best thing'.

He is, of course, the true lost child (or youth) of Roeg's film. He represents that moment of black and white reconciliation (emotional, as well as to do with practical salvation) that so many of the lost child narratives promise, and yet which turn out to be transient. The two codas to *Walkabout* suggest that Roeg is instinctively alert to the cultural tradition in which he is working. First he cuts to Sydney, where the girl has become a young wife. She stands chopping liver while her boorish husband, in his electric blue suit, talks of promotion and material rewards: 'in two years we'll be holidaying on the Gold Coast and shopping in Vaucluse'. This is the fate for which she has been saved. In a dream sequence with which the film ends, a vision of what might have been (but in the long history of lost child stories in Australia never was the outcome), the Aborigine and the two children are joyously naked, laughing, swimming, united. This is not emotional fakery by Roeg, but rather indicative of an acute awareness of an idyllic possibility that in real life, in the stories of lost children, would seldom be.

Picnic at Hanging Rock

The heroines of Shakespeare's late romances are variously endangered. Some are believed lost forever, like Miranda in *The Tempest* or Perdita in *The Winter's Tale*; others are threatened with the loss of their chastity and perhaps their lives – Imogen in *Cymbeline* and Marina in *Pericles*. None is a child. Marriage is the imminent fate which is at some stage promised for each of them. Miranda, daughter of the magician and exile Duke of Milan, Prospero, she who wonders at a 'brave new world that has such people in it' (being not much acquainted with people), is the fated name borne by one of the lost girls in Joan Lindsay's novel, *Picnic at Hanging Rock* (1967). So suggestive does Lindsay take the name to be, that her Miranda is given no other.

Miranda is a student at Mrs Appleyard's College for Young Ladies, 'an architectural anachronism in the Australian bush – a hopeless misfit in time and place'. The time is 1900, cusp of an old and new century, whatever one's millennial figuring. The place is Mount Macedon, north of Melbourne. On St Valentine's Day, most of the students of the college set out on a picnic to nearby Hanging Rock. Miranda remembers having been shown 'a picture of people in old-fashioned dresses having a picnic at the Rock. I wish I knew where it was painted'. That inquiry is easily answered. Lindsay supplies a footnote. The painting in question is William Ford's 'At the Hanging Rock', which was first shown in 1875 at the Intercolonial Exhibition in Melbourne.

Ford, who was born in England in 1820, came to Melbourne as an immigrant in September 1871, settling in St Kilda. His best-known painting featured a fashionable, and innocuous activity at a site which was available to many Victorians once the railway from Melbourne had reached Woodend. Horses and buggies took thousands of excursioners to the nearby Hanging Rock, not far east of the town. They picnicked. Ford's painting shows fifteen of them, mainly women and children, altogether unsuitably attired for the heat of the day. They have chosen their picnic spot in a clearing not at the base, but some way up the rock. Thus the eucalypts overtop the formations in stone. The viewer is afforded a glance through the trees to the horizon. The picnickers have broken, insouciantly, into groups. Yet all of them appear to be imposed upon, rather than comfortably part of this setting. At the same time, all are untroubled, it seems, by a place that Lindsay would inject with so much implicit menace.

As Frederick McCubbin had done before her in his painting 'Lost' (1907), which used the landscape around his home, Fontainebleau, on Mount Macedon, close to Hanging Rock. One surmises that Lindsay knew of the connection when she wrote her novel. Her work harkens back to a past time which it archly re-imagines, as well as to the nineteenth-century commonplace of children lost in the bush. Lindsay's novel is an unusual, because decadent, instance of the lost child topos in Australian literature, a remystification of material that still had power to chill the heart, but was here turned to an aimless guessing game.

The novel introduces us to Miranda, Marion Quade (seventeen years old and a mathematician), the heiress Irma Leopold (whose parents own mines in Brazil) and the school dunce, Edith. Glimpsed at their picnic, they are as incongruously imposed on the landscape as their counterparts in Ford's painting:

> the drowsy well-fed girls lounging in the shade were no more a part of their environment than figures in a photograph album, arbitrarily posed against a backcloth of cork rocks and cardboard trees.

The four of them wander away from the rest of the school party. They cross a creek. Doing so, they summon up essential memories of lost child narratives of the nineteenth century. The difference, so far as one can infer it, is that these girls have responded to, sought out or half recognised, a sexual enticement, rather than the pre-pubescent bewitchment to which their younger predecessors in fiction had been subject.

As the girls cross the creek at noon, watches stop. Another picnicker at the Rock, and a visitor from England, the Honourable Michael Fitzhubert, takes his chance coincidentally to ponder the strangeness of time and place in the antipodes:

> He reminded himself that he was in Australia now: Australia, where anything might happen. In England everything had been done before: quite often by one's ancestors, over and over again.

But in Australia, the possibilities for romance have not been exhausted. As the girls venture on, with 'every step the prospect ahead grew more enchanting'. Irma is also sensible, 'for a little while, of a rather curious sound coming up from the plain. Like the beating of far-off drums'.

For whatever reason and means, it is as if the four girls are put under a spell. They are 'suddenly overcome by an over-powering lassitude'; fling themselves onto the rocks 'in the shelter of the monolith' and fall into a deep sleep. It is when they awaken that three of them – Miranda, Marion and Irma – leave Edith behind and move quickly out of sight 'behind the monolith'. They leave no tracks. Strangely, and

As in the novel, which the film script closely follows, the girls cross a creek. They are observed by Michael (Dominic Guard), who will soon be implicated in their story, and by Albert (John Jarratt), who would be in the manservant role if Australia was an 'old' rather than a 'new' country. The girls vanish from view and then they reappear, climbing the rock, passing through a spot that recalls the picnic ground of Ford's painting. Edith whinges that 'there is nothing here. I never thought it would be so nasty or I wouldn't have come'. It is a lack of imagination which hampers her, a fearful or at least unresponsive attitude towards the mysteries that this brooding landform may harbour. For her part, Miranda peers through two dark rocks, then enters an opening between them. Her face is filled with a dreamy sexual yearning. Together with Irma (Jane Vallsi) and Marion, she removes her boots and stockings. The four girls lie down to sleep. When they wake, Edith asks 'when are we going home?' but the other three pass through a cleft in the rocks and vanish. Edith goes screaming down the hill. The mystery of Hanging Rock has begun, and in a sense has also already ended.

Weir's structural problem is how to sustain interest in the film, by more prosaic narrative means, while at the same time continuing to tease us with interpretation of the inexplicable. Thus he presents various consequences of the disappearance: the search, the investigation of the mystery and speculation about it, besides the sub-plot with Sara (Margaret Wilson) and the disintegration of Mrs Appleyard. In his essay on 'Fantasy' in *The New Australian Cinema*, Adrian Martin was full of praise for the film's unresolved insinuations (for instance of the relations between Miranda and Mlle de Poitiers, Mrs Appleyard and Miss McCraw):

> Such details are left in abeyance, and this suspends the audience in what the French call *signifiance* – traces of meaning, fragments of sense, but never a coherent, fixed, final truth – delivered easily to us by the film's end.

It is better, however, to take the film in an Australian rather than the French way. One of the lost children, Irma, is found after a few days, 'intact'. Does this mean that the other two have had a strange sexual initiation, so that they can never return to the world which they left? Or has the land swallowed them up, in whatever spirit, for whatever reason? And what of the character who does not fit the pattern of lost child stories – the adult, spinster Miss McCraw – has she too sought a kind of climax at the Rock?

On the one hand the film, and the novel before it, would have us believe that there is a meaning in and an explanation for (however obscure or improbable) the loss of three people at Hanging Rock.

Yvonne Rousseau wittily marshalled a number of theories in her book *The Murders at Hanging Rock* (1980), perhaps to suggest the absurdity of the enterprise. On the other hand, Lindsay and Weir surrender to a mystification of the Australian landscape, which invests it with a power to enchant and lure that is deliciously fatal. Lost children in nineteenth-century stories felt that enchantment, but the landscape was the indifferent scene rather than the agent of their perils. Both novel and film of *Picnic at Hanging Rock* want the human dimension of the lost child story to be reduced to a puzzle without an answer, to the scrabbling of people across a vast, animate, indecipherable landscape, or their disappearance into it. And yet in doing so, Lindsay and then Weir have perhaps returned the story of lost children that they tell and retell to its symbolic origins: to the anxious suspicion that Europeans do not belong in this country; that therefore they should go back to England, or escape into another time, or simply vanish. And in vanishing, whatever else they have intended or accomplished, or been compelled to do, these lost children have forever escaped from childhood.

Manganinnie

Shot on a budget of less than $500 000, the Tasmanian-made film, *Manganinnie*, opened there on 10 July 1980. Beth Roberts's novel, published the year before, was scripted for the screen by Ken Kelso. Tasmanian-born composer Peter Sculthorpe wrote the score and John Honey directed. As the film opens, Manganinnie – an Aboriginal woman in middle age – blows on a fire stick whose custodian she is. Possessing 'the secrets of things that burn', she is 'the red fire woman'. Other Aboriginal figures now appear in silhouette on the horizon. They are 'dark figures in the sky'. Or that is how they are recalled by the narrator, Joanna Waterman, whose childhood epiphany is the substance of the story. She relives what adults who survive being lost in the bush seldom seem or wish to bring back from memory: the causes and circumstances of their transforming ordeals.

Honey cuts from the campfire of the Singing River People to whom Manganinnie belongs, to the Waterman house. The father reads to his family the account of the creation in the Book of Genesis and prays that God will 'defend us from all dangers and perils of the night'. In a pointed juxtaposition, we witness Manganinnie explaining an Aboriginal tale of origins, telling fellow members of the tribe how fire fell from the sky. This episode is followed by one in which an army officer outlines to Mr Waterman a matter altogether less wondrous. This is 'the sensible plan' of the Black Line, which is intended to round up all the Aborigines still alive on the mainland of Tasmania. The officer reminds Waterman that 'They're a treacherous lot', but the landowner takes a much more liberal view: 'there are not many people who'd be prepared to be removed from their own land'.

Across grey-brown country in the Lake District of the Central Highlands of Tasmania, the Singing River People are chased and dispersed by whites on horseback. Manganinnie's husband is shot. She eludes capture. Pondering the prelude to her own adventures, Joanna laments how she had never had the chance to see Manganinnie 'in happiness among her own people'. Soon after that happiness ends (because of the whites' attack), Joanna will begin her journey with Manganinnie. It happens this way: Waterman and Joanna are wandering by a waterfall. He puts flowers in her red hair and declares 'you look like an Indian princess'. Then the father is called away. Joanna pauses by a stream, thus entering the liminal space of lost child stories of the nineteenth century (which the film, of course, also purports to be). Manganinnie is on the other side. She attracts (rather than lures or entices) the child to her, and touches Joanna's face. Evidently, and crucially, 'the child had returned'. That is, the white girl with 'fire in her hair' is a surrogate for Manganinnie's own lost child.

Joanna's bonnet, which has floated down stream, is found, and she is presumed by most of those searching to have been drowned. Only her father refuses to believe that she is dead. Meanwhile, Manganinnie and the child keep to a cave near the waterfall. When Joanna steps outside it, she appears to be ensnared by the bush, entrapped within thicker undergrowth than her similarly dressed counterpart in McCubbin's painting 'Lost' (1886). Gradually Joanna becomes a less incongruous figure in this landscape. Manganinnie dresses her in animal skins and is able to persuade the child to blend into the bush and to hide with her when a white man on horseback passes by.

Because 'the time of cold had returned', Manganinnie sets off from the Great Water, taking Joanna with her. It is the Aboriginal woman's intention to find 'her people again on the shores of the sea'. So they travel to the coast, where Manganinnie looks in vain for others from the Singing River tribe. We are thus confronted starkly with two kinds of loss, and with the corresponding searches that they occasion: for the vanished child and for the scattered Aboriginal tribe. These are temporally connected, but are more profoundly entwined as well. The European child, Joanna, is 'lost'. By one reckoning, she has been abducted by the Aboriginal woman, Manganinnie. Yet the woman cares for, teaches and loves Joanna. The long forgotten Tasmanian novel, Mrs Thrower's *Younah!* (1898), has its resonances here, but more importantly and more generally, the relationship of Manganinnie and Joanna proclaims reconciliation between the races, a possibility of an order that makes

'Manganinnie': the liminal moment – creek crossing
Tasmanian State Archives

unimportant how they came to be together. At the same time, the tribal, cultural and familial world of Manganinnie herself has been irrevocably lost, as in despair she senses. Nor will she survive the lost child story in which, at first, and then at its ending, she had the principal agency.

The next section of Honey's film is the least convincing. While trying to steal fire from them, Manganinnie is captured by a group of runaway convict desperadoes, in prison garb, replete with the broad arrow insignia. With the aid of a dog, Joanna effects an unlikely rescue. Manganinnie – and this is the critical point as well as the symbolic consequence of the encounter – sustains a wound from which eventually she will die. Before that, she guides the lost child home. While checking his horses, Mr Waterman comes upon Joanna, who retreats into a corner

IN THE TWENTIETH CENTURY – BOOK INTO FILM

'Manganinnie': Joanna and Manganinnie at the cave
Tasmanian State Archives

in fear of him. Early the next morning, the dog leads Joanna to Manganinnie's body. Mr Waterman guesses, rightly, that 'this poor creature has been the guardian of our child all this time' and wants to give her a dignified burial. Joanna persuades him that, according to Aboriginal custom, the body must be burned. In the cremation of Manganinnie, Waterman's barn accidentally catches fire. He lets it go, sitting and watching with his daughter. And that is where the grown-up Joanna concludes her story: 'I remember it as if I was dreaming. Fire in the wind and dark figures in the sky'.

This beautiful and neglected telling in film of a lost child story from the colonial past of Van Diemen's Land, sought a contemporary, healing reference as well. Tom Haydon's film, *The Last Tasmanian* (1978) included a scene wherein the Tasmanian Premier, Doug Lowe, cast the ashes of Trugannini, the last full-blooded Tasmanian Aborigine, onto the waters of the D'Entrecasteaux Channel. Two years later, Honey's film, gently appropriating perhaps the most familiar narrative of the Australian frontier, the lost child story, also emphasised Aboriginal loss. Manganinnie had both filled a conventional role in this lost child story, as Aboriginal saviour of a European child, but also a premonitory one, as an agent of healing that might and ought to have come to be.

Fortress

Fortress (1980), first of the thrillers that Gabrielle Lord has written in a successful, single-minded and enduring career, begins with its heroine contemplating an abortion. She is a country schoolteacher called Sally Jones, made miserable by an unwanted pregnancy, and by the strains of a three year stint in a bush school at Sunny Flat, 500 kilometres west of Sydney. The ordeal that Sally is about to endure involves her in the protection, eventually through violence, of the children in her care. Lord took as the basis for her novel the kidnapping in 1972 of the pupils and teacher at the Faraday School, north of Melbourne, by John Francis Eastway and his accomplices. That incident ended without bloodshed, although remarkably Eastway would repeat his crime at another school some years later. *Fortress* envisages an altogether bloodier outcome from the kidnapping.

Sally's class – which is to say the whole school – is taken by men in masks: Mac the Mouse, Father Christmas and Daffy Duck. Their motives are obscure to her: 'None of us rich or famous. Instead of sons or daughters of the wealthy, they are taking a whole small school, thirteen souls'. And she is rightly 'chilled' by the thought of other kidnappings, in which the victims were dead before ransom had ever been negotiated. Driven away from the school, harried and disoriented, the children and Sally are entombed by their kidnappers. In a manner that recalls Rider Haggard's romance *King Solomon's Mines* (1885), they escape through an underground river. Later they think they have found safety at a nearby farmhouse, only to be recaptured. No doubt with the best of intentions, Sally endeavours to keep the children's spirits up by singing 'Now I lay me down to sleep/Pray thee, Lord, my soul to keep'. Thus it is 'Hansel and Gretel's prayer', whose 'slow, formal melody shaped itself around the barn'. They sing a tune of ill omen.

The children escape again, at first, it appears into a benign realm familiar from children's fiction. Their place of refuge literally recalls Nan Chauncy's Tasmanian novel *They Found a Cave* (1948, released as a film in 1963). The escape of boys and girls from adult persecution is also reminiscent of many moments in the stories of Enid Blyton. But Lord sours her Blyton with William Golding. Sally and the children plot revenge against their kidnappers and persecutors: 'Such creatures had no right to walk on the good earth'. At first the men's motives are more menacing because unclear. One of the boys, Derek, asks Sally 'why do people do this sort of thing?' She answers as conventionally as can be:

IN THE TWENTIETH CENTURY – BOOK INTO FILM

'Fortress': Christmas comes early
Photograph supplied courtesy of Crawford Productions

'No one knows ... an unhappy childhood, or [they] had parents who were harsh with them, or didn't love them'. The leader's motive is mundanely explained by the author soon afterwards. Unhappy at this same school, then graduating from petty crime to armed robbery, Jim Marsh (Father Christmas) 'had thought of the kidnap of his Alma Mater'.

What this might signify – for instance as the symbolic and vengeful recapture of a lost childhood – does not delay the narrative. Instead Lord offers another revenge fantasy, the counterpart of Jim's, in which the children destroy the adults who prey on them. Sally not only joins in the killings, with 'wild triumph soaring through her body', but she is on hand to moralise as well. Narelle wonders if God will punish their group for what they have done. Sally responds: 'Remember that savagery and barbarity are the other side of love. That we loved each other and fought for and defended each other from enemies'. Without exploring, or perhaps suspecting, all the implications of its story, *Fortress* presents the most disturbing, pre-emptive strike of children against the older generation that Australian fiction has to show.

The film which appeared five years later, a Crawford Production, with a script by Everett de Roche based on Lord's novel, made the children's revenge more violent, explicit and – in its own terms – sanctified. This *Fortress* (1985) translated the kidnapping from western New South Wales to the Grampians and the Buchan Caves, that is, to Victoria, albeit to disparate locations far from Faraday (and from each other). In the film's opening, one of the O'Brien boys wants to shoot a predatory fox in the family's chicken coop. Sally (Rachel Ward) boards with the O'Briens and walks to school with the children. It is only two weeks from the end of the school term, but the children's will finish early. Four kidnappers, identifiable only by their different masks, set upon the class: Father Christmas, who tells them that 'we be goin' on a picnic', Mac the Mouse, Pussy Cat and Daffy Duck.

The story closely follows the novel. After a drive through a blank landscape, void of passing traffic, the children and their teacher are forced to descend into a cave. Sally tries to be consoling: 'I think children we are going to have an adventure'. Her role is curious. That line is Blytonesque, yet Blyton's children's stories very often hinged on the absence of protective, natural parents, whose role was usurped by malevolent and criminal surrogates. As their teacher, Sally stands *in loco parentis* for the children, but she will dissolve the differences and distance between them. Most importantly, she will be a full and equal participant in the vengeance that they exact upon their kidnappers.

Stripping to her underwear, Sally swims the underground river and finds the way of escape. 'We beat them didn't we', one child prematurely proclaims. But the homestead that they glimpse, then enter, offers only an illusory promise of refuge and safety. They are soon enough kidnapped, hence lost again. But not for long. These kidnappers are vicious but inept. The police are nowhere to be seen. Sally and the children will have to find their own way home.

As in the novel, they do so murderously. In September 1986, a *Cinema Papers* critic, Tony Drouyn, unkindly titled his review of the film 'Mutton Dressed as Rambo'. He missed both the darker and older reverberations of this treatment of a story of lost children, and its modern, twentieth-century inflections. Human agents are to blame for this 'loss'. The motives of Father Christmas and his associates may have begun as mercenary, with a ransom in mind, but after the thwarting of their plans, their intentions become purely homicidal. The children, however, fight back. For once – and exceptionally – they best and kill adults who have made patent their own murderous plans. Sally, the teacher, is complicit with the children. In print and in film, *Fortress* enunciates a wish fulfilment that is seldom ventilated in the late twentieth-century body of Australian narrative that much more usually, if discomfortingly, portrays the death or ruin of children, rather than their triumph by violence.

Lord has returned to the theme of the lost child in modern Australia in several of her later novels. *The Sharp End* (1998) features a part-Aboriginal hero, the Dog Squad detective Harry Doyle, who was one of the 'stolen generation'. The novel relates the kidnapping of his daughter by a homicidal former friend of Doyle's. *Whipping Boy* (1992) deals with paedophilia and child pornography. Like *Fortress*, this novel was made into a film: a tele-movie for Channel Ten that was released in 1996, directed by Di Drew, with Sigrid Thornton in the lead role. Once opened, such seams of horror as violent paedophilia represent appear to spread, implicating everyone, whether they are innocent or guilty. This has the disruptive power to turn a novel or film on such subjects into a documentary or a crusade, not that either kind of approach is likely in any event to be altogether absent. Lord's solution is to make the obsession her heroine's. After her success in exposing Customs rorts in Melbourne, lawyer Cass Meredith is appointed to head a child porn investigation in Sydney. Her private demons prejudice her impartiality. She believes that her father betrayed her mother and deserted the family, while her own estranged husband Otto (a playwright who drinks and lives in Melbourne) is trying to obtain custody of their son Moses, or Moz. Thus Cass inveighs against

> the whole monstrous regiment of killers and abusers, the ones who have no hearts. The men. The fathers. The killers. Betrayers and murderers. She thought of the men who said they loved children.

Her inquiries give Cass ample independent warrant for such an opinion.

Whipping Boy begins with the making of what accidentally turns into a snuff movie. Leo, a young addict, dies during the filming of a bondage session, which has been staged and recorded for the benefit of male authority figures who thus gravely abuse their power. They are named for their occupations: Policeman, Headmaster, Judge, Doctor. It is the former who dismisses the loss of the child, Leo, as a thing of no importance: 'they're only temporary Australians, these street kids. One day they fall over and stay there. Look at the track marks'. At first anguished, the Headmaster comes to console himself that 'there is no one to care about such a boy'. He is an exemplary hypocrite: 'a family man with three grown-up children, two grandchildren, and a loyal wife – not to mention the thousands of boys who had passed through his hands'. It is a chilling life story in miniature.

'Chicken hawks' such as the Policeman, the Headmaster and their ilk find fodder for their sordid fancies everywhere at hand. They recruit eight-year-old alcoholics, or draw on 'Satanist groups whose children are available for abuse in their rituals', or even use their own children. This is the kind of urban prospect which provides for their needs, as Cass observes it one morning in inner Sydney:

> Already, near the station entrance, a group of child alcoholics was sitting with flagons, cigarettes and guitars. Several of them were Koori and one of them, not more than eleven or twelve, was attempting a dreary country-and-western song.

And they are catered for off the street as well. Cass has to track an informant called Saphra who strips at a club for paedophile tastes that is cloyingly named Babes. At first blinded by the darkness downstairs, Cass then thinks that she has interrupted a crime, 'because lying along the front of the bar opposite, with her eyes staring up into the darkness, was a naked child, like an offering'. It is a hologram, a child ghost, an image – maybe – that gloats over so many children already and actually lost. Cass sees

> golden children everywhere. Babes in the wood. Babes everywhere. Their images covered every surface like wallpaper. Naked, partly clothed, teasing, simpering, pouting, thrusting – posed children, aping adult affectations; young faces with dead eyes.

If one phrase – 'Babes in the wood' – returns us to the world of fairytale, innocence, happy endings and a century other than this, the last detail turns that world over. Not the lost children of fairytale, but the memories of real victims inform these grisly images. What Cass sees, passing in horror through the holograms, illuminated by them, is an abridged version of the whole trajectory of stories of lost children in Australia. It has come to this: 'young faces with dead eyes', a blighted generation, many of whom are virtually dead in life, and whose veritable deaths beckon.

Evil Angels

Fred Schepisi's film, *Evil Angels* (1988), like Weir's *Picnic at Hanging Rock*, is about a vanishing near a rock monolith; it depicts a mystery that summons old, folk memories of children lost in the bush. Neither the fictional girls, Miranda and Marion, nor the actual baby Azaria Chamberlain, were ever found. Nor have the circumstances and causes of their disappearances ever been unambiguously established. The Chamberlain case is one of the most notorious and controversial episodes in Australian public life, not only of the last two decades, but in this century. An outline can be offered, but no answer to the mystery.

In the winter of 1980, Seventh Day Adventist Minister Michael Chamberlain, his wife Lindy, their two sons Aidan and Regan, and their nine-week-old daughter Azaria set off from Mt Isa to central Australia for a camping holiday. By Sunday 17 August they were at Ayers Rock. That night, the baby Azaria disappeared from the family tent. Her mother alerted the other campers, crying distractedly that a dingo had taken her baby. The night search failed to find any trace of the child, who was therefore presumed to have died. A week later, articles of the baby's clothing, a jumpsuit, singlet and booties, were recovered near the base of Ayers Rock.

On 15 December, the first of several judicial inquiries into Azaria's disappearance began. This was the coronial inquest at Alice Springs, before the local magistrate, Denis Barritt. On 20 February of the next year, Barritt brought down a televised judgment in which he deemed that the child had indeed been taken by a dingo. In consequence, no charges were brought against the Chamberlains. But police were not satisfied. Their investigations continued until purportedly they found new forensic evidence which pointed to the Chamberlains' guilt. The first verdict was quashed by the Supreme Court of the Northern Territory in December 1981 and a new inquiry was opened.

On 2 February 1982, Chief Magistrate Gerry Galvin found sufficient cause to commit both Chamberlain parents for trial: the mother for the murder of her child, the father as an accessory after the fact. The trial began in Darwin in September. At the end of October, both Michael and Lindy Chamberlain were found guilty as charged. She received a mandatory life sentence; he was given an eighteen-month suspended sentence. The trials of the Chamberlains were by no means done. They appealed to the Federal Court, but the verdict of the Northern Territory Supreme Court was upheld at the end of April 1983. In February of the next year, the High Court also rejected the Chamberlains' appeal, albeit in a split decision. A Chamberlain Innocence Committee was established in 1985, but its approaches to the Northern Territory government were rejected.

A crucial and unexpected piece of evidence turned up on 2 February 1986. A matinee jacket (an article of clothing that Lindy Chamberlain always claimed that her daughter had been wearing) was found not far from the spot where the other clothing had been located in August 1980. Five days later, Lindy Chamberlain was released from Berrimah

Gaol in Darwin on licence. Subsequently a Royal Commission was appointed to re-examine the forensic evidence in the case. Its report was not released until 2 June 1987, but Justice Morling argued that – based on the evidence before the Royal Commission – a judge would have been bound to have directed the jury towards acquittal of the Chamberlains. More than four years later, and almost eleven years after Azaria's disappearance, the Northern Territory government paid compensation to the Chamberlains and to the Seventh Day Adventist Church. The legal aspects of the case came to an end in December 1995, when Northern Territory Coroner John Lowndes, presiding over a second inquest, concluded that: 'The cause and manner of Azaria's death cannot be determined, and must remain unknown'.

The most impassioned and tendentious account of the case, John Bryson's *Evil Angels*, was published in 1985, just months before Lindy Chamberlain's release. The finding of a matinee jacket 150 metres from where the baby's other clothes had been discovered nearly six years before, was the stroke of fortune that – by the reckoning of Bryson's book – enabled an injustice belatedly to be undone. *Evil Angels* is the most ambitious Australian essay in the New Journalism. Painstaking reconstruction of a sensational series of public events is a key element of Bryson's method. At the same time he deploys fictional techniques, freely entering the consciousness of his characters, presuming their motives, sketching their emotional responses.

Bryson begins with an account of the Seventh Day Adventist movement's origins in the United States last century, and of the kind of censure and innuendo to which its members have long been subjected. Then he cuts to the days before the tragedy. He has stories to tell of a child bitten by a dingo and of the concerns of Ayers Rock ranger Derek Roff at how fearless and predatory the animals which live by the Rock were becoming. A stranger's recollection of having nursed Azaria, taking the baby from a 'dauntingly cautious' mother, is cited. Bryson has signalled where his judgment of the case will fall. We are only 40 pages into the book before one of the century's most harrowing exclamations is reported: 'My God. My God. The dingo's got my baby!'

There is a place for Aborigines in this 1980 lost child story. The tracker Minyintiri is called in the next day and a dingo's trail is followed, without anything being found. The Aborigines seem reticent, if not evasive. Later, at the first coronial inquest, the court is told the story of 'the Luritja's dreaming of dingoes and children'; of the warning of how 'children who leave the camp, the Dingo Spirit will get them'; of how the weaker of twins is often left in the bush, supposedly for the dingoes to take. Magistrate Barritt was berated later by an Aboriginal woman for having allowed such private and sensitive business to be aired in open court. But he was exercised by the need to find whether there were any solidly corroborated instances of Australian children being lost to dingoes.

He learned of the disappearance of a two-year-old boy from a verandah at Gympie about a century before, the child having allegedly been taken by a dingo. Other stories of attacks would be forwarded, in later stages of the affair, of an Aboriginal child killed and carried off at Tennant Creek in the 1960s, and a *Sydney Morning Herald* report from 1902 of a two-year-old white boy from a family called Ford, who was carried 35 miles by a dingo to feed her young. The stories were old or dubious or unsubstantiated. At the core of Australian disbelief in Lindy Chamberlain's innocence, it seems, was the refusal to credit dingoes with such active and malign agency as she had ascribed to one of them.

In the *Illustrated Melbourne Post* engraving of a dying bushman, 'Lost in the Bush' (25 October 1865), the dingoes are waiting for their prey to become helpless, or indeed to be dead. It is menacing, but at a distance. By blaming the dingo for Azaria's loss, the Chamberlain defence set itself against the body of nineteenth-century Australian narrative of children lost in the bush. Much too young to wander off, thence to perish, this child had allegedly been stolen away by a bush creature. The outback, no longer indifferent to, however unwelcoming of, the European presence, was now conceived as purposefully destructive. The Chamberlains therefore confronted a deep reserve of Australian folk memory, called up unexpectedly and disturbingly by the loss of their child. Such remembering was almost bound to be sceptical of their story. Indeed, as Michael Chamberlain himself said to reporters, people doubted them because such an event had not been reliably recorded before.

The trial would see some conflicting testimony concerning what dingoes could do and had done to children. But the purported role of the dingo is a part of Bryson's story that, understandably, he finds intractable. Most of the book – the last 500 pages after Azaria's loss – is bound up with the legal proceedings. These were increasingly occupied by battles between rival teams of forensic scientists over blood samples, and not with canine behaviour. One alleged culprit, the dingo itself, nearly disappeared from the story. At the same time, the loss of Azaria became incidental to public and legal fixation upon her mother.

One of Lindy Chamberlain's problems – exemplified deftly and without comment by Bryson early in his book – was of talking too much. Earnestly, nervously, she reconstructed what she thought she had seen as well as imagining what might have happened by the tent that night. Telling and retelling, trying to form a stock version of events that yet will not hold its shape, this is a core element of lost child narratives. The bereaved one, in particular, is compelled to such iteration, whether she is Maggie Head talking in private to strangers in Lawson's story 'The Babies in the Bush', or Lindy Chamberlain, arraigned in public, speaking to police, testifying in court.

Evil Angels hurries to an ending which its author no doubt hoped would be provisional, rather than conclusive. Against the expectation of most professional observers, but not against the drift of public sentiment, Lindy Chamberlain was found guilty of the murder of her child. The characteristic late twentieth-century story of why children are lost in Australia – that is, through human, and often parental agency – was accepted by the jury. Rejecting the dingo as perpetrator, it refused a mystification of the outback, although one which – as it happened – was not congruent with the tales of lost children that were remembered and retold in the nineteenth century.

Frank Moorhouse had been an interested spectator at the Chamberlains' trial, present because of a professional curiosity that would lead him to write the script for the first film treatment of the story. Directed by Judy Rymer and produced by Michael Thornhill, *Disappearance of Azaria Chamberlain* was shown on Australian television in 1984. The film involved separate shootings of the defence and prosecution versions of what had allegedly transpired after dark on 17 August 1980. The deliberate awkwardness of this method pointed to the irreconcilability not only of the two sets of stories, but of the evidence contested between them. Beyond that it showed Australian public opinion divided and entrenched in a manner that recalled, incongruously, the Vietnam War.

Fred Schepisi's film version of *Evil Angels* (1988) concentrated on that last matter: the strident dispute between the partisans of Lindy Chamberlain's guilt or innocence. American distributors preferred a more plaintive and unambiguous title (if one less congruent with Schepisi's treatment). This was *A Cry in the Dark*, a title which was also derived from Bryson's book. Justice Muirhead had summed up the case in a way that seemed to favour the defence case, not least by emphasising the testimony of Sally Lowe that she had heard Azaria cry out from the tent. Reporting the trial for the *Sydney Morning Herald*, Malcolm Brown said 'So the case ends as it begins, with a cry in the dark'.

Schepisi cast Hollywood stars Meryl Streep and Sam Neill as the Chamberlains, although the latter – like Michael – had been born in New Zealand. His film opened with the christening, in Mount Isa, of Azaria Chantel Lauren Chamberlain. A truckie, driving by, expresses resentment at the supposed wealth of the Seventh Day Adventists. It is the first of many pointed moments in an unsubtle film which is determined to indict what Schepisi judges to be a censorious, often brutish and ignorant Australian community.

But there are signs of the Chamberlains' oddities as well. Lindy prefers black baby clothes. Pastor Michael processes through his church with a small coffin and calls for cigarettes to be thrown into it. The events of 17 August are rehearsed once more. The Chamberlain boys play on Chicken Rock (one of the lower slopes of the monolith). A dingo makes a threatening appearance. Michael photographs the sunset while Lindy bathes the baby. At a barbeque, the Chamberlains meet the Lowes, from the Hobart suburb of West Moonah. Lindy primly chips Greg Lowe for climbing the Rock with a baby in harness and a six pack of beer. He is unimpressed with her vegetarian sausage: 'Jesus! Feed the man meat'. These cultural differences are soon dispelled by Lindy's own cry in the dark.

From the beginning no-one is in any doubt about the child's fate. Greg warns the father to expect the worst and Michael coolly, or distractedly, replies: 'I've seen what dogs do to lambs mate'. An Aboriginal tracker turns up with a torch and judges: 'the baby's bin here. Finished you know'. At the camp-fire, Michael tells searchers and sympathisers that while he realises that his daughter is lost, he and Lindy will see Azaria at the resurrection.

While assuming the Chamberlains' innocence, Schepisi depicts those reactions in them – an emotional distance, a refusal of conventional modes of response to bereavement – which would come to isolate them from public sympathy. They soon have to face another kind of predator than the dingo. Just as in the nineteenth century, the role of the press is crucial in the dissemination and crystallisation of this lost child story. Both Chamberlains unguardedly speak to the press: first to the ABC, and then in an interview by Lindy with *Woman's Day*. Publicising their reactions, they open themselves – in Schepisi's telling – to the contempt and disbelief of lumpen Australia. A pub audience responds scornfully, but typically: 'a dingo, they must think we came down in the last shower'. One of its number staggers around with a bucket of sand, of the baby's supposed weight, in his mouth to prove the point.

Schepisi turns from the investigation of Azaria's disappearance to an anatomy of Australian prejudice, across class lines. It is an unrelenting attempt to make sections of the public the true culprit for the fate of the Chamberlains. In its way, this is disingenuous, in so far as the film profits from a slanted rehashing of the same events. The disparagement of a hoon world, of the lack of civil discourse, becomes Schepisi's preoccupation. The adult Chamberlains, like the baby, disappear from view. They are, of course, back for the court case. As in Bryson's book, much of the film is that overly familiar entertainment, 'the court-room drama'. Interpolated scenes show the Chamberlains as the point of heated debate at dinner parties, in pubs, at social games of tennis. Lindy's pertinent complaint, to a legal counsel who tells her to 'try and be more demure', is that 'I can't cry to order and I won't be squashed into some dumb act for the public'.

The verdict comes with brutal swiftness and the sentence is mandatory: she is 'imprisoned with hard labour for life'. Poignantly, the film draws to its conclusion with an image of another lost child. This is Lindy Chamberlain's second daughter, Kahlia, who is born in Berrimah gaol, but must be surrendered by her mother almost at once. A guard tells her that 'she's yours to hold for one hour, but that's all I'm afraid'. *Evil Angels* concludes with a series of postscripts, that summarise the stages of legal argument and appeal which followed. Schepisi, unlike Bryson, is able to announce the release of Lindy Chamberlain, though not convincingly to end the most contentious of all lost child stories in Australian history, and the one that most curiously mingles and confounds the nineteenth and the twentieth-century master narratives of such tragedy.

True Stories

In the colonial period, journalistic witnesses to actual lost girls and boys found dead, or providentially saved, intersected with and influenced artistic versions of the topos of the lost child. But those were tragedies without a human perpetrator. Since the benchmark date of 1960, the Australian media has reacted to the circumstances of children stolen rather than strayed, to losses which cannot be accounted as a possible, if shocking consequence of life in the bush, but rather as an arbitrary terror that might be visited upon any dweller in a modern Australian city. When schoolboy Graeme Thorne was taken from a street corner in Bondi in July 1960, it became the first kidnapping for ransom recorded in Australia. Nearly six weeks after his abduction, the boy was found dead. In January 1964, two fifteen-year-old girls, Marianne Schmidt and Christie Sharrock, were mutilated and murdered. Their remains were left at Wanda Beach, in Sydney's south. On 26 August 1970 the Mackay children of Townsville, Judith aged seven and Susan, five, were taken on their way to the Aitkenvale State School. Two days later their bodies – raped, stabbed and strangled – were found in the dry bed of Antill Creek, south-west of Townsville. (More than 28 years later, on 3 December 1998, 86-year-old Arthur Brown, who worked at the school as a carpenter, was charged with the girls' murders.) The three Beaumont children – Jane, Arnna and Grant – who disappeared from Glenelg Beach in Adelaide on 26 January 1966, were never seen again. The loss of all these children, and of many others, underlined how insecure suburban life in Australia could be, however beguiling its appearance of, and reputation for safety and ease. Even the typical site of innocent Australian hedonism and recreation – the beach, not the bush – invited predators. Yet perhaps worse than the arbitrary cruelties inflicted by strangers, were the stories of abuse of children within their own families.

In 1993, 32-year-old Paul Aiton was convicted in Melbourne for the systematic bashing and eventual murder of the infant Daniel Valerio. In her account of the trial and the events that led up to it, Helen Garner asked: 'What sort of man would beat a two-year-old boy to death?' Garner's coverage of the story for *Time* won her a Gold Walkley Award. It was one of the pieces collected in her book, *True Stories* (1996). Aiton, de facto husband of Daniel's mother, Cheryl Butcher, was – Garner noted – 'a very big man', yet in the dock 'he looked oddly like a child himself':

> On his heavily muscled body, with its overhanging belly and meaty hands, sat the round, hot-cheeked face of a boy who'd been sprung, who was in serious trouble, but who glared back at the world with eyes that sometimes threatened to pop out of his head with indignation and defiance.

Something about Aiton, Garner judged, 'persistently called to mind the word infantile'. But what baffled her even more than his behaviour was that of Daniel's mother. On the night after Daniel died, she agreed to marry the man who – as events would prove and as she must at least have suspected – had killed him. Daniel was not the first child whom Cheryl Butcher had lost. Two others, Candice and Benjamin, seven and four respectively at the time of the trial, had been taken from her and given into the custody of her previous de facto, Michael Valerio, Daniel's father.

Garner related the failure of all the many people who had 'noticed the boy's afflictions' – 'neighbours, tradesmen, social workers, teachers, family, friends, doctors, nurses, police, a photographer' – and yet who did not intervene in time to prevent his death. The hideous injuries that Aiton had inflicted on the child for months, evidently with pleasure, because he boasted to work mates of what he had done, make this failure all the more strange and lamentable. For 'the boy was adrift. The people with the power to save him strolled, fumbled and tripped; and Aiton got there first'. Oddest of all, for Garner, was Cheryl Butcher's fabrication of reasons for the child's injuries:

> What deal did she make with herself to allow her child to suffer the brutality of her boyfriend Aiton in exchange for his company, his pay packet – for the simple fact of not being manless?

Finally Garner judged that the killing of Daniel 'stirs up deep fears about ourselves, and makes us frightened and ashamed'. It is not possible, she contended, to comprehend the meaning of Daniel's story 'without acknowledging the existence of evil'.

That view is a humane and necessary, but perhaps not a sufficient way in which to understand a true story such as Daniel Valerio's, and the others which are analysed in this final section of the book. Some of them are stories of abortion; some of abduction. There are instances of the callousness of individual adults and others of the institutionalised abuse of children. Peter Carey's account of an abortion and its consequences begins the section, with its melancholy witness to a loss then deemed unavoidable. Stories of kidnapping and killing of children follow, from the murder of Graeme Thorne in 1960, to the murder of Jaidyn Leskie in 1997. The bizarre and destructive episodes of recovered memory in the 1990s signal a fightback by adults against their parents, and the exposure of the abuses which allegedly they endured in childhood. The state (that is, the British and Australian governments, as well as those of the Australian states) was also instrumental in systematic, wholesale ill-treatment of the young. Many Australian mothers surrendered their illegitimate children for adoption, in a modern kind of baby-farming. Willingly and otherwise, many British families relinquished their children to church and charitable institutions which then arranged for their passage to Australia. Some of these 'orphans of the empire', who never lost their memories, have begun to tell their stories. And so have Aboriginal men and women, members of the 'stolen generation', who as children were forcibly removed from their families, if for well-intentioned reasons, to be put in orphanages or brought up by white parents. This book is not principally about their stories, individual and collective, despite their great moral import for Australia. Yet it ends with them, not as an after-thought, but as the appropriate last word. In the tale of the 'stolen generation', the narrative of the lost child in Australia reaches a conclusion which may – against odds and expectations – bring about a racial healing that has been too long delayed.

Peter Carey's Testaments

Peter Carey's first child, Sam, was born in the United States on 13 September 1986. One of the author's responses was to write about the experience. 'A Letter to Our Son' was first published in the magazine *Granta* in 1988, and reprinted by the University of Queensland Press in 1994. Carey begins with the story of how he fell in love with Alison Summers, who would become Sam's mother. After Summers fell pregnant, Carey listened to the child's noises in her stomach. He struggles for the right simile to transport him to a familiar, more comfortable elsewhere. Thus the sound is 'like soldiers marching on a bridge ... like a short-wave radio ... like the inside of the sea'. The author desired such distraction because of ante-natal complications. These induced in him worries that he could not share, precisely because of his own vocation: 'I have made a whole career out of making my anxieties get up and walk around, not only in my own mind but in the minds of readers'. The very act of authorial will by which he invented Herbert Badgery, the 'Illywhacker' (in the 1985 novel of that name), or set a glass church in motion up river in *Oscar and Lucinda* (1988), or imagined the weather, history, architecture of a fictitious place such as Efica in *The Unusual Life of Tristan Smith* (1994), was unavailing now. Carey cannot impose his will on the birth to come, nor can he safeguard the health of either mother or child. But both lived. The child is born safely, and is calm, with big eyes, reminding the author (and father) of generations of his ancestors on both the mother's and father's sides of the family which Sam has joined.

Carey would set a hazardous birth almost at the end of *The Tax Inspector* (1992). Miraculously, Maria Takis's child survives his basement birth with the psychopath Benny Catchprice as midwife. *The Unusual Life of Tristan Smith* opens with the birth of its eponymous hero. Felicity Smith, former soap opera star and now actor-manager of the radical Feu Follett theatre in Efica's capital, Chemin Rouge, approaches her child's birth with a soon-to-be reproved insouciance. Her labours begin at an ill-omened time, 'at the end of a full rehearsal' of *Macbeth*, the Shakespeare play traditionally regarded as unlucky by actors so superstitious that they will not speak its name. The child is not expected to live long, being lipless, crippled, intestinally wrecked. To those who see him, he appears to be a monster. The boy is christened Tristan, a given name that recalls the arabesques of Laurence Sterne's comic novel, *Tristram Shandy* (1760-7), besides the hero of legend and Wagnerian opera. In the milieu of Efica that Carey constructs so painstakingly, but with an enviable impression of naturalness and legerity, the boy has in fact been named 'after Tristan Devalier, the leader of the calamitous strike at the Imperial Dye Works in 137 E.C.'

It is hard not to feel that Carey's anxieties before the birth of his own son have been channelled into the description of Tristan. Most of any parent's tormented 'what ifs?' receive their worst answer here (not that Tristan's mother will behave at all despairingly). Of course Tristan Smith is, metaphorically, Carey's child. As such – but in a manner put to suggestive, probing, comic effect – he is a self-portrait as well. Like the self-confessed lair and liar, Herbert Badgery, in *Illywhacker*, Tristan is given the chance to tell his own story in the first person. Up to the point where he escapes from Voorstand (Efica's dominant neighbour) to Bergen in Norway, promising readers that the most unusual part of his life is yet in store, much of Tristan's story concerns the assertion of his own implacable will to become an actor, despite the most demoralising of physical circumstances. Every author's deep desire for an audience, and his or her dread of rejection, is dramatised in Tristan. How much of personal investment there is in this portrayal, only Carey could say, and probably did.

A fuller answer to such an issue was afforded by Carey in the next year. His essay in the *New Yorker* on 25 September 1995 also did something to explain the intensity of the apprehension with which he awaited the birth of his first son. For Sam was by no means the first of Carey's children to be conceived. 'A Small Testament' begins with a revelation:

> Lately when I think of my children I have begun to remember not just the four-year-old who is rattling on my doorknob as I write, or the eight-year-old whom I will take to a swimming lesson this afternoon, but those other children I have spent a long time trying to forget.

Now he takes the chance to remember them, and to relate how they came to be lost.

In 1961, when Carey was eighteen years old, his first girlfriend – whom he calls H – became pregnant. This was in Victoria, but – Carey insists – in a moral and cultural place so different from the present as to be imagined only with difficulty by those who remembered it, with incredulity by a younger generation:

> In Melbourne in 1961, the bars closed at six o'clock at night. The White Australia Policy was still in force. You could be arrested for having an abortion or reading James Joyce's *Ulysses*.

Yet the couple had determined to end H's pregnancy. The humiliations and terrors that the preliminaries occasioned are harrowingly recalled. Mendacious and cowardly doctors and chemists turned out to be much less helpful than the zoology professor from whom they borrowed 50 pounds, or indeed H's mother. The abortion completed, the pair found that 'Our hearts were not broken, and we went on to our new young marriage, and our new young lives'.

The consequences of the abortion, however, continued to affect those lives. Pregnant again, H was delivered prematurely of a dead baby: 'we did not know that the fifty pounds the strawberry-blond woman counted so carefully had also procured an "incompetent cervix" '. So the ordeal was repeated: 'Like all nightmares, the repetition was not exact. This time there were twins, and when the labour was over they were alive'. But not for long – 'a boy and girl, with perfect little hands and faces' – died too. They were cremated, unnamed. That would become the author's deepest regret, however often thereafter he could name characters in his fictions and would name his two sons. 'A Small Testament' – words instead of material remembrance – ends with this reflection on a long past time and on the losses that Carey and H had sustained:

> Looking back on Australia in 1961, I feel I grew up in a dark and ignorant time: a racist immigration policy, great works of English literature banned, abortions performed furtively, illegally, not always well. When I look back now on how our story went, H's and mine, I don't really see that it could have gone any differently. I wish only that we had honoured those children with a plaque, a name. I will always wish that, forever.

Such losses of children, as Carey grievingly knows, can never be made good. In the very act of writing them, the author acknowledges how little difference his words , this 'small memorial', can make.

Abductions

The case of eight-year-old Graeme Thorne, as newspaper editorials and letter-writers soon agreed, was Australia's first genuine kidnapping. At 8.30 a.m. on 7 July 1960, the schoolboy disappeared from Wellington Street, Bondi, where he had been waiting for a lift to Scots College in Bellevue Hill. Two hours later, his parents, Bazil and Freda Thorne, received a phone call at their flat from a man with a European accent. Claiming to have Graeme, he demanded a ransom. Five weeks earlier, on 1 June 1960, Bazil Thorne had won the first prize of 100 000 pounds in the Sydney Opera House Lottery. At that time, the addresses of lottery winners were routinely published. The kidnapper had no trouble finding, then stalking the Thornes. In this instance at least, there was a mercenary motive for the cruelty that was being inflicted on a child.

In a statement produced in court on 5 December 1960, the accused man, Stephen Leslie Bradley, allegedly gave this version of events to police. The spelling and expression was Bradley's: 'I have told the boy that I am to take him to the school. He sed why, where is the lady. I sed she is sick and can not come today'. He then put the child in his blue Ford sedan, drove to a public phone box near the Spit Bridge and rang the Thornes:

> I talked to Mrs Thorne and to a man who sed he was the boys father. [He was in fact a detective]. I have asked for £25 000 from the boys mother and father. I told them that if I didnt get the money I feed him to the sharks and I have told them I ring later.

By the end of the day, Graeme Thorne was already dead. The nation's biggest manhunt to that time continued fruitlessly for weeks, until the boy's body was discovered, wrapped in a rug, at Frenchs Forest.

The novelty of this crime against a child deeply agitated many Australians. There were calls for the death penalty for convicted kidnappers, although it was pointed out that this would make them indifferent to the survival of their victims. The American kidnapping in 1932 of the baby of the famous aviator Charles Lindbergh was the horrible precedent most often invoked. Now such crime had come to Australia. But via Europe: Bradley, an electroplater with a poker machine manufacturer who lived in Manly, was born Istvan Baranyay in Hungary. He had arrived in Australia in 1950 and was now naturalised, as was his second wife, Magda, who had endured years in the concentration camp at Auschwitz. In what Carey would inveigh against as 'a dark and ignorant time', there were some xenophobic overtones in press reports of Graeme Thorne supposedly in the hands of two swarthy Maltese men. More practically, the father's appeals to the kidnappers were broadcast in three languages besides English – German, Italian and Greek – those most commonly spoken then by 'new' Australians.

According to the New South Wales government medical officer who examined the body in August, Graeme Thorne died of asphyxiation or a blow to the head or both. Bradley asserted, in his statement, that the boy had suffocated in the boot of his car, that is, had died by accident. The forensic trail and his own incompetence eventually led to Bradley's apprehension, but not before he, his wife and three children had got as far as Colombo, on the cruise liner *Himalaya*. Bradley was arrested on 10 October and extradited from Ceylon the next month. Magda Bradley and the children continued on another ship, to Tilbury in England, although first there was a further twist in this strange tale. For Magda was not the mother of Bradley's daughter, Helen. That child's grandfather, Dr Franz Laszio, a lecturer in engineering at the University of Melbourne, attempted to gain custody. His daughter, Helen's mother and Bradley's first wife, had been killed in a car accident. Laszio flew to meet the ship at Aden, in what would be an unavailing attempt at what he regarded as the rescue of a child.

Bradley was convicted and sentenced to life imprisonment for murder on 29 March 1961. On the same day, the Australian cricket team sailed for a six-month tour of England. Richie Benaud's men travelled on the *Himalaya*, the same ship on which Bradley had nearly escaped, six months earlier. His conviction brought an astonishing outburst from many of the women in the court. The verdict was cheered and then – remembering Bradley's threat to the Thornes – they chanted 'Feed him to the sharks. Feed him to the sharks'. Bradley appealed unsuccessfully. In October 1968, aged 45, he died of a heart attack in Goulburn gaol. Fortunately Bradley's actions did not lead to copycat crimes. Kidnappings in Australia, such as Eastwood's abduction of the school children of Faraday in 1972, have remained very rare. But the disappearances of children, many of whom have been presumed to have been murdered, have been tragically common. In these cases, money has nothing to do with the kidnappers' motives. They take the young to abuse and kill them. Sometimes parents had the partial comfort that the discovery of a body affords. Often they did not. In the most notorious of these cases – the loss of the three Beaumont children – the bodies were never found, for all the weird and continuing speculation as to where they might be.

At 10 a.m. on Australia Day, 26 January 1966, Jane, Arnna and Grant Beaumont alighted from a bus at the Jetty Road/Moseley Street stop in Glenelg. Unsupervised by their parents, they had gone to play at the beach. The children were aged nine, seven and four respectively. There were no witnesses to how they came to go missing, although a couple of reports had them playing with a tall, blond surfie. There was no ransom demand. A massive search was mounted. The Glenelg boat haven was drained. However no clue to the disappearance was found. Superintendent J. A. Vogelsang established the police search headquarters at Glenelg. It was more than two decades since his comic moment of cultural infamy, the trial of *Angry Penguins* editor Max Harris on the grounds of having published obscene material. On that occasion, Detective Jacobus Vogelsang solemnly informed the court that while he did not know what 'incestuous' meant, 'I think there is a suggestion of indecency about it'.

While the police search continued in South Australia, on the other side of the world a man was having visions. The 57-year-old Dutch clairvoyant, Gerard Croiset, claimed to have seen sites associated with the children. Adelaide businessmen paid for him to come to Australia in November 1966. While convinced that the Beaumonts were dead, Croiset claimed confidently that 'the children died accidentally, they were not murdered'. He believed that they were buried in the city, but changed his mind about where. First it was near Minda Home in North Brighton, then under a warehouse in Wilton Avenue, Paringa Park. An extensive, expensive excavation revealed nothing, but the case was not so easily closed. As recently as 1996 another warehouse floor was dug up and there were reports of skeletons found in a cargo ship in Singapore and of one of the Beaumont girls alive and living in Canberra under another name.

In truth, the children had vanished. They were lost forever. They had disappeared not into trackless bush, but from a benign, suburban beach in the middle of the day towards the end of the summer school holidays. Just over a decade later, between 23 December 1976 and 12 February 1977, seven girls and young women (although the latter description hardly does justice to the savage abridgement of their adult lives) went missing from various locations in Adelaide. All of them turned out to have been abducted and murdered. Most of the bodies were located in the bush at Truro, north-east of Adelaide, which grisly burial place gave the case its name. Two men were found to have been responsible. When one of them, Christopher John Worrell, was killed in a car accident, the killings stopped. His partner, James William Miller, was subsequently found guilty on six of seven charges of murder.

The mother of one of his victims was Anne-Marie Mykyta. She wrote the story of the death of her daughter, Juliet, and of the others, in *It's a long way to Truro* (1981). Juliet went missing on 22 January 1977. The confirmation of her death would come much later. In the intervening months, the mother tormented herself with questions: 'Why would she run away? Would she run away?' Trying to be consoling, the mother of Anne-Marie Mykyta said that 'I pray for her all the time. Poor babe in the woods'. At once a poignant memory of childhood was triggered. Anne-Marie remembered the song that her mother had sung to her, and which still made her cry:

> My dear, don't you know, how a long time ago,
> Two poor little children, whose names I don't know,
> Were taken away, on a bright summer's day,
> And left in the woods, I've heard people say.

They die, 'poor babes in the wood', but the palliative context of nursery rhyme, which by repetition lulls words out of significance, is not available to Anne-Marie Mykyta, or to the six other mothers of lost girls. Why has the recall of the song made the author cry throughout her life? She wonders 'Did I have some premonition that my own babe would be taken away?'

After the recovery and identification of Juliet's body, the Mykytas stayed with friends – Isobel, an artist, and her husband John, in a town north of Adelaide. There Isobel confided how 'I lost a baby too'. This is what had happened: 'she had given birth to twins, and one had died, no one knew why. Now her dreams were haunted, and her little girl, now three, could not speak'. There was no funeral. There is no grave: 'they just took the body away'. Anne-Marie Mykyta's husband, Irush, who is gravely silent through much of this narrative, and indeed the whole book, now speaks: 'the death of children is particularly hard to bear because we bury not only them, we bury our future'. He, at least, has been able to bury his child. His mother-in-law's funeral notice for Juliet in the Adelaide *Advertiser* asked for respite: 'Poor babe in the woods: rest in peace'. Others whom the Mykytas encounter in their ordeal have not even had the consolation of a body to bury.

In haunting ways that seem to be among their inevitable consequences, one story of lost children summons or provokes others. An acquaintance, Les Ratcliffe, called the Mykytas to explain to them that they were entitled to the compensation due to 'people who have suffered as the result of a crime'. He and his wife have already done so. On 25 August 1973, during a football match at the Adelaide Oval, their daughter Joanne, aged eleven, and Kirste Gordon, aged four and the child of friends, had disappeared after going to the toilet. As Mykyta relates the incident:

> the families had searched, and finally Les went to the office and asked the officials to broadcast an appeal for anyone who might have seen the two little girls. The officials refused to do this during a match. Later, someone claimed to have seen a man dragging a little girl away, with another older child following, but he had done nothing; after all, it was probably her father.

Despite the efforts of police and clairvoyants (as in the Beaumont case) no traces of these children were found either. Had the same man killed all of them – and perhaps others? As much would be suspected, and alleged.

It's a long way to Truro contains chilling variants of the familiar business of lost children in Australia. Seven young females were killed. The scale and the capriciousness of the slaughter is modern. Another decade or so later, and the murders of at least seven backpackers – their remains buried, not at Truro, but in the Belanglo State Forest in New South Wales – would exercise a public imagination that was still, happily, not jaded by such horrors. Ivan Milat would be convicted for those murders. The numbers of killings, in both states, meant that to an extent the individual losses were subsumed by the sensational extent of the crimes. Juliet Mykyta's grandmother would not have it that way. She remembered her grand-daughter and comforted herself by thinking of Juliet in terms of fairytale, as a lost babe in the woods. Yet the witness of Anne-Marie Mykyta's book was that – of cruelties to the young in Australia – there appeared to be no end.

'Little boy lost in a lost town'

At first it seemed that the disappearance of fourteenth-month-old Jaidyn Leskie, in June 1997, from a house in Moe in the Gippsland region of Victoria, where he was being minded by his mother's boyfriend, would remain a mystery. The twenty-day search mounted for this lost boy was on a scale not seen in the state since the Prime Minister, Harold Holt, went missing in the sea off Portsea in December 1967. Despite Chinese submarine theories and other crack-brained surmises, the open coronial verdict on Holt was 'presumed drowned'. For weeks it appeared that similar uncertainty would attend the fate of Jaidyn Leskie. Had he been abducted, and if so, by whom? Had he been murdered, and if so, why and by whom and where was the body? The search, which involved the partial draining of Lake Narracan, revealed nothing.

The adult principals, his mother, Bilynda Murphy (then aged 22), her partner, Greg Domaszewicz (28) and the child's father, Brett Leskie (25), together with their companions of a similar age, resembled children themselves, being desperate, uneducated, without resources, irresponsible, occasionally violent, and heedless of the consequences of their actions. The childhoods and young adult lives of those involved with Jaidyn mark them not so much perhaps as a lost or stolen, but as an abandoned generation, members of a lumpen proletariat consigned to a kind of internal exile in Gippsland, without much hope of employment, or the will to find it, indeed with scant hope of anything. However, their stories lack the terrible outcome of Jaidyn's, whose body was at last found on 1 January 1998, in the Blue Rock Lake twenty kilometres north of Moe. Some months earlier, notwithstanding the absence of a body, Domaszewicz had been charged with Jaidyn's murder.

The metropolitan press, and in particular the *Age* and the *Sunday Age* in Melbourne, developed and appeared to relish the picture of a deprived social and regional group that the loss of Jaidyn Leskie had brought to national attention. The relations between the main characters and the course of their daily lives were set forth carefully, more perhaps for titillation than to move readers to sympathy. Thus one learned that Brett Leskie had been married in October 1992 to Kadee (formerly Katie) Murphy with whom he had a daughter Shannan, who was subsequently diagnosed as suffering from leukaemia. Kadee already had one child, and would later have another by a third man. This occurred several years after Brett had left her, in the middle of 1993, for her younger sister Bilynda. Evidently Kadee waited patiently for the chance of revenge on Brett, rather than Bilynda. The means that she found was the unemployed motor mechanic Greg Domaszewicz, with whom Leskie had once worked. She told *Sunday Age* reporter Andrew Rule that 'I stooged Brett with his best mate'. When Domaszewicz's and Bilynda Murphy's affair became public, Leskie left Moe to work in Kalgoorlie. Thus, when Bilynda and Kadee went for a night's partying and drinking at a private house and then at a pub in Traralgon, 30 kilometres from Moe, Jaidyn was left in the care of Domaszewicz. Just before two o'clock on the morning of Sunday 15 June, Domaszewicz drove to Traralgon to pick up Bilynda after having received a phone call from her. Either when they met, or during an earlier call, he told her that Jaidyn had been burned in a domestic accident, and was in hospital. She did not believe him, and asked to be driven to Kadee's house, where her other child, Brehanna, was staying. By her subsequent admission, Bilynda was very drunk. At 5 a.m., Domaszewicz returned to Kadee's house with a different story. Jaidyn was missing. Soon afterwards, the Moe police were informed.

This modern lost child narrative looked to be the first episode in a grisly abduction tale. Yet already there were perplexing extra pieces of evidence that complicated the story. While Domaszewicz drove to Traralgon, his home was vandalised. Windows were smashed and a pig's head was thrown on to the lawn. For a blessedly brief period – until this event was proven to be unrelated to the disappearance of Jaidyn – it seemed as though cults, sects and witchcraft might be part of the little boy's story. Indeed Domaszewicz was reported to be obsessed with the possibility of abduction by aliens. As it turned out, the vandals were local rather than extra-terrestrial: Kerry Penfold ('known to police') and his sister, Yvonne. Theirs was another act of sexual revenge, for Domaszewicz had dumped Yvonne for Bilynda Murphy, and had allegedly damaged Yvonne's car. Seeking an appropriate symbolic embellishment of the window-breaking, Penfold butchered his small black and white pig Darren (named in honour of the Collingwood footballer Darren Millane who had been killed in a car accident several years before). The pig's body went into the freezer for later consumption. Its head went over Domaszewicz's fence.

This strand of Jaidyn's story has already had several sordid and sentimental sequels. On 28 January 1998, Bilynda Murphy was fined $1500 for assault and harassment of Yvonne Penfold. She had written in lipstick 'Yvonne where the fuck were you fucking slut' on Penfold's workplace window. Purportedly this was a response to Yvonne's taunting question, 'where is Jaidyn?' At his committal hearing, Domaszewicz would accuse Penfold of kidnapping the child. Domaszewicz apparently coached Murphy with the prose, although two weeks before this she had written a poem of her own as a funeral tribute for her son. Other poems have followed, as Murphy – who is under contract to a women's magazine and a television network – completes a book of verse to be called 'My Story'. On 5 April 1998, the *Sunday Herald-Sun* broke the news that Domaszewicz and Murphy were engaged. A $3000 ring was brought into prison by Domaszewicz's mother. After a warder saw the exchange, she was banned from visiting for three months. The women's magazine regularly reports and illustrates the vicissitudes of Murphy's relationship with Domaszewicz, her visits to Jaidyn's grave, the comfort which she gains from her dog called Justice.

For several weeks, the loss of Jaidyn was treated as a disappearance, rather than as a murder. Police interrogated Domaszewicz extensively, but he was not charged until 16 July, a month after Jaidyn went missing.

Police diver recovers Jaidyn Leskie's clothes and a crowbar
Blue Rock Lake, north of Moe
Theo Fakos, *The Herald & Weekly Times*

It would be another five and a half months, New Year's Day 1998, before a Tasmanian picnicker, thirteen-year-old Sam Payne, came across a body in the Blue Rock Lake. A few days later it was identified as Jaidyn's on the basis of a lock of ginger hair which Domaszewicz had allegedly shaved from the top of the boy's head, to give the infant the semblance of his own bald spot. Next day police found a two metre long crowbar, a bottle, bib and baby's boots near the site where the body had been discovered. The autopsy revealed that Jaidyn had suffered a broken arm and severe head injuries. 'Mystery turns to tragedy', the *Age* proclaimed on 3 January. In fact this lost child story had run to its most predictable, frightful conclusion. Greg Domaszewicz was tried for the murder of Jaidyn Leskie in the Supreme Court of Victoria. On 4 December 1998, after more than three days of deliberation, the jury found Domaszewicz not guilty of either murder or manslaughter.

In their coverages of Jaidyn's disappearance a week after the event, the *Age* (21 June) and the *Sunday Age* (22 June) had set the tone of their articles with a single, resonant adjective. For the *Age*, Jaidyn Leskie was 'a little boy lost in a lost town', while the feature the following day in the *Sunday Age* was boldly titled 'Lost Girls of the Valley'. The girls in question were not just the women in Jaidyn's story, but others of their age, living in poverty, anger and despair in the La Trobe Valley. The privatisation of the State Electricity Commission led to heavy job losses and to consequent long-term unemployment in Gippsland. The *Age* report quoted the opinion of Nina Burke, of the organisation People Together, that the Victorian government had a deliberate policy of dumping single mothers in Moe because of its abundance of cheap housing. The existence of such a policy is not likely to be confirmed, but newspaper photographs gave plenty of glimpses of the style of life in Moe, of its housing, clothing and recreational habits. Moe, it seemed, was a town where the moccasin reigned. Newspaper and magazine stories evoked a ghetto of the abandoned, of young people without work or prospects, culturally and economically deprived. Members of the fabled under-class that economic rationalism had created in Australia, they belonged to a lost white generation which was now rawly exposed for a predominantly middle-class readership whose own insecurities might thus temporarily and selfishly be assuaged by the prospect of so many worse off than they were.

Helen Garner contended that Daniel Valerio's story could only be comprehended by acknowledging the existence of evil. Yet for the Leskie case at least, such an assertion pre-empts the necessary inquiry into the social dimensions and the causes of the tragedy. The lost and murdered Jaidyn was the child of parents who were themselves lost children. The second meaning of 'lost' that the *Oxford English Dictionary* records bears on the physical condition of being lost, and speaks more specifically to the case of nineteenth-century narratives of lost children: '2. Of which some one has been deprived; not retained in possession; no longer to be found. Also, of a person or animal: Having gone astray, having lost his or its way'. The sense of the word given first place defines a yet more desolating abandonment, and applies more directly to the Murphys, Leskies, Penfolds and Domaszewiczs, to young people whose behaviour appeared to be beyond their powers to amend. The primary sense of 'loss' has it this way: '1. That has perished or been destroyed; ruined, especially morally or spiritually; (of the soul) damned'.

Talk of the Devil

The recall to remembrance of childhoods long ago 'lost' because of abuse, and the concomitant attempt to seek restitution from parents who were held to be responsible, is another variation in the history of lost children in Australia. It is one that reveals unusual kinds of damage. In this country, the phenomenon has been critically analysed by Richard Guilliatt in *Talk of the Devil* (1996). There he summarises his subject as 'the recovery by adults of entirely forgotten memories of childhood sexual abuse'. While Guilliatt's researches were primarily local, he was alert to and encouraged by the reaction against 'Repressed Memory and the Ritual Abuse Witch-Hunt' (the sub-title of his book) that had already occurred abroad when his inquiries into Australian cases began. In the United States, a sceptical address to the issue was led by the feminist Elaine Showalter, whose *Hystories* (1997) indicated the scope of its investigation in a polemical sub-title: 'Hysterical epidemics from alien abduction to recovered memory'.

Guilliatt's theme, and Showalter's, was the perverse, destructive, expert-assisted recovery (or fabrication) of lost, because ruined, childhoods, and the consequent suffering of bewildered parents at the hands of their now adult children. In 'The Mindsnatchers' (*New York Review of Books*, 25 June 1998), Frederick Crews's demolition of 'ufology' argued that reports of abduction by aliens

> began multiplying just when, in the 1980s, false memories of 'repressed' or 'dissociated' incest trauma became a national epidemic [in the United States]. Abduction memories and memories of 'forgotten' childhood sexual abuse are conjured in exactly the same way, by applying unsubstantiated psychodynamic theory to the images unearthed by hypnotherapy, dream analysis, and assorted techniques for stimulating and guiding fantasy.

Both, according to Crews, are playing 'the same noxious game', although specialists in sexual abuse 'see recollections of alien contact as screen memories for incest while the abductionists take the opposite view'.

The epigraphs to Guilliatt's book signal his stance. The first, which furnished the title, is from Desiderius Erasmus: 'Talk of the Devil and he'll appear'. Alonzo Salazar de Frias, Grand Inquisitor of Spain, provided the second in a comment he made in 1610: 'there were neither witches nor bewitched until they were talked about'. The witch-hunt analogy is elaborated later. The demons who have been especially summoned by modern denunciations of abuse are paedophiles: the men (almost always) who prey upon and molest children. Inevitably, some so labelled have been falsely, carelessly or vindictively accused. Guilliatt attempts to explain such demonising:

> A witch-hunt is not a meaningless or random event. It reflects the latent fears of the society that spawned it. It is nurtured by those who wield political power and intellectual influence. As one historian has noted of the mass witch-burnings of the Middle Ages, it was a conflagration in which the experts – the judges, the lawyers, scholars and clergy – commanded the field.

While he has no intention of denying actual, indeed manifold cases of child abuse (for instance involving the notorious Newcastle paedophile ring) Guilliatt's interest is with a narrower business. 'The satanic ritual abuse hysteria of the past fifteen years', he contends, followed the pattern of medieval witch-hunts:

> It began with scattered recollections of therapy patients. It acquired intellectual weight through the advocacy of psychotherapists and doctors. It finally became a political cause célèbre through the agency of feminism and state child protection authorities. In the course of that journey, ritual abuse came to share some remarkable similarities with the satanic hysteria of an unenlightened past.

A similar group of experts, whose negligence Garner exposed in her account of the death of Daniel Valerio, are here seen to have engaged in the unjust persecution of parents in the guise of the protection of those who had long ceased to be children and – had their stories been true – had not anyway been cared for at the time of their abuse in childhood.

For Guilliatt does not believe those stories. He asserts that notwithstanding 'hundreds of massive police investigations in Europe, the United Kingdom, the United States and Australia over the past decade', it is the case that 'virtually no material evidence has ever emerged to support the existence of ritual or satanic cult abuse'. Guilliatt's book concentrates on one story in particular, the allegations made to police in Bunbury, Western Australia, by 29-year-old 'Barbara Emmett', against her father, 'Clive Moore'. The desolating and unresolved consequences of this case are examined in detail. But Guilliatt is concerned with a wider social hysteria, one that has been assisted and exploited by some psychiatrists, whether credulously or cynically:

> The contemporary psychiatric literature of satanic abuse – with its elaborate explanations of how entire classrooms of three-year-olds might be raped, tortured and kidnapped without anyone noticing – carries a disquieting echo of those credulous church documents which detailed the paranormal facility of wicked old women with broomsticks. Paediatric reports from the 1980s, in which infant genitalia are examined in microscopic detail, hark back to a time when the 'secret parts' of witches were scrutinised for their physical abnormalities.

Guilliatt emphasises that three generations, not just two, suffer from such a process: 'hundreds of children' (or more exactly, grandchildren) are damaged as well.

Indeed, as he concludes, 'hysteria has only ever harmed the cause of protecting children'. An indictment follows about the misdirected uses of both the powers of the state and of the reputation of many of the professionals who were involved with supposed cases of ritual or satanic abuse:

Every false allegation of child abuse absorbs the resources of a system which is already struggling to protect children in genuine danger. Every repressed memory allegation which is investigated and found to be baseless reinforces the hardened scepticism of the police. Every well-meaning therapist who 'validates' a byzantine story of satanic abuse to authorities erects a hurdle in front of women who, in the future, will struggle harder to have their stories believed.

The recovered memory syndrome has created innocent victims in late middle age, while doing little to relieve the real (however fanciful) pain of their accusers – that is to say, their children. The suspicion of some members of a younger generation that its parents resented their very being was analysed, if from a different standpoint and in other kinds of story, in the fiction of Frank Moorhouse. In the actual instances that Guilliatt investigated, that suspicion was expressed and entrenched through allegations of ritual and satanic abuse. *Talk of the Devil* eloquently documents an hysterical phenomenon and the injustices which it occasioned. More widely, it exposed an intensification of the suffering of children, brought on themselves by adults who terribly seek, or are induced, to lose their childhoods afresh as, falsely and self-destructively, they contrive to remember them.

Orphans of the Empire

In late July 1998, the British House of Commons Select Committee on Health completed its inquiry into the welfare of up to 10 000 former child migrants who were sent to Australia between 1947 and 1967. Indicting especially the Christian Brothers and the Sisters of Mercy in Perth, the committee concluded that large numbers of these children had been treated with 'quite exceptional depravity'. In seeming to shift the blame for the children's initial and continuing suffering to the Australian institutions which received them rather than the British ones from which they were despatched, the Committee did not show much sensitivity to the complexities of these cases, or to the investigations begun into them in Australia some time before.

For example, in 1993 the Christian Brothers order had apologised for abuse and offered out-of-court compensation for victims. Individual brothers have gone through criminal prosecution for paedophilia and child abuse. The testaments of their victims have begun to be published. Two of these appeared in book form in 1998. Ivor Knight's *Out of Darkness* is the story of an Australian boy who was declared a 'neglected child' in 1938, at the age of four, and who thereafter endured years of punishment and sexual molestation in the Western Australian Catholic orphanages Castledare, Clontarf and Tardun. Flo Hickson's *Flo: Child*

Migrant from Liverpool, is the story of a little English girl who came under Barnardo's care before she was five and then, two years later, in 1928, was sent to the Fairbridge Farm at Pinjarra in Western Australia. Its founder, Kingsley Fairbridge, was a philanthropist who sought to mould abandoned and unwanted children on farm schools, both at Pinjarra and at Molong in New South Wales. His aim – expressed in the Fairbridge song – was to produce 'Boys to be farmers and girls for farmers' wives'. British-born David Hill, later managing director of the Australian Broadcasting Corporation, was perhaps the most famous alumnus of the Fairbridge experiment. Flo Hickson's sad experiences may have been more typical. Her autobiography, with its attestations of abuse, was requested as evidence by the House of Commons Committee. When – in June 1987 – she returned for a reunion with past farm school friends and entered the Church of the Holy Innocents: 'the well that was around my heart broke as the horror of so many children being deprived of home and family was brought home to me'.

The fullest account of what he calls the 'Shocking Story of Child Migration to Australia' is Alan Gill's *Orphans of the Empire* (1997, 1998). His subject is the large-scale relocation of 'institutional' children from Britain to Australia, Canada and New Zealand. This began as long ago, for this country, as 1834, when 29 children, sponsored by the London-based Children's Friend Society, came out on the *James Pattison* and were put ashore in Western Australia. Many thousands would follow, particularly in the two decades after the end of the Second World War. Gill documents the fates of many of them – not just their ordeal in private and church institutions – but the consequent impairment of their adult lives.

The second release of *Orphans of the Empire* (the first made much less of an impact than it deserved because of the collapse of his publisher in the week when Gill's book appeared) was attended by fulsome praise. Chair of the Literature Board, Father Edmund Campion, for instance, stated his belief that Gill 'has befriended a lost tribe and given them a voice. His honest book gives a new edge of meaning to the phrase "stolen generation"'. For Geraldine Doogue, 'the image of the lone, isolated child produces almost primal responses in all of us at levels we hardly know'. The adjective with which the principals in the Jaidyn Leskie tragedy were characterised tolls again. This is a story of the 'lost', but it refers not only to individual children here, but collectively, to thousands.

In Britain and in Australia, Gill instructs us, 'the sending and receiving agencies were for the most part Christian charities'. If children had typically come into their care because of poverty, illegitimate birth, or the collapse of families as a result of the desertion of a parent:

both the sending and receiving agencies deliberately deceived children in their care by telling them that their parents were dead, or (if the story tellers were nuns) offering fanciful accounts of human bundles being left on doorsteps.

Thus the human ties with living relatives were callously severed. In the belated reconstitution of their identities, many of these transplanted children have sought to be re-united with surviving relatives overseas. Flo Hickson, for instance, finally met a long lost brother in England in 1991. People seeking such reunions (which were frequently not welcomed by those long since left behind, and surprised or resentful at the attempt at reconnection) have often been helped by the Child Migrants' Trust. Its director, Margaret Humphreys, speaks of them as 'a kind of lost tribe – defenceless and exploited as children, abandoned as adults. Now they demand the right to come home and find their roots'. But, as Gill puts it: 'Not every person welcomes the discovery of, or being discovered by, a "lost" or perhaps totally unknown relative in the antipodes'.

To describe them as once 'exploited', as Humphreys had, is to use too tame an adjective for the plight of many of these children. That they were the victims of systematic and personal cruelty, is amply demonstrated by Gill. As he notes, the scale of child migration and resettlement in Australia and other British Commonwealth countries has been scantly known until the last decade. Thus what the children went through is still to be fully appreciated. Part of the reason for this was isolation: 'In Australia, as in Britain, many of the institutions were away from centres of population, walled in, and away from prying eyes'. That is, child abuse could occur more freely.

The central section of *Orphans of the Empire* documents many alleged and proven instances of abuse, by church groups such as the Methodists and Salvation Army, and above all by the Christian Brothers, and by individuals, such as the eugenicist and vegetarian fanatic, L. O. 'Daddy' Bailey. He established Hopewood House at Bowral in New South Wales. There women gave birth and then surrendered their illegitimate children. Bailey and his staff brought them up under a strict dietary and disciplinary regimen that was intended to produce a superior Australian stock. A favourite technique of punishment was the 'bowel wash', or enema. Gill describes the vile 'Daddy' Bailey 'sitting on a toilet naked, masturbating and/or defecating while fingering a child's rectum or administering a "bowel wash" '. Bailey eventually died of bowel cancer.

His abuse of children was shocking but not, it seems, to anything like the extent of that of the Christian Brothers. Gill relates the activities, in particular, of Brother Francis Paul Keaney, who ran several of the Brothers' institutions in Western Australia, notably Bindoon. These places were substantially built by the labour of their boys. Many remember Keaney as 'the beast of Bindoon'. He would take boys into his bed to warm his feet, have them massage gel into his hair or – when the mood took him – beat them senseless. Some of these 'orphans' objected to the softening of Keaney's portrayal by Bill Hunter in the television mini series, *The Leaving of Liverpool* (1992). One survivor of Bindoon, Paddy Dorrain, illegitimate son of a Catholic Irish woman, told Gill simply that: 'I've been inside. I've been in gaol. I would prefer thirty years in gaol compared to what I went through in Bindoon'.

Yet, curiously, some Bindoon boys sought to, or succeeded in joining the Christian Brothers. As Gill remarks, 'the compulsion to return to a disliked environment is often commented upon by psychologists'. Reinstitutionalisation may have prolonged, for some, the sufferings of their childhoods. There were many other costs for the child migrants in their later lives: lack of education, low paid jobs, unstable marriages, insecurities in dealing with their own children. Gill commented eloquently: 'there was also a sense of a foreshortened future – for instance, a victim does not expect to have a career, marriage, or children, or a long life'. The cultural history of Australia has long been gloomily fascinated with the figure of the lost child, of boys and girl suffering from want and cruelty, from abandonment and abuse. The child migrants from Britain whose stories are told by Gill, came to a land unhappily, but well fitted, to intensify the loneliness and misery of their plight.

The Stolen Generation

Necessarily without much elaboration, Alan Gill's *Orphans of the Empire* observed how 'the parallels between child migrants and the [Aboriginal] Stolen Children has been noticed by many people'. Indeed some of them – British and Aboriginal waifs forcibly taken from their families – ended up in the same institutions (such as the Christian Brothers orphanages in Western Australia, Castledare and Tardun) and were subject to the same abuse and want of care. Made to feel unwanted and rejected, often told falsely that their parents were dead, cut off from their cultural roots, these children shared a bond of suffering and – all too frequently – damaged and diminished adult lives.

The difference between the children's experiences is that Australian authorities had full responsibility for what was done to the 'stolen generation' of Aborigines. Allowing their stories to become known is a preliminary, but vital step in any moral or material reparation that might be made for them. The 'loss' of these Aborigines – some removed from their mothers at birth, others when they were of school age – was judicially, not accidentally occasioned. The intention was not simply to protect boys and girls who might loosely and conveniently be designated as 'neglected'. Part-Aboriginal children in particular were fostered out to white Australian couples or put in institutions so that over time they might marry and 'merge' with the non-indigenous population. Thus they would be absorbed, or assimilated. The problem of Australia's indigenous peoples would, in this manner, eventually disappear.

This was the theory. The practice was far from benign. Evidence about it has only recently begun to be published. In 1989, Coral Edwards and Peter Read edited *The Lost Children*, which contained the stories of thirteen Aboriginal men and women who had been taken from their natural parents while children, and who were now endeavouring to find them again. In 1994, the Going Home Conference, held in Darwin, gave the opportunity for delegates from every state and territory to tell stories of the 'stolen generation' across Australia and to devise strategies to meet the present needs of the survivors and their families. A year later, the Commonwealth Attorney-General, Michael Lavarch, requested the Human Rights and Equal Opportunities Commission to prepare a report on the plight of the 'stolen generation' of Aboriginal children. The HREOC hearings were held before its President, Sir Ronald Wilson, and the Aboriginal and Torres Strait Islanders Commission's Social Justice Commissioner, Mick Dodson.

The 'Report of the National Inquiry into the Separation of Aboriginal and Torres Strait Islander Children from their Families' was delivered in 1997. In a spirit of hope, it was titled *Bringing Them Home*. The report begins abruptly, as if in the present time: 'So the next thing I remember was that they took us from there and we went to the hospital...'. The deponent, in this – Confidential Submission 318 – was one of eight siblings removed in the 1960s from Cape Barren Island in Bass Strait. On the 'split the litter' principle, all were fostered separately on the mainland of Tasmania. As a matter of government policy, a family was thus twice sundered: children lost their parents, and their brothers and sisters. This was an individual tragedy, but one that was indicative of a much more massive dislocation of Indigenous families. The report concluded, 'with confidence', that 'Nationally ... between one in three and one in ten Indigenous children were forcibly removed from their families and communities in the period from about 1910 until 1970'.

That gives a sense of the scale of government intervention, whether – in the terms of the report – the means employed were compulsion, duress or undue influence. The poignancy of this history lies in the testimonies of individual survivors. One, from Victoria, asserted that 'the stolen years that are worth more than any other treasure are irrecoverable'. Another, from New South Wales, was a woman removed from her family together with her three sisters in the 1940s and sent to the Cootamundra Girls' Home:

> Most of us girls were thinking white in the head but were feeling black inside. We weren't black or white. We were a lonely, lost and sad displaced group of people ... They were simply a lost generation of children. I know. I was one of them.

Most controversial perhaps, although with warrant in international law, was the conclusion of the inquiry that such practices as it documented were tantamount to 'genocide'. For, the authors argued, 'when a child was forcibly removed, that child's entire community lost, often permanently, its chance to perpetuate itself in that child'. This was akin, if to a much more devastating extent, to the effects on their nineteenth-century communities of white children lost in the bush. The land took those white children. The Aboriginal children were taken from their families and from their land. As Lynne Datnow, of the Victorian Koori Kids Mental Health Network commented: 'the removal of these children creates a sense of death and loss in the community, and the community dies too'.

On 20 January 1996, soon after the National Inquiry had been established, the Melbourne *Age* quoted the hope of Sir Ronald Wilson that its result would be 'to produce a healing, a reconciliation, and enable this nation to go forward as one'. Politicians have not unanimously taken Wilson's cue. The name and policies of Pauline Hanson's One Nation Party have contaminated his optimistic and anti-racist rhetoric. The Liberal Prime Minister of the time, John Howard, would not apologise for what had been done to the 'stolen generation' when the report was presented to federal parliament. Yet *Bringing Them Home* can mean a bringing of hope as well. It could still become a means of reconciliation and recompense by Europeans to Indigenous Australians. It is clear that some Aborigines, who endured the process of being removed as children from their parents, are prepared to be reconciled.

Charlie McAdam's *Boundary Lines* (1995) is dedicated – with a curious echo of Ethel Pedley's *Dot and the Kangaroo* – not only to his own children, but to all 'future generations of Australians – Aboriginal and non-Aboriginal'. Born near Springvale Station in the Kimberley Region of Western Australia, McAdam was nearly lost at birth. As he relates the incident: 'When I was born my white father [the station owner James McAdam] wanted my mother to knock me on the head because he didn't want me'. He was spared, only to be taken as a child – in 1943 or 1944 – by a Native Affairs officer, who removed him to the Moola Bulla Station. A few years later, in 1947, 'they loaded us coloured kids up on the back of this truck and headed off to Beagle Bay' (north of Broome and now an Aboriginal Settlement). Those who ran the mission there believed, paternalistically, that 'Aborigines needed to be protected from European exploitation ... and that their salvation lay in conversion to Christianity'. The words are those of Elizabeth Tregenza, who throughout the book studiedly interpolates – with no impression of trespass – details of history, topography and culture pertinent to McAdam's story. From McAdam we learn that his wife, Val, had also suffered an uprooting by 'welfare' authorities.

And yet in neither of them does there appear to be a legacy of bitterness. Before 'white' Australia should too readily seek consolation thereby, its peoples should recognise that McAdam is offering reconciliation on his terms. In this polyvocal, collaborative story, McAdam is refusing the status of lost Aboriginal child as victim which he might easily have assumed. Instead, his 'lost' childhood generates a healing narrative. As such, it may mark the beginning of the end of one crucial strand of one of the oldest and most disturbing bodies of story that European Australians have told, to express their anxiety in the land to which they came more than two centuries ago, and in the urban society which they have made here. It may be that some lost children, at least, and at last, can find peace.

List of Works Consulted

Astbury, Leigh, *City Bushmen. The Heidelberg School and the Rural Mythology*, Melbourne: Oxford University Press, 1985
The Australian Babes in the Wood, London, 1866
Barnes, John, *The Order of Things. A Life of Joseph Furphy*, Melbourne: Oxford University Press, 1990
Bentley, Eric, *The Life of the Drama*, London: Methuen, 1965
Bird, Carmel, *Automatic Teller*, Sydney: Random House, 1996
—— *The Bluebird Café*, Sydney: Vintage, 1990
—— *Red Shoes*, Sydney: Vintage, 1998
Bird, Carmel (ed.), *The Stolen Children. Their Stories*, Sydney: Random House, 1998
Boake, Barcroft, *Where the Dead Men Lie, and Other Poems*, Sydney: Angus & Robertson, 1897
Brady, Veronica, *South of My Days*, Sydney: Angus & Robertson, 1998
Bringing Them Home (Report of the National Inquiry into the Separation of Aboriginal and Torres Strait Islander Children from their Families), Sydney: Human Rights and Equal Opportunities Commission, 1997
Bruce, Mary Grant, *Glen Eyre*, London: Ward, Lock, 1912
—— *Gray's Hollow*, London: Ward, Lock, 1914
Bryson, John, *Evil Angels*, Melbourne: Penguin, 1985
Carey, Peter, *Illywhacker*, St Lucia: University of Queensland Press, 1985
—— *A Letter to Our Son*, St Lucia: University of Queensland Press, 1994
—— *Oscar and Lucinda*, St Lucia: University of Queensland Press, 1988
—— 'A Small Testament', *New Yorker*, 25 September 1995
—— *The Tax Inspector*, St Lucia: University of Queensland Press, 1992
—— *The Unusual Life of Tristan Smith*, St Lucia: University of Queensland Press, 1994
Chatwin, Bruce, *The Songlines*, London: Jonathan Cape, 1987
Chauvel, Charles, *Uncivilised*, Sydney: Bookstall, 1936
Clarke, Marcus, *His Natural Life*, Melbourne: G. Robertson, 1874
—— *Holiday Peak and Other Tales*, Melbourne: G. Robertson, 1873
Crews, Frederick, 'The Mindsnatchers', *New York Review of Books*, 25 June 1998
Croft, Julian, *The Life and Opinion of Tom Collins. A Study of the Works of Joseph Furphy*, St Lucia: University of Queensland Press, 1991

Davis, Mark, *Gangland. Cultural Elites and the New Generationalism*, Sydney: Allen & Unwin, 1997
Drewe, Robert, *The Savage Crows*, Sydney: Collins, 1976
Edwards, Coral and Read, Peter (eds), *The Lost Children*, Sydney: Doubleday, 1989
Farmer, Beverley, *Home Time*, Melbourne: Penguin, 1985
Ferrar, William Moore, *Artabanzanus: The Demon of the Great Lake; An Allegorical Romance of Australia*, London: Elliot Stock, 1896
Fitzpatrick, Peter, *'After the Doll'. Australian Drama Since 1955*, Melbourne, 1979
Furphy, Joseph, *Such is Life*, Sydney: Bulletin Newspaper Company, 1903
Galbally, Ann, *Frederick McCubbin*, Melbourne: Hutchinson, 1981
Garner, Helen, *True Stories*, Melbourne: Text Publishing, 1996
Gill, Alan, *Orphans of the Empire*, Sydney: Random House, 1997
Gould, Alan, *The Tazyrik Year*, Sydney: Sceptre, 1998
Grenville, Kate, *Dreamhouse*, St Lucia: University of Queensland Press, 1986
Guilliatt, Richard, *Talk of the Devil*, Melbourne: Text Publishing, 1996
Haggard, Henry Rider, *She*, London: Longmans, Green & Co, 1887
Hardy, Thomas, *Tess of the D'Urbervilles*, London: Macmillan, 1891
—— *Jude the Obscure*, London: Macmillan, 1895
Hibberd, Jack, *Memoirs of an Old Bastard*, Melbourne: McPhee Gribble, 1989
—— *Perdita*, Melbourne: McPhee Gribble, 1992
—— *A Stretch of the Imagination*, Sydney: Currency Press, 1973
Hickson, Flo, *Flo: Child Migrant from Liverpool*, Warwick: Plowright Press, 1998
Holden, Robert, 'Lost, Stolen or Strayed', *Voices*, Autumn 1991, National Library of Australia
Hughes, Robert, *The Art of Australia*, Melbourne: Penguin, 1970
Jenkins, William Stitt, *The Lost Children: in Perpetual Remembrance of Jane Duff*, Geelong: Advertiser, 1864
Keneally, Thomas, *Bring Larks and Heroes*, Melbourne: Cassell, 1967
—— *A Family Madness*, London: Hodder & Stoughton, 1985
—— *Passenger*, London: Collins, 1979
—— *The Survivor*, Sydney: Angus & Robertson, 1969
—— *Woman of the Inner Sea*, London: Hodder & Stoughton, 1992
Kiernan, Brian, *Images of Society and Nature: Seven Essays on Australian Novels*, Melbourne: Oxford University Press, 1971
Kingsley, Henry, *The Recollections of Geoffry Hamlyn*, London: Macmillan, 1859
—— *The Lost Child*, London: Macmillan, 1871
Knight, Ivor, *Out of Darkness*, Fremantle: Fremantle Arts Press, 1998
Kociumbas, Jan, *Australian Childhood. A History*, Sydney: Allen & Unwin, 1997
Lawler, Ray, *Summer of the Seventeenth Doll*, Sydney: Angus & Robertson, 1957
Lawson, Henry, *Joe Wilson and His Mates*, Edinburgh: Blackwood, 1901
Leakey, Caroline, *The Broad Arrow*, London: Bentley, 1859
Lindsay, Joan, *Picnic at Hanging Rock*, Melbourne: Penguin, 1967
Lord, Gabrielle, *Fortress*, Sydney: Aurora Press, 1980
—— *The Sharp End*, Sydney: Sceptre, 1998
—— *Whipping Boy*, Sydney: McPhee Gribble, 1992
McAdam, Charlie, *Boundary Lines*, Melbourne: McPhee Gribble, 1995
McEwan, Ian, *The Child in Time*, London: Jonathan Cape, 1987
McGregor, Russell, *Imagined Destinies. Aboriginal Australians and the Doomed Race Theory, 1880–1939*, Melbourne: Melbourne University Press, 1997
MacKenzie, Andrew, *Frederick McCubbin 1855-1917: 'The Proff' and his art*, Melbourne: Mannagun Press, 1990

McLintock, Anne, *Imperial Leather*, London: Routledge, 1995
Mahler, Gustav, *Kinder-Totenlieder*, New York: International Music Company, n.d.
Maiden, Jennifer, *The Terms*, Sydney: Hale & Iremonger, 1982
────── *Play With Knives*, Sydney: Allen & Unwin, 1990
Malouf, David, *The Great World*, London: Chatto & Windus, 1990
────── *An Imaginary Life*, London: Chatto & Windus, 1978
────── *Johnno*, St Lucia: University of Queensland Press, 1975
────── *Remembering Babylon*, Sydney: Random House, 1993
Marshall, James Vance, *Walkabout*, London: Penguin, 1961
Martin, Arthur Patchett (ed.), *Over the Sea. Stories of Two Worlds*, London: Griffith, Faran, 1891
Matthews, Brian, *The Receding Wave. Henry Lawson's Prose*, Melbourne: Melbourne University Press, 1972
Mellick, J. S. D., *The Passing Guest. A Life of Henry Kingsley*, St Lucia: University of Queensland Press, 1983
Moffitt, Ian, *The Colour Man*, Sydney: Collins, 1983
────── *Death Adder Dreaming*, Sydney: Pan, 1988
Moorhouse, Frank, *The Americans, Baby*, Sydney: Angus & Roberston, 1972
────── *The Electrical Experience*, Sydney: Angus & Robertson, 1974
────── *The Everlasting Secret Family*, Sydney: Angus & Robertson, 1980
────── *Forty-Seventeen*, Melbourne: Viking, 1988
────── *Futility and Other Animals*, Sydney: Angus & Robertson, 1969
────── *Grand Days*, Sydney: Macmillan, 1993
────── *Room Service*, Melbourne: Viking, 1985
────── *Tales of Mystery and Romance*, Sydney: Angus & Robertson, 1977
Mulvaney, D. J., *Cricket Walkabout. The Australian Aboriginal Cricketers on Tour 1867–8*, Melbourne: Melbourne University Press, 1967
Murray, Scott (ed.), *The New Australian Cinema*, Melbourne: Nelson, 1980
Mykyta, Anne-Marie, *It's a long way to Truro*, Melbourne: Melbourne University Press, 1981
Nemerov, Howard, *Poetry and Fiction Essays*, New Brunswick and New Jersey: Rutgers University Press, 1963
Pedley, Ethel, *Dot and the Kangaroo*, London: Burleigh, 1899
Pierce, Peter, *Australian Melodramas. Thomas Keneally's Fiction*, St Lucia: University of Queensland Press, 1995
Powell, Craig, 'Rumpelstiltskin, or being available to our children', unpublished paper.
Praed, Rosa, *The Bond of Wedlock*, London: Chatto & Windus, 1887
────── *Fugitive Anne*, London: J. Long, 1903
────── *Mrs Tregaskiss*, London: Chatto & Windus, 1895
Roberts, Beth, *Manganinnie*, Melbourne: Macmillan, 1979
Roderick, Colin, *Banjo Paterson. Poet by Accident*, Sydney: Angus & Robertson, 1993
────── *In Mortal Bondage. The Strange Life of Rosa Praed*, Sydney: Angus & Robertson, 1948
Rousseau, Yvonne, *The Murders at Hanging Rock*, Melbourne: Sun Books, 1980
Salusinszky, Imré (ed.), *The Oxford Book of Australian Essays*, Melbourne, 1997
Scott, Margaret, *The Baby-Farmer*, Sydney: Angus & Robertson, 1990
Slotkin, Richard, *Regeneration Through Violence. The Mythology of the American West 1600–1800*, Middletown: Wesleyan University Press, 1973
Sperling, Leone, *Coins for the Ferryman*, Sydney: Pan, 1981
────── *Mother's Day*, Sydney: Wild & Woolley, 1984

Stewart, Ken (ed.), *The 1890s*, St Lucia: University of Queensland Press, 1996
Strutt, William, *Cooey: or, the Trackers of Glenferry*, Canberra: National Library of Australia, 1989
Tandy, Sophia, *The Children in the Scrub: a Story of Tasmania*, Hobart, 1878
Thrower, W. I., *Younah! A Tasmanian Aboriginal Romance of the Cataract Gorge*, Hobart: *Mercury*, 1894
Timms, O. F., *Station Dangerous: or, The Settlers in Central Australia, A Tale Founded on Facts*, Sydney, 1866
Tournier, Michel, *Gilles et Jeanne*, Paris: Editions Gallimard, 1983; London: Methuen, 1987
Twain, Mark, *Huckleberry Finn*, London: Chatto & Windus, 1884
Wells, T. E., *Michael Howe. The Last and Worst of the Bushrangers of Van Diemen's Land*, Hobart: Andrew Bent, 1818
Westbury, Atha, *Australian Fairy Tales*, London: Ward, Lock, 1897
White, Patrick, *Big Toys*, Sydney: Currency Press, 1978
—— *A Cheery Soul*, London: Eyre and Spottiswoode, 1965
—— *The Ham Funeral*, London: Eyre and Spottiswoode, 1965
—— *Netherwood*, Sydney: Currency Press, 1983
—— *A Season at Sarsaparilla*, London: Eyre and Spottiswoode, 1965
—— *Signal Driver*, Sydney: Currency Press, 1983
—— *The Tree of Man*, New York: Viking, 1955
—— *The Vivisector*, London: Jonathan Cape, 1970
Whitehead, Anne, *Paradise Mislaid*, St Lucia: University of Queensland Press, 1997
Whitfield, Jessie, *The Spirit of the Bush Fire*, Sydney: Angus & Robertson, 1898
Wilding, Michael, *Studies in Classic Australian Fiction*, Sydney: Shoestring Press, 1997
Window, Carolin, *Dim*, Sydney: Vintage, 1996
Young, David, *Making Crime Pay*, Hobart: Tasmanian Historical Research Association, 1996

Index

Aboriginal cricket team 22, 38
Aborigines *see*
 Aboriginal cricket team
 Aborigines in art
 black trackers
 Dick-a-Dick
 reconciliation
Aborigines in art 10, 20, 67
Adams, Francis 42
Advertiser (Adelaide) 187
Age (Melbourne) 189, 191, 200
Age Book of the Year Award 122
'Alice' ('In Memoriam. The Lost Children of Daylesford') 38–9, 65
Archibald, J. F. 86
Argus (Melbourne) 17, 41, 48, 52, 53, 55
Ashcroft, Johnny and Withers, Tommy ('Little Boy Lost') 97
Astbury, Leigh (City Bushmen) 60
Australasian Sketcher 37, 48–53
Australian Babes in the Woods, The 17–20
Australian Illustrated Magazine 22
Australian Journal 45
Australian Sketchbook 19

Babe 152
baby-farming 115, 145, 181
Back of Beyond, The 153–6
balladists 65–71
'Barnard Eldershaw' xiii

Barnes, John (*Order of Things, The*) 86
Barrie, James (*Peter Pan*) 80
Baynton, Barbara ('Scrammy 'And') 7
Beaumont children, the 95, 136, 179, 186
Bentley, Eric (*The Life of the Drama*) 100
Bird, Carmel 95, 98, 114, 115, 116, 128, 143–6
 Automatic Teller 145–6
 Bluebird Café, The 143–4, 145
 In Her Father's House 145
 Red Shoes 114, 115, 145–6
 Stolen Children. Their Stories, The 145
black trackers xii, 8, 10–11, 21–2, 25–7, 34, 49, 51, 65, 67, 68, 69, 72, 84, 88–9, 95, 161, 174, 177
Blyton, Enid 168, 170
Boake, Barcroft 6, 65, 69–71
 'At Devlin's Siding' 65, 69, 70–1
 'Babes in the Bush, The' 69–70
 Where the Dead Men Lie 6, 69
'Boldrewood, Rolf' 11
Bolger, James xvi
Bond, Edward 156
Boomerang 65
Boulter, Alfred 9, 29–34, 89
Brady, Veronica (*South of My Days*) 97
Brennan, Christopher 121
Bringing Them Home 199–200

INDEX

Bruce, Mary Grant xiii
  Glen Eyre xiii
  Gray's Hollow xiii
Bryson, John 153, 174–6, 178
  Evil Angels 153, 174–6
Buckley, William 8, 147
Bulletin 6, 68, 79, 86
bunyips 8, 15, 44
Burroughs, Edgar Rice (*Tarzan of the Apes*) xiii
bushrangers 13–14
Buzo, Alex (*Norm and Ahmed*) 113

Cameron, Mary 77–9
Carey, Peter 181–4, 185
  Illywhacker 182
  'Letter to Our Son, A' 181–2
  Oscar and Lucinda 182
  'Small, Testament, A' 183–4
  Tax Inspector, The 182
  Unusual Life of Tristan Smith, The 182–3
Carroll, Lewis (*Alice in Wonderland*) 63
Calvert, Samuel 5, 9, 29–30, 36, 37, 53–4
  'Alfred Boulter' 30
  'Children Lost in the Bush' 5
  'Finding the Remains of the Daylesford Children' 36, 37, 53–4
captivity narratives xvi–xvii, 8
Chamberlain, Azaria 4, 95–6, 143, 153, 172–8
Chatwin, Bruce (*Songlines, The*) xi, 98
Chaucer, Geoffrey 64
Chauncy, Nan (*They Found a Cave*) 168
Chauvel, Charles (*Uncivilised*) xiii
Chekhov, Anton 100, 101
Chevalier, Nicholas 19, 20, 23
  'Lost Children, The' 19, 20
Cinema Papers 170
Clarke, Marcus 6, 11, 14, 39, 40–6, 49, 50–1, 89, 126
  His Natural Life 14, 45–6
  Holiday Peak 40
  'Pretty Dick' 39, 40–5, 49, 50–1, 89
Clipper 79
Collinson, Peter 153

Colonial Monthly 40
'coming race, the' see 'young Australia'
creeks, creek-crossing 15, 42–3, 50–1, 160, 165, 166
Crews, Frederick 193
Croft, Julian (*Life and Opinion of Tom Collins, The*) 88, 90–2
Crosbie, Clara 9, 46–54, 95, 99
Cry in the Dark, A see *Evil Angels*

Dark, Eleanor xiii
Davis, Mark (*Gangland*) 98
Dawn 65
Daylesford boys 5, 34–40, 42, 53–4, 91
Daylesford Mercury 34–7
Demidenko, Helen (*Hand That Signed the Paper, The*) 98
Dermody, Susan 151
Dick-a-Dick 22, 38
Dickens, Charles 15, 45
dingoes 4, 25, 68, 173–5
Dodds, Peter 27, 151
Dodson, Mick 199
Dot and the Kangaroo (book) see Pedley, Ethel
Dot and the Kangaroo (film) 63, 152
Drewe, Robert (*Savage Crows, The*) 115
Duff children 5, 11, 16–29, 53, 54, 55, 148, 151
Duigan, Virginia 151
Dumas, Alexandre 12
Dunblane massacre xvi, 146
Dutroux, Marc xvi

Earthling, The 153
Edwards, Coral and Read, Peter (*Lost Children, The*) 199
Edwards, Pat ('Lost in the Bush') 27
Egg, Augustus 60
Eliot, George (*Adam Bede*) 70
Evil Angels (book) see Bryson, John
Evil Angels (film) 95, 153, 172–8

fairytales 9, 17, 49, 58, 60–4, 129, 132, 172, 188
Farmer, Beverley 115, 116, 128, 133–5
  Home Time 133–5

Ferrar, William Moore (*Artabanzanus*) 64
Fitzpatrick, Peter (*After 'The Doll'*) 101
Ford, William ('At the Hanging Rock') 159
Fortress (book) *see* Lord, Gabrielle
Fortress (film) 95, 153, 170–1
Fraser, Eliza 8, 147
Frith, W. P. 60
Furphy, Joseph, xii, xv, 6, 10, 11, 39, 49, 64, 86–92, 96, 126
   Buln Buln and the Brolga, The 86
   Rigby's Romance 86
   Such is Life xii, 49, 86–92, 96

Galbally, Ann (*Frederick McCubbin*) 54, 57–8, 59, 64
Garner, Helen 98, 180, 192, 194
   First Stone, The 98
   True Stories 180
Geelong Advertiser 20
Gill, Alan 181, 196–8, 200
   Orphans of the Empire 181, 196–8
Gill, S. T. 9, 10
   'Duff Children, The' 19
Gilmore, Dame Mary 78
Golding, William 168
Gordon, Adam Lindsay 6, 42, 81
Gould, Alan (*Tazyrik Year, The*) 116
Granta 181
Grenville, Kate 95, 115
   Dreamhouse 115
Grimm brothers xv, 17, 49
Gross, Yoram 152
Guilliatt, Richard (*Talk of the Devil*) 192–5

Haggard, Rider 71, 73, 168
   King Solomon's Mines 168
   She 71
Hardy, Thomas 140–1
   Jude the Obscure 140–1
   Tess of the D'Urbervilles 140–1
Harpur, Charles ('Creek of the Four Graves, The') 16
Haydon, Tom 167
Head, Walter 77–81
Hemingway, Ernest 125
Hennings, John (*Fairy Home of the Waratah*) 9

Heyer, Janet 153
Heyer, John 153–6
Hibberd, Jack 7, 115–16, 118
   Memoirs of an Old Bastard 115, 118
   Perdita 116
   Stretch of the Imagination, A 7
Hickson, Flo (*Flo: Child Migrant from Liverpool*) 195–6
Holden, Robert ('Lost, Stolen or Strayed') 19, 27
Honey, John 164, 166, 167
Horsham Times 27–9
Hughes, Robert (*Art of Australia, The*) 59–60
Hugo, Victor (*Hunchback of Notre Dame, The*) 146
Hummer 78

Ibsen, Henrik 100, 102
Illustrated Australian News 10, 17, 19, 20, 36–9, 52–3, 68
Illustrated London News 37
Illustrated Melbourne Post 4–8, 16, 19, 29, 31, 36–7, 53, 87, 175

Jenkins, William Stitt (*Lost Children, The*) 18–19
J. M. H. ('Tribute') 28
Johnson, A. J. 60

Kelso, Ken 164
Keneally, Thomas 95, 114, 115–21
   Bring Larks and Heroes 116
   Chant of Jimmie Blacksmith, The 116
   Family Madness, A 116–17
   Passenger 114, 116, 119–21
   Survivor, The 116, 119
   Woman of the Inner Sea 116, 117–8
kidnapping xiv, xvi, 8, 95, 135, 179, 181, 184–8
Kiernan, Brian (*Images of Society and Nature*) 114
Kingsley, Charles 13, 16
Kingsley, Henry, xii, 6, 11–16, 19, 41, 44, 50–1, 53, 58, 73, 126
   Lost Child, The 16, 73
   Recollections of Geoffry Hamlyn, The xii, 11–16, 19, 41, 44, 50–1, 58, 73
Knight, Ivor (*Out of Darkness*) 195
Kociumbas, Jan (*Australian Childhood*) 3

Lambert, G. W. 62
Last Tasmanian, The 167
Lawler, Ray 95, 98, 99–104, 113
  Summer of the Seventeenth Doll 99–104, 113
Lawson, Henry xv, 6, 7, 10, 39, 49, 55, 64, 65–6, 77–86, 124–5, 126, 156, 176
  'Babies in the Bush, The' (poem) 49, 79–81, 85
  'Babies in the Bush, The' (story) 49, 55, 79, 81–6, 90, 176
  'Babies of Walloon, The' 65–6
  'Bush Undertaker, The' 7
  Joe Wilson and His Mates 81, 85, 125
  'Union Buries Its Dead, The' 87
Leakey, Caroline (*The Broad Arrow*) 14
Leaving of Liverpool, The 198
Leichhardt, Ludwig 6, 38, 74
Leskie, Jaidyn 181, 188–92, 196
Lindsay, Joan (*Picnic at Hanging Rock*) 59, 152–3, 159–64
Lord, Gabrielle 115, 116, 128, 136, 153, 168–72
  Fortress 153, 168–70
  Sharp End, The 171
  Whipping Boy 136, 171–2
Lost in the Bush 27, 151
Lost White Woman of Gippsland, The 8

McAdam, Charlie (*Boundary Lines*) 200–1
McCubbin, Frederick 9, 54–60, 151, 160, 165
  'Bush Idyll' 59
  'Childhood Fancies' 58
  'Found' 55, 57
  'Gathering Mistletoes' 55
  'Lost' (1886) 54, 55, 56, 59, 165
  'Lost' (1907) 54, 57, 58, 59, 160
  'What the Little Girl Saw in the Bush' 58
McEwan, Ian (*Child in Time, The*) xvi
McGregor, Russell (*Imagined Destinies*) 23
Mackay children 179
MacKenzie, Andrew (*Frederick McCubbin*) 55
McLeod, William 9, 67, 68

McLintock, Anne (*Imperial Leather*) 23, 37
Mad Max: Beyond Thunderdome 153
Mahler, Gustav (*Kinder-totenlieder*) xv, xvi
Mahony, Frank 63
Maiden, Jennifer 98, 115, 116, 128, 136, 138–43
  'Blood Judge, The' 143
  Play With Knives 136, 139–43
  Terms, The 138–9
Malouf, David 114, 115, 146–50
  Fly Away Peter 147
  Great World, The 146, 147
  Imaginary Life, An 147, 150
  Johnno 146–7
  Remembering Babylon 114, 147–50
  12 Edmonstone Street 147
Man 122
Manganinnie (book) *see* Roberts, Beth
Manganinnie (film) 95, 153, 164–8
Marshall, James Vance (*Walkabout*) 152, 156–7
Martin, Adrian 163
Martin, Arthur (*Over the Sea*) 71
Martineau, Robert 60
Matthews, Brian (*Receding Wave, The*) 83
Meanjin 97
Melbourne Review 71
Mellick, Stan (*Passing Guest, The*) 16
Mercury (Hobart) 31–2, 33
Milat, Ivan 188
Moffitt, Ian 98, 115, 116, 128, 135–8
  Colour Man, The 135–8
  Death Adder Dreaming 135
  Presence of Evil 135
Moorhouse, Frank 95, 115, 121–8, 176, 195
  Americans Baby, The 123, 125
  Death of Azaria Chamberlain 176
  Electrical Experience, The 123–4
  Everlasting Secret Family, The 122
  Forty-Seventeen 122, 124–8
  Futility and Other Animals 122, 126, 127
  Grand Days 125
  Room Service 124
  Tales of Mystery and Romance 123, 127

Mulvaney, D. J. (*Cricket Walkabout*) 22
Mykyta, Anne-Marie (*It's a long way to Truro*) 187–8

Nemerov, Howard (*Poetry and Fiction Essays*) 129–30
New Australia 77, 79, 81
New Australia 77, 79, 81
New Australian Cinema, The 151
New Yorker 183

Ogilvie, Will 65, 68–9
  'Black Trackers, The' 68–9
'orphans of the empire' *see* Gill, Alan
Oxford Companion to Australian Literature, The 156

Paterson, A. B. ('Banjo') ('Lost') 65, 66, 68
Pedley, Ethel 6, 58, 63–4, 126, 152, 200
  Dot and the Kangaroo 58, 63–4, 152, 200
Penton, Brian xiii
Picnic at Hanging Rock (book) *see* Lindsay, Joan
Picnic at Hanging Rock (film) 95, 153, 162–4, 172
Pierce, Peter (*Australian Melodramas*) 116
Pitt, M. A. (*Australian Second Book*) 27
Playboy 122
Powell, Craig 132
Praed, Rosa, 6, 39, 48, 60, 71–7
  Bond of Wedlock, The 74
  Fugitive Anne 71
  Mrs Tregaskiss 48, 73–7
  'Sea-Birds' Message, The' 71–3

reconciliation of Aboriginal and European Australians xiii, xiv, 4, 11, 69, 158–9, 165–6, 168, 187, 200–1
Richardson, Henry Handel (*Fortunes of Richard Mahony, The*) 85
Roberts, Beth (*Manganinnie*) 153, 164
Robinson, Roland 153
Roderick, Colin 65, 66, 73, 79
  Banjo Paterson 66
  In Mortal Bondage 73

Roeg, Nicolas 98, 152, 156–9
Rousseau, Yvonne (*Murders at Hanging Rock, The*) 164
Rueckert, Friedrich xv, xvi

saga literature xiii, xiv, 106
Salusinszky, Imré (*Oxford Book of Australian Essays, The*) 9
Schepisi, Fred 98, 172, 176–8
Scott, Margaret (*Baby-Farmer, The*) 115
Scott, Sir Walter 12
Scribe, Eugene 100
Sculthorpe, Peter 164
searches, search parties xii, xvii, 7–8, 14, 16, 17, 21, 25, 29, 34–5, 38, 44, 49, 51–2, 68, 69, 72, 80, 83–4, 88, 89, 90, 91, 95, 150, 153, 159, 165, 171, 182–6
Searchers, The xvii
Seymour, Alan 100, 113
  One Day of the Year, The 113
Shakespeare, William 98, 115, 118, 159, 182
  Cymbeline 159
  I Henry IV 98
  Macbeth 182
  Pericles 159
  Tempest, The 159
  Winter's Tale, The 115, 118, 159
Shoobridge, Peter 33–4
Showalter, Elaine (*Hystories*) 193
Slotkin, Richard (*Regeneration Through Violence*) xvi–xvii
Southey, Robert (*Botany Bay Eclogues*) 63
Sperling, Leone 115, 116, 128–33
  Coins for the Ferryman 128
  Mother's Day 128–33
  Oasis 128
Squire 122
Stacey, W. S. (*Australian Pictures Drawn in Pen and Pencil*) 54
Stein, Gertrude 123
Stephens, A. G. 69
Sterne, Laurence (*Tristram Shandy*) 182
Stewart, Douglas 153
Stewart, Ken (*1890s, The*) 87
'stolen generation' xiv, 96, 181, 198–201

Strutt, William 9, 19, 22–7, 32–3, 72–3
  'Black Thursday, 6 Feb. 1851' 23
  Cooey: or, the Trackers of Glenferry 23–6, 32–3
  'Found' 72–3
  'Found, Mr Duncan, Roderick, Bella and David' 26
  'Little Wanderers, or The Lost Track, The' 23
Sunday Age 189, 191
Sunday Herald-Sun 190
Sydney Mail 62, 66
Sydney Morning Herald 46–7, 175, 176

Table Talk 55
Tandy, Sophia (*Children in the Scrub, The*) 20
Tasmanian Democrat 79
Thorne, Graeme 95, 96, 179, 181, 184–5
Thrower, Mrs W. I. (*Younah!*) 8, 165
Time 180
Timms, O.F. (*Station Dangerous*) 19
Tompson, Charles ('Blacktown') xiv, 3–4
Tournier, Michel (*Gilles et Jeanne*) xv
Truro murders 95, 186–8
Twain, Mark (*Huckleberry Finn*) xvii

Ulitarra 143

Valerio, Daniel 180, 192, 194
Van Diemen's Land 12–14

Walkabout (book) *see* Marshall, James Vance

Walkabout (film) 95, 152, 156–9
Wall, Stephen 97
Wanda Beach murders 179
Weir, Peter 153, 162–4, 172
Wells, T. E. (*Michael Howe*) 13
Westbury, Atha (*Australian Fairy Tales*) 60–2
White, Patrick 95, 98, 99, 100, 102, 104–13, 114, 115
  Aunt's Story, The 111
  Big Toys 106, 109
  Cheery Soul, A 108–9, 111
  Ham Funeral, The 106–7, 112
  Netherwood 111–13
  Riders in the Chariot 107
  Season at Sarsaparilla, A 107–8
  Signal Driver 109–11, 112
  Tree of Man, The 104–7, 114
  Vivisector, The 104
  Voss 107
Whitehead, Anne (*Paradise Mislaid*) 78
Whitfield, Jessie (*Spirit of the Bushfire, The*) 62–3
Wilding, Michael (*Studies in Classic Australian Fiction*) 42, 46
Williams, Tennessee (*Glass Menagerie, The*) 102
Wilson, Sir Ronald 199, 200
Window, Carolin (*Dim*) 116
Woman's Day 177
Worker 78–9
Wright, Judith ('Precipice, The') 97

'young Australia' 8, 14–15, 19, 53, 82, 86–8, 90
Young, David (*Making Crime Pay*) 45